Modern World History

for SEG syllabus B

DAVID FERRIBY • DAVID HANSOM • STEVE WAUGH

Heinemann

Heinemann Educational Publishers
Halley Court, Jordan Hill, Oxford, OX2 8EJ
a division of Reed Educational & Professional Publishing Ltd
Heinemann is a registered trademark of Reed Educational & Professional Publishing Ltd

OXFORD MELBOURNE AUCKLAND

JOHANNESBURG BLANTYRE GABORONE

IBADAN PORTSMOUTH NH (USA) CHICAGO

First published 2000

ISBN 0 435 30847 5

02 01 00

10 9 8 7 6 5 4 3 2 1

Designed and typeset by Hardlines, Charlbury, Oxon

Printed and bound in Spain by Edelvives

Photographic acknowledgements

The authors and publisher would like to thank the following for permission to reproduce photographs:

Cover photograph: © Hulton Getty

AKG London: 133O, 144E, 147H, 148A, 161E, 164H, 166I, 167J, 170O; Associated Press: 24E; Bath Chronicle: 202A; Malcolm Brown: 200A; Centre for the Study of Cartoon and Caricature: 79I; Corbis: 10C, 57A, 63C, 82A, 94F, 229A; Corbis/Sygma: 87B, 92D; Daily Mail: 48D; David King: 107D, 112L, 114M, 119E, 121H, 122I, 124M, 127D, 130H, 132J, 135Q, 136B, 169N; Bob Lavin: 53J; David Low/Solo Syndication: 17C, 21C, 23D, 32K, 33L, 37A; Detroit Free Press: 68A; Hoover Institute: 111K; Hulton Getty: 8A, 54K, 84E, 139A, 146G, 197N, 200C, 231A, 251D, 253H, 255K, 260D; Imperial War Museum: 153G, 181D, 191D, 234B, 236C, 238G, 249A; John Frost: 204F; Krauze: 98H; Les Gibbard: 91B; Magnum: 83C, Mary Evans: 229B; New Statesman: 62A, 69A; New York Magazine: 215D; Peter Newark:78G, 207D, 208F, 209G, 212B, 213C, 218G, 223D, 227A; Philadelphia Bulletin & Jerry Doyle: 221B; Popperfoto: 33M, 58B, 100A; Punch: 15A, 28B, 52H, 76E, 156J; Simplissimus: 216E; Topham Picturepoint: 48B, 73B, 74C, 229C; US Navy: 257C; War Illustrated 1917: 203C; Whitney Museum of American Art: 206C

Contents

Paper 2 topics

Coursework or Paper 1 topics

CHAPTER 1

Peace to war, 1919–39

Introduction

When the First World War ended in November 1918, Europeans were weary of war, and horrified by the cost in human lives and other damage. The peace treaties of 1919–20 were intended to guarantee that wars could be avoided in future. The terms involved a major redrawing of the boundaries of Europe and the abolition of several empires. New democratic governments replaced them, and there were high hopes that this would be a new period of international co-operation. Overseeing all this was to be the League of Nations.

The Wall Street Crash of 1929 had devastating effects on industry, employment and international trade. During the depression of the 1930s, the League of Nations was clearly incapable of maintaining international law or world peace. Japan's invasion of Manchuria (1931) and Italy's invasion of Abyssinia (1935) both showed that aggressive dictatorships could over-ride the League of Nations. The League was powerless to enforce its wishes, especially without help from the USA.

Hitler took full advantage of this situation in Europe. First of all, he used criticisms of the Treaty of Versailles to justify his policy of expansion. Then he sought international support over the Sudetenland. Finally, he used simple aggression – and other countries woke up to the fact that the policy of trying to maintain the peace had failed. When Hitler invaded Poland on 1 September 1939, the Second World War had begun.

1919 Treaty of Versailles

1923 French invasion of the Ruhr

1926 Germany allowed to join League of Nations

1929 Wall Street Crash

1931 Japanese invasion of Manchuria

1933 Hitler begins policy of re-armament

1935 Italian invasion of Abyssinia

1936 Germany reoccupies the Rhineland

1938 Germany joins with Austria (March)
Germany gains the Sudetenland (September)

1939 Germany takes over the rest of Czechoslovakia (March)
Nazi–Soviet Pact (August)
Germany invades Poland (September)

The Paris peace settlement of 1919–20

The First World War, 1914–18

In 1914 the great powers of Europe went to war. Britain, France and Russia (the Allies) found themselves in conflict with Germany, Austria-Hungary and Turkey (the Central Powers). By 1917 both Italy (joined the war in 1915) and the USA had joined the war on the Allies' side. Although there was fighting worldwide, the main campaigns took place in eastern Europe (the Eastern Front) and in France and Belgium (the Western Front).

The last stages of the First World War, 1917–18

The main focus of the war was on the Western Front. Both sides poured millions of men into this area in a desperate bid to win the war. The names of the major battles, such as Ypres, Verdun and the Somme, are famous in history for their huge numbers of casualties. But by 1917 there still seemed no end in sight. When the British attacked the Germans at Passchendaele in that year, they lost 250,000 men in gaining just 750 metres of waterlogged land.

However, 1917 can be seen as a turning point for the war. In April the USA declared war on Germany. President Woodrow Wilson had persuaded the US Congress that 'the world must be made safe for democracy'. The British and French were about to get huge supplies of equipment and troops. Germany would have to win the war quickly before the balance tipped against it.

It appeared at the end of 1917 that Germany had a good chance of success. A communist revolution in Russia in November 1917 led to Russia leaving the war. In the Treaty of Brest-Litovsk in March 1918 Russia signed a peace agreement, and gave Germany land that included a quarter of Russia's population, farming land and three-quarters of its iron ore. Germany could now concentrate on fighting on the Western Front.

The alliances of the First World War.

Germany's gamble fails

In March 1918, the Germans threw all their resources into one final major attack on the Western Front. They attacked where the Allies were weakest and, after years of stalemate, they made great gains. However, the Allies managed to stop the advance and then in late July counter-attacked. By now US soldiers were beginning to arrive in France in substantial numbers, and these fresh troops gave great heart to the Allied soldiers fighting against exhausted German troops.

At the same time, conditions in Germany were becoming desperate. A blockade of German ports by the Royal Navy was preventing food entering Germany and thousands were starving. Many more were dying in a huge influenza outbreak. Soon Munich and Berlin were in the hands of revolutionaries who wanted the German government overthrown. In October 1918 the German navy mutinied in Wilhelmshaven and some soldiers on the Western Front refused to fight.

The German Emperor, Kaiser Wilhelm II, and his government ministers realised that they had to end the war, particularly as Germany's allies (Bulgaria, Turkey and Austria-Hungary) had all surrendered by early November. So on 9 November 1918 the German Kaiser stood down to allow his government to surrender. Germany surrendered at 11 a.m. on 11 November 1918. The Kaiser fled to Holland and a new government was set up in Germany.

The impact of the war

Casualties in the war had been huge. Nearly two million Russian soldiers had been killed in the fighting. Germany had lost almost as many. France and Austria had lost over a million each, and Britain nearly a million. In addition, at least 20 million soldiers had been wounded – many of them were still suffering the consequences of their wounds long after the war had ended.

France

Most of the fighting in western Europe had taken place in France. Over 2 million French people had to flee from their homes. Three-quarters of a million homes were destroyed. So were many roads and railways, and many places where people had worked, such as factories. Huge areas of good farming land had been turned into mud – and there was the constant danger of unexploded shells.

Belgium

The Germans had occupied most of Belgium for four years, taking the country's resources, such as machinery and crops, to help their own war effort. The part not occupied by the Germans had been the scene of bitter fighting and widespread devastation. For example, the old city of Ypres was in ruins.

Britain

The British had not suffered serious damage at home, although air attacks had killed over 1000 people. Many families had lost relatives or friends. Life would be totally different after the war compared with before 1914. Also the country was very heavily in debt because of the war, and owed nearly £1 billion to the Americans.

Italy

Having been promised land from Austria after the fighting was over, the Italians had joined the war in 1915 on the side of the Allies. There were over half a million dead Italian soldiers, and the Italians believed they had made a significant contribution to the war and deserved what they had been promised.

Germany

Very little fighting had taken place on German soil, but the country was suffering very badly by the end of 1918. There was widespread starvation, made worse by the British blockade of German ports. Many German people could not believe that they had lost – and so quickly. German politicians had told the German people of military successes in the spring of 1918; the retreats had not been so well publicised! Some Germans suspected their leaders of treachery.

Russia

The Russians suffered very heavy casualties in the war, even though they had ceased to fight after the new Bolshevik (communist) government took over in November 1917. This new government signed the Treaty of Brest-Litovsk with the Germans in March 1918. Russia gave up huge areas of land on its western borders, in Finland, Poland and the Ukraine, and on the Baltic coastline. What should happen to these areas after the war?

Austria-Hungary

Defeat in the war led to the downfall of the Austrian monarchy and the break-up of the Austro-Hungarian Empire. By the time the peacemakers met at Versailles, the new states of Austria, Hungary and Czechoslovakia had already come into being.

SOURCE A

Destruction of the city of Ypres, Belgium.

The main personalities and their attitudes to the defeated countries

In January 1919 people from the Allied countries met in Paris. The leaders of America, France and Britain dominated the detailed discussions. Each had his priorities, and they did not always agree. Yet they were under pressure to reach a peaceful settlement to Europe's problems. The defeated countries were not allowed to join them, nor was Russia, as the western allies did not trust communism.

Woodrow Wilson, President of the USA

The American President was an idealist – he believed in finding perfect solutions. He had great plans to make sure that war never happened again. To achieve world peace in the future, nations would have to co-operate. He made his views clear in January 1918, before the end of the war. His Fourteen Points set out principles that he believed should guide peacemaking once the war had finished. The most important was self-determination – people of different national groups had the right to rule themselves.

Some of these points were easy to argue in 1919. Others were acceptable in theory, but were difficult to apply in practice, such as self-determination of peoples. The peoples of eastern Europe were scattered across wide areas. Some people were bound to end up being ruled by people from another group who had a different language and culture.

Wilson believed that Germany should be punished, but not too harshly. If the peace treaty was too harsh, Germans would be resentful and demand revenge. Instead Wilson wanted all countries to join a League of Nations, which would resolve disputes peacefully. He believed that Germany should lose some territory, but should not be made to pay the cost of war damage.

It was easy for him to take this lenient attitude as the USA had not suffered much from the war. After all, it did not join until April 1917, and American soldiers did not reach Europe until late 1917. Americans could take a more detached attitude than Europeans, who had suffered the full horrors of the war.

The Fourteen Points

1. No secret treaties
2. Free access to the seas in peacetime and wartime
3. Free trade between countries
4. Disarmament
5. Colonies to be able to have a say in their own futures
6. German troops to leave Russia
7. Independence for Belgium
8. France to regain Alsace-Lorraine
9. Frontier between Austria and Italy to be adjusted
10. Self-determination for the peoples of the Austro-Hungarian Empire
11. Serbia to have access to the sea
12. Self-determination for the people in the Turkish Empire
13. Poland to become an independent state with access to the sea
14. A League of Nations to be set up to keep the peace

SOURCE B

I consider it a distinguished privilege to be permitted to open the discussion in this conference on the League of Nations. We have assembled here for two purposes – to make the peace settlements, and also to secure the future peace of the world. The League of Nations seems to me to be necessary for both of these purposes.

From a speech by President Woodrow Wilson to the Paris Peace Conference, January 1919.

SOURCE C

Woodrow Wilson, Georges Clemenceau and David Lloyd George.

David Lloyd George, Prime Minister of Britain

David Lloyd George had been involved in politics for nearly thirty years and was very experienced. He understood that there would have to be many compromises in the peace talks, otherwise a settlement would never be reached.

He wanted Germany to be punished, but not too harshly – like Wilson, he did not want Germany to seek revenge in the future. This conflicted with the view of most British people. Indeed, Lloyd George's government had won an election in December 1918 promising to 'squeeze the German lemon until the pips squeak'.

Lloyd George also wanted to protect British interests at sea, and therefore disliked Wilson's idea of 'freedom of the seas'. He was keen for Germany to have only a limited navy. Yet at the same time he knew that Britain was primarily a trading nation, and it was important that Germany was not crippled too much, so that the two countries could start trading again.

Georges Clemenceau, Prime Minister of France

Georges Clemenceau had had a long career in French politics, and he was aged 77 when the peace talks began. He had become Prime Minister in November 1917, promising to win the war for France and to ensure that Germany could never do the same to France again. After all, Germany had invaded France before in 1870, and had taken Alsace-Lorraine. Now this must be restored to France.

Clemenceau was under great pressure from the French people to make Germany pay for the suffering that they had endured. They argued that this should take the form of money and land. If Germany lost land on the French–German border, this would help to make the French feel more secure from possible future attack. With Clemenceau as their leader, the French people had a tough politician who would argue their case strongly.

QUESTIONS

1. What did Clemenceau want France to get from the peace settlement?
2. Did Lloyd George want the same for Britain?

The Treaty of Versailles, June 1919

On 28 June 1919 the leading politicians from the victorious countries left Paris and went by train to Versailles, 16 kilometres away. There, in the famous royal palace, they signed the Treaty of Versailles. It dealt only with Germany, but it was over 200 pages long, with over 400 separate sections, or clauses. Two representatives of the new German government were summoned. The Germans had been allowed no say in the discussions; they were simply invited to sign in humiliating circumstances. They had no choice.

Territorial changes

The map shows the main changes that Germany was forced to accept at Versailles.

- Alsace and Lorraine were returned to France. (They had been French before 1871.)
- Eupen and Malmédy went to Belgium.
- North Schleswig went to Denmark.
- Germany lost land to the newly recreated country of Poland. This included West Prussia, Posen and part of Upper Silesia. (East Prussia was now separated from the rest of Germany by Polish land.)
- Memel was lost to the new country of Lithuania.
- Germany lost control of the Saar coalfields for 15 years. The League of Nations gave them to France.
- Danzig was made a free city under League of Nations control. Poland could use its port for trade and had a corridor of land to the sea.
- Germany lost all the land taken from Russia in the Treaty of Brest-Litovsk in 1918. (Estonia, Latvia and Lithuania became independent states.)
- Germany was forbidden to unite with Austria.
- Germany lost all its colonies. The League of Nations gave them to victorious countries as mandates. These countries were intended to govern the territories until they were able to rule themselves.
  In Africa, the colonies were given to Britain, France and South Africa. New Guinea was given to Australia. Samoa was given to New Zealand. Several islands in the Pacific were given to Japan.

The territorial terms of the Treaty of Versailles.

Military restrictions

The Treaty of Versailles restricted Germany's armed forces to a level far below what they had been before the war.

- The army was limited to 100,000 men.
- Conscription was banned; all soldiers had to be volunteers.
- Germany was not allowed tanks, submarines or military aircraft.
- The navy could have only six battleships.
- The Rhineland became a demilitarised zone. This meant that no German troops were allowed into this area near the French border. It included all the land west of the River Rhine and an area 50 km wide on the east bank. The Allies were to keep an army of occupation on the west bank for fifteen years.

War guilt

The War Guilt Clause (Clause 231) forced Germany to accept responsibility for the war.

This provided the reason for punishing the German people in the peace settlement.

SOURCE D

The Allied governments affirm, and Germany accepts, the responsibility of Germany and her allies for causing all the loss and damage to which the Allied governments and their peoples have been subjected as a result of the war.

The War Guilt Clause.

Reparations

The Allied powers agreed that Germany had to pay for the damage caused by the war. These payments were called reparations (payments). The sum was not fixed in the Treaty of Versailles, but was later set in 1921 at the huge figure of £6600 million. Germany was supposed to pay a certain amount each year – originally for 42 years. (In fact, the amounts were modified during the 1920s and then, in 1930, Germany stopped paying altogether.)

SOURCE E

It is a people's treaty because it achieves the liberation of peoples. Not one foot of territory is demanded by the conquerors. The time has come when the peoples of Europe will not consent to live under masters, but to live under governments that they choose themselves. This is the fundamental principle of this great settlement.

From a speech by President Woodrow Wilson at Pueblo, Colorado, on 25 September 1919. This was part of his campaign to get US support for the Treaty of Versailles. The next day he collapsed through exhaustion.

The League of Nations

The League of Nations was set up to keep international peace in the future. The Covenant (binding agreement) was included at the beginning of each of the peace treaties. It meant that the League was made responsible for maintaining the details of the peace settlement as the central part of its job. (For details on the League of Nations, see pages 18–27.)

QUESTIONS

1. Which terms of the Treaty of Versailles would Clemenceau be happy with? And which would he not be?
2. Would Lloyd George's views be the same?
3. Look at Source E. Do you think that the Treaty of Versailles reflects what Wilson was claiming?

The other treaties – the main territorial changes

Each of the other four defeated countries had a peace settlement imposed on it. The map below shows how Austria-Hungary was broken up.

Austria: The Treaty of St Germain, September 1919

In addition to the territorial losses made at St Germain, Austria was told to pay reparations, and its army was limited in size.

The treaty tried to give each national group self-determination. However, this was impossible, and most of the new states contained minorities who were unhappy being in the 'wrong' country. The new countries were also weak and trying to establish order where often there was economic chaos.

Hungary: The Treaty of Trianon, June 1920

This completed the break-up of the Austro-Hungarian Empire. About 3 million Magyars (Hungarians) were unhappy to be outside the boundaries of the new Hungary. Hungary also had to pay reparations and was limited to a small army.

Bulgaria: The Treaty of Neuilly, November 1919

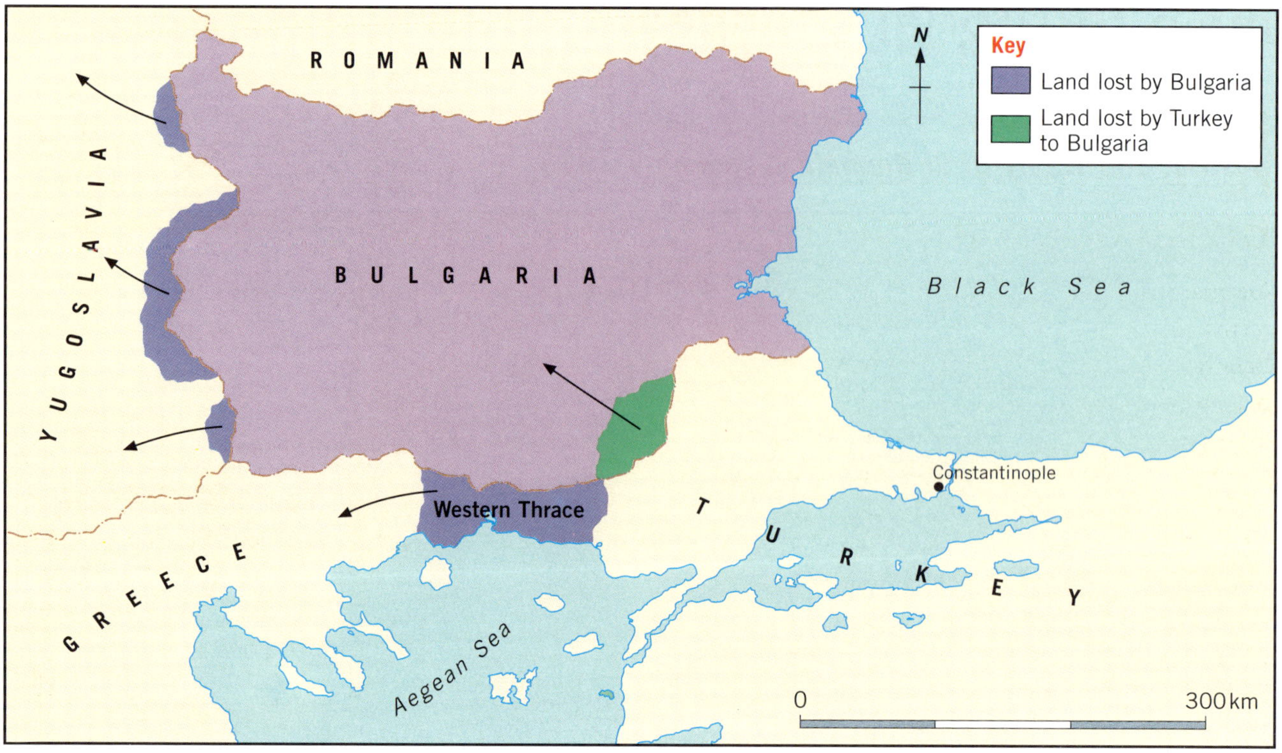

Bulgaria was treated less harshly than the other defeated countries, but it still lost some territory. It was also told to pay reparations and was limited in the size of its army.

Turkey: The Treaty of Sèvres, August 1920 (amended by the Treaty of Lausanne, July 1923)

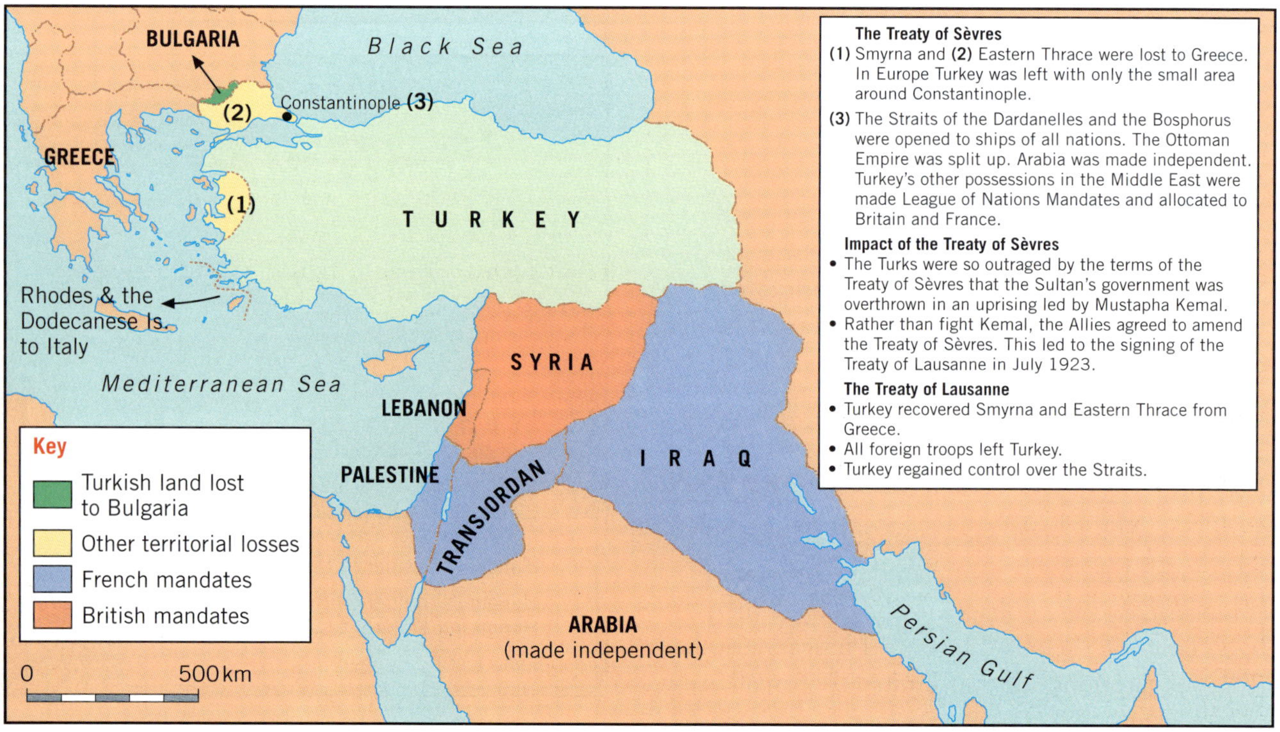

Problems associated with the peace settlement

Reasons for resentment and bitterness in Germany

Germans were horrified when they discovered the terms of the Treaty of Versailles. They did not believe that they had started the war, and saw no reason why they should be blamed. They did not even believe that they had lost the war. The Germans had agreed to an armistice – a cease-fire – but they expected there to be negotiations. Many Germans were outraged when Germany was not even represented at the discussions to sort out a peace settlement. The Allies were blaming Germany for the war, but the person who could be held responsible, Kaiser Wilhelm II, had fled the country, which now had a new democratic government (known as the Weimar Republic). Surely the Allies would want to support this, especially with the possible threat of communism spreading from Russia.

SOURCE A

THE FINISHING TOUCH.

A cartoon from *Punch*, 1919.

November Criminals

Many Germans did not want their new government to sign the peace settlement. They believed that they had been stabbed in the back by the 'November Crimimals' – those who had agreed to the end of the fighting in November 1918. They were happy to believe that their country had been betrayed by cowards or by those whom many thought might be disloyal to the country, such as the Jews.

Land and population

Under the terms of the treaty, Germany was to lose 10 per cent of its land, all its overseas colonies, 12.5 per cent of its population; 16 per cent of its coalfields, and half of its iron and steel industry. The losses in land were made much worse by what Germans saw as the unfair way in which the Fourteen Points were applied to Germany. There were millions of Germans living in other countries. But the way that the principle of self-determination was

applied was always to Germany's disadvantage. The loss of all its colonies was not justified by the Fourteen Points at all; it was all determined by the attitudes of other victorious countries that had empires themselves. It seemed that disarmament was only for defeated countries.

Germans ignored the fact that Austria-Hungary and Turkey were later treated even more harshly. They also overlooked how harshly Germany had treated Russia when it signed a peace treaty at Brest-Litovsk in March 1918.

War guilt

The losses in land and materials were made even worse by the War Guilt Clause. Germans felt that this took away their pride and left them humiliated. This was reflected in a patriotic German newspaper, the *Deutsche Zeitung*, published on the day that the treaty was signed (see Source B). Its front-page comment appeared surrounded by a black mourning band.

SOURCE B

Vengeance! German Nation!

Today in the Hall of Mirrors at Versailles a disgraceful treaty is being signed. Never forget it! On the spot where, in the glorious year of 1871, the German Empire in all its glory began, today German honour is dragged to the grave. Never forget it! There will be vengeance for the shame of 1919.

From the front page of the Deutsche Zeitung, *28 June 1919.*

The situation in Germany

The Allied blockade of German ports had caused serious food shortages in Germany. Many Germans were near starvation. To make the situation worse, an outbreak of so-called Spanish influenza killed over half a million people. All this was happening at a time when the new German government (the Weimar Republic) was trying to establish itself amid riots and there was a risk of full-scale civil war breaking out in Germany. (See Chapter 5 for details.) So it is not surprising that most Germans felt full of despair and ready to blame anyone or any group that seemed a likely scapegoat.

The question of reparations payments

The Treaty of Versailles had stated that Germany was guilty of starting the war and must therefore pay for the damage. The exact amount was to be calculated by a special commission called the Reparations Commission.

The new commission found its task difficult. One problem was calculating the amount. Another was the argument being voiced by some people that Germany could not afford to pay. One of these people was John Maynard Keynes, a famous British economist. He said that if Germany were to be made to pay, its economy would be ruined and this would also have an adverse effect on Britain's economy.

Most people disagreed, especially the French. Germany had not been as badly damaged as France and Belgium. So Germany must pay, otherwise Germany would become strong while they remained weak.

In 1921 the Reparations Commission announced how much Germany had to pay – £6600 million in 42 yearly instalments. The Germans were horrified and claimed that they could not possibly afford this.

Occupation of the Ruhr

In fact, Germany did manage to make a small first payment in 1922, but asked for a two-year delay in making the second one. The French refused this. When Germany failed to make its next payment in 1923, the French decided to take it for themselves by invading the Ruhr Valley, which was the richest part of Germany. This area produced four-fifths of all the country's iron, coal and steel.

The German government replied by ordering workers in the Ruhr to go on strike. As the government had to provide for the people who were not working, and as it had no money to pay them with, it printed more paper money. The result was hyperinflation, and the collapse in value of the German mark. In January 1923 a loaf of bread cost 250 marks. By November 1923 it cost 201,000,000,000 marks.

However, a new German government under Gustav Stresemann worked with the Allies to rescue the situation. A new German currency was introduced, and Germany agreed to make a small payment of reparations.

SOURCE C

A cartoon from the *London Star*, January 1921.

Dawes Commission

An international committee, chaired by an American, Charles Dawes, looked into the question of reparations payments and Germany's ability to pay. In 1924 the Dawes Commission recommended the scaling down of payments to 2500 million marks per year, which were to be paid over a longer period. The USA would provide 800 million gold marks in loans to Germany to help stabilise its currency and develop its industry and trade. In return, Germany would pay the USA a proportion of its industrial output each year. The French agreed to withdraw their troops from the Ruhr.

Over the next five years, 1924–9, Germany began to prosper (see Chapter 5). Resentment and bitterness about the Treaty of Versailles went to the back of most people's minds. In 1929 the Young Plan further reduced the reparations payments to 2000 million marks a year, extending them until 1988. However, payments ceased in 1930. By then the effects of the 1929 Wall Street Crash were being felt fully in Germany. With a catastrophic drop in trade and huge unemployment, Germany suspended payments in 1931. When Hitler became Chancellor of Germany in January 1933, he refused to make any more payments.

QUESTIONS

1. List the terms of the Treaty of Versailles that would be hated by most Germans. Give reasons for your answer.
2. Germans hated the idea of reparations. Why then didn't they just refuse to make the payment in 1922?
3. The USA had decided to stay out of world affairs after 1919. So why should the US government agree to give huge loans to Germany in the 1920s?

The failure of the League of Nations

The League of Nations was formed in 1919–20 as part of the peace treaties. Indeed, the Covenant setting out the aims of the League was included in each of the treaties. The League was the idea of Woodrow Wilson, who had included such a body in his Fourteen Points. It would, he believed, ensure that there was no repeat of the First World War. In fact, almost everyone wanted no repetition. The only question was whether the League of Nations would work. Most people thought (or hoped) that it would, with the USA taking a leading role. Even those who had doubts had nothing else to offer as an alternative.

The powers, membership and peace-keeping role of the League

The Covenant was a set of 26 Articles or laws that all members agreed to follow. These encouraged countries to co-operate in trade and in improving social conditions. They also encouraged nations to disarm. However, the most important Article was Article 10, which said that members of the League would act together to ensure any member threatened with war was protected by the other members. This became known as collective security.

Initially, 42 countries joined – by the 1930s this had become 59. However, defeated countries were not invited to join; nor was Russia because it was communist. This gave the League the appearance of being a club for the victorious countries.

The USA fails to join

Woodrow Wilson confidently expected the USA to join the League of Nations. But many Americans hated the idea. Many had been against US involvement in the war, and they certainly did not want the USA to get entangled in European affairs after 1919. They did not want to be involved in what they saw as petty squabbles in Europe that could cost Americans a lot of money. Also, within the USA there were millions of recent immigrants from many European countries, including Germany and the Austro-Hungarian Empire.

SOURCE A

We have interests of our own in Asia and in the Pacific which we must guard. The less we play the part of umpire in Europe, the better for the United States ... I must think of America first. I love only one flag, and cannot give affection for that mongrel banner invented for a league. The United States is the world's best hope, but if you tie her in the interests and quarrels of other nations, if you tangle her in the intrigues of Europe, you will destroy her power for good.

From a speech made in August 1919 by the US Senator Henry Cabot Lodge, a leading opponent of Woodrow Wilson's arguments.

Woodrow Wilson campaigned vigorously for Congress (the US parliament) to support him. In spite of poor health (leading to a stroke), Wilson toured the country by train and spoke in many cities and towns. However, when the vote was taken, American politicians voted for the USA to be isolated. When Americans voted for their next President to take office in 1921, they voted for a leader, Warren Harding, who promised a return to 'normalcy'. In other words, he promised a policy of isolationism to keep Americans out of European political affairs. This greatly weakened the League of Nations.

THE ASSEMBLY

Every country in the League sent a representative to the Assembly. It could recommend action to the Council and could vote on the budget, admitting new members, and so on.

It met once a year at the League's headquarters, Geneva in Switzerland. Decisions made by the Assembly had to be unanimous – that is, they had to be agreed by all members of the Assembly.

THE COUNCIL

This was a smaller group that met several times a year and for emergencies. It included permanent members. (In 1920 these were Britain, France, Italy and Japan. The fifth was meant to be the USA). It also included non-permanent members, elected by the Assembly for three-year periods.

Each of the permanent members had a veto. That meant that one vote against could stop action being agreed.

If persuasion did not work against a wrongdoer, the Council had powers to act (see page 20).

THE SECRETARIAT

This was like an international civil service. It kept records of meetings and prepared reports. Many of its staff were linguists. English and French were the main languages used.

THE PERMANENT COURT OF INTERNATIONAL JUSTICE

This was intended to help settle disputes peacefully. The Court was based at the Hague in the Netherlands. It was made up of judges from the member countries. However, it had no way of enforcing its rulings.

SPECIAL COMMISSIONS

There were a number of commissions that aimed to tackle major world problems. Some of these were:

MANDATES COMMISSION – set up to make sure that Britain and France were ruling the colonies given to them as mandates in the interests of the peoples of those territories.

INTERNATIONAL LABOUR ORGANISATION (ILO) – aimed to improve the conditions of working people throughout the world. It tried to persuade member countries to adopt its suggestions.

REFUGEES COMMISSION – tried to help refugees return to their own country after the end of the First World War.

HEALTH COMMITTEE – attempted to reduce the problem of dangerous diseases and to educate people about health and sanitation.

SOURCE B

A British cartoon from 1920.

genuinely wanted to avoid conflicts like the one just ended, and they believed that this could be done. Most of the major countries had joined; others would surely do so, and defeated countries would be allowed to enter later on. Better communications by the 1920s (including international flights and the telephone) seemed to make it easier to act when conflict threatened.

Powers of the League

The Covenant of the League set out three ways in which the League could act to settle disputes:

- A hearing by an impartial, neutral country.
- A ruling by the International Court of Justice.
- An inquiry by the Council.

If these did not work, and a country ignored the League's decision, then the League could take action:

- It could put pressure on the guilty country, bringing world opinion against it (moral pressure).
- Members of the League could refuse to trade with the guilty country (economic sanctions).
- The armed forces of member countries could be joined together and used against an aggressor (military force).

Strengths of the League

When the League was set up in 1919–20, there was almost total goodwill towards it from ordinary people and from most governments. People

Weaknesses of the League

Yet the League had a number of weaknesses. The USA's unwillingness to join undermined the League from the start. The organisation of the League relied on goodwill and persuasion; the League had very little real power and did not have a permanent army. In addition, disarmament was still a hope, not a reality. The Disarmament Commission tried, but found it impossible to achieve success. For example, the French regarded disarmament as a threat to their security, while the failure of other nations to disarm enabled the Germans to claim that they had a right to re-arm to protect themselves. There was still a lot of hatred left over from the war. International suspicion and traditional rivalries remained.

It is therefore all too easy to blame the League of Nations for its 'failure' to prevent the Second World War. It is also easy to forget that the League did solve some political disputes in the 1920s. These attracted little attention at the time simply because they were solved. In 1921 there was a dispute between Sweden and Finland over the Aaland Islands. Then, following an incident in 1925 on the border between Bulgaria and Greece, the Greeks reacted by invading Bulgaria. In both cases the League of Nations restored order.

However, the very treaties that created the League of Nations also contained the explosive issues that later destroyed it. In the 1930s, the League proved to be powerless to act against the dictatorships of Japan, Germany and Italy. Goodwill on the part of the League of Nations was not enough in itself to keep the peace.

QUESTIONS

1. Read Source A on page 18. Explain why the arguments used by Henry Cabot Lodge would appeal to many Americans.
2. We know that the League of Nations failed. However, most people in the 1920s thought it had an excellent chance of solving disputes. Explain why.

Japanese expansion into Manchuria and China

Effects of the Wall Street Crash

In the 1920s the world economy was thriving. There was a boom in world trade, centred on the USA. Japan benefited as well as Europe. But in 1929 economic disaster struck. In the USA, in October 1929, there was a spectacular collapse of the New York Stock Exchange (known as the Wall Street Crash), as a result of which millions of people lost their jobs. In the USA, many banks went bankrupt. As confidence disappeared, world trade was very badly affected. Countries put up tariffs (trade barriers) to try to protect their own industries. The USA did this against Japanese goods, and with less trade Japan could not afford to import food. Japanese industrial production and employment fell by 30 per cent between 1929 and 1931.

SOURCE C

A cartoon from the *London Star*, November 1920.

The Japanese army

The depression gave Japan's army leaders the chance to voice their opinions to a sympathetic people. They were not happy with the way Japan was treated by the other powers. Japan had not gained as much as it had hoped in the Paris peace settlement. It also appeared that its government allowed itself to be pushed around by the western world leaders. For example, in the Washington Naval Agreements (1922), Japan had agreed to have only three ships to every five built by Britain and the USA. Now it appeared that the Japanese government was unable to act effectively against the results of the Wall Street Crash. Japanese army leaders believed that the only possible policy to show Japan's strength and solve its economic problems was territorial conquest.

Manchuria

Manchuria was an area over which Japan already had some influence. It was a province of China and had raw materials, such as coal and iron ore, that Japan lacked. China was weak at the time. The last Emperor, aged six, had been overthrown in a revolution in 1911. China had collapsed into chaos as rival warlords divided the huge country between them and created mini-kingdoms.

Japan had already taken advantage of this. The Japanese had an army stationed in southern Manchuria to protect the territory that had been gained from Russia in 1905. The Japanese also owned the South Manchurian Railway. The Japanese military leaders saw this as the perfect opportunity to seize full control of Manchuria, while the Chinese government was in no position to act.

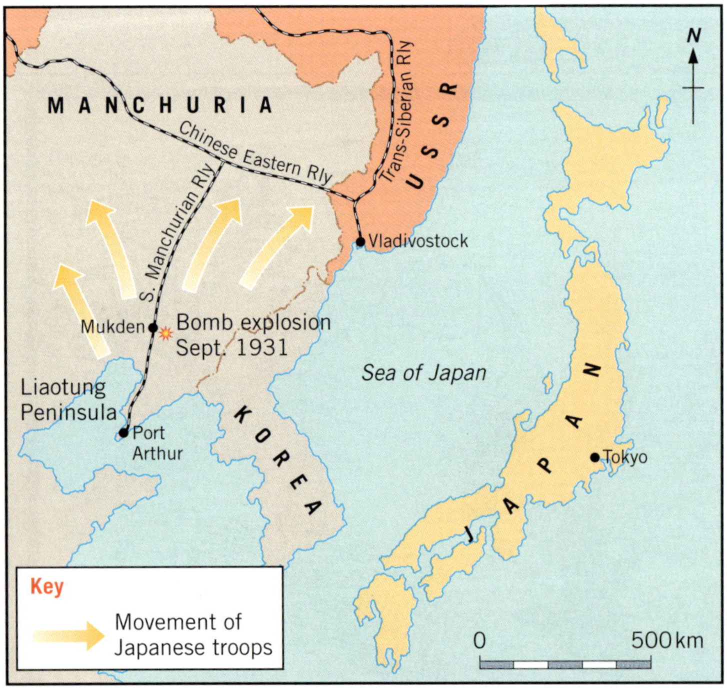

The Japanese invasion of Manchuria.

The Japanese takeover of Manchuria

In September 1931, an explosion occurred on the South Manchurian Railway just outside the city of Mukden. The Japanese claimed that this was sabotage by the Chinese, who wanted to be rid of the Japanese. There was a Chinese army in the area, but the Chinese claimed that all their soldiers were in their barracks at the time. Whatever the truth of the matter, the Japanese turned events to their advantage. They argued that the Chinese had sabotaged the line, which provided an excuse for Japan to take over the area. This was done within months, and the Chinese forces were forced to withdraw.

In February 1932 the Japanese set up a puppet government in Manchuria (that is, a government under the control of the Japanese). The area was renamed Manchukuo and the last Emperor, Pu Yi, was put in control.

The reaction of the League of Nations

China appealed to the League. Japan claimed it was taking control of Manchuria simply because the area was getting out of hand. China had previously agreed that Manchuria should be a Japanese sphere of interest with long-standing economic rights.

The League had to act carefully. There was some truth in Japan's arguments, and Japan was a leading member of the League of Nations with a permanent seat on the Council. On the other hand, it appeared that the Japanese army had used military aggression to get what it wanted. The League told Japan to withdraw its troops from Manchuria. Instead, the Japanese gained firmer control by taking over more territory.

The League decided to set up a Commission of Inquiry under Lord Lytton. It was sent to the area to gather information and produce a report. The slow journey by sea took months, and the report was not published until September 1932 – a full year after the initial incident.

The Lytton Report was thorough, but its conclusion was most definitely in favour of China. Japan had acted unlawfully, and Manchuria should be returned to China. All countries in the League, except Japan, accepted the report. The Japanese response was simple. They ignored the report and left the League in March 1933.

The Japanese invade China

Japan announced the intention to invade more territory. In 1933 it started to invade the Jehol province, and in 1937 it began a major invasion of China. This showed the weakness of the League. Economic sanctions would have been useless, as Japan's main trading partner was the USA, which was not a member of the League. Britain was worried about taking any further measures against Japan, in case British trade in Asia was further harmed. Although people tried to make excuses for the League, nothing could really hide the truth. When an aggressive dictator wanted to invade neighbouring territories, the League was powerless to prevent it.

QUESTIONS

1. Was the League of Nations powerless to act against Japan in Manchuria mainly because the USA was absent from the League?
2. Why do historians consider the Manchurian incident to be so important?

SOURCE D

A cartoon from the *London Evening Standard*, 19 January 1933.

The Italian conquest of Abyssinia

The background

Abyssinia was a poor and undeveloped country in north-east Africa. It was one of very few areas of Africa not under European control, and it was next to the Italian colonies of Eritrea and Somaliland. Italy had tried to conquer Abyssinia in 1896, but the Italians had been beaten at the Battle of Adowa.

Now the Italian dictator Mussolini was keen to avenge that defeat and to gain access to the country's mineral resources and fertile lands. He wanted the glory to be gained from military victory. In spite of the treaty of friendship signed in 1928 between Italy and Abyssinia, it was clear that Mussolini was preparing for war.

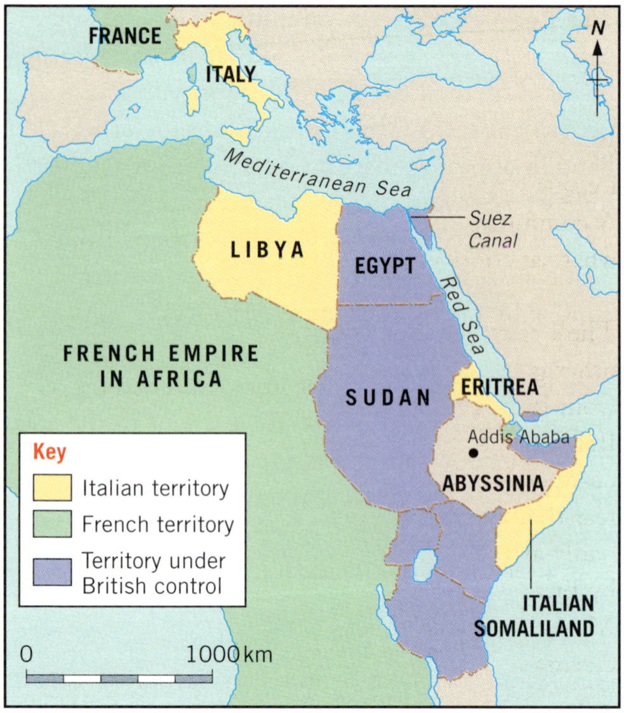

Foreign possessions around Abyssinia, 1935.

Mussolini and the League of Nations, January–October 1935

The League was anxious to avoid a clash with Mussolini. Britain and France believed that he was their best ally against the growing threat of Hitler. They signed the Stresa Pact with him. Meanwhile, Mussolini hoped that Britain and France would allow him to do what he wanted in Abyssinia. The League talked of collective security to protect Abyssinia, but it had little intention of taking decisive action against Mussolini.

Italy attacks Abyssinia, October 1935

In October 1935 the Italians attacked Abyssinia after a clash between Italian and Abyssinian troops at the oasis of Wal-Wal in Abyssinia. The Italians used modern weapons, including tanks, planes and poison gas. The Abyssinian army was mostly infantry and cavalry and was no match for the Italians. The only hope for their Emperor, Haile Selassie, seemed to be in the size of the country, the state of the roads and an appeal to the League of Nations.

SOURCE E

Destruction caused by an Italian bombing raid on Abyssinia in December 1935.

The League's response

There seemed to be no excuse for the League not acting. This was clearly an unprovoked invasion of the weak by the strong. The Covenant of the League laid down what should happen – sanctions. A committee of the League was set up to agree what sanctions to impose.

The League banned the sale of arms and some other goods to Italy, all loans to Italy and imports from Italy. However, it did not ban oil exports to Italy because it feared that the USA would not co-operate. Neither did it ban coal exports for fear that the British mining industry would be badly affected. The Suez Canal, which was owned by Britain and France, was not closed to Mussolini's ships because they were afraid that closing it would provoke a full-scale war with Italy. This decision was important, as the canal was Mussolini's main supply route to Abyssinia.

The Hoare–Laval Pact

Behind the scenes, in December 1935 the British and French foreign ministers, Hoare and Laval, were preparing a plan that they hoped would end the fighting. They proposed to divide up Abyssinia, with Italy getting the best areas for agriculture and minerals, and Abyssinia being limited to the barren mountainous areas. The plan was never presented for discussion. It was leaked to the press and there was an outcry. Hoare and Laval were forced to resign.

This episode showed that British and French politicians were willing to put the interests of their country before that of the League of Nations. This badly damaged the League's reputation.

Mussolini triumphs

Meanwhile the Italians continued their invasion of Abyssinia. In May 1936, Italian troops entered the Abyssinian capital, Addis Ababa, in triumph. Just before this, the Emperor, Haile Selassie, fled the country and travelled to Geneva. He spoke to the League of Nations on 30 June 1936. He protested against the failure of the League of Nations to protect his country from aggression.

SOURCE F

I, Haile Selassie, Emperor of Abyssinia, am here today to claim that justice which is due to my people, and the assistance promised to it eight months ago, when fifty nations asserted that aggression had been committed in violation of international treaties.

Emperor Haile Selassie speaking to the League of Nations, 30 June 1936.

The end of the League of Nations

This was really the end of the League of Nations. The USA was disgusted with the ditherings of the League. In March 1936, Hitler had already sent German troops into the Rhineland in violation of the Treaty of Versailles, and the League had done nothing. In October 1936, Hitler and Mussolini signed an agreement of their own, known as the Rome–Berlin Axis. Nobody took the League seriously after this, even though it existed formally until 1946.

SOURCE G

The real death of the League was in 1935, not 1939 or 1945. One day it was a powerful body imposing sanctions, seemingly more effective than ever before; the next day it was an empty sham, everyone scuttling from it as quickly as possible. Hitler watched.

The historian A. J. P. Taylor, writing in 1966.

SOURCE H

After seeing what happened first in Manchuria and then in Abyssinia, most people drew the conclusion that it was no longer much use placing their hopes in the League.

The historian James Joll, writing in 1976.

The reasons for and the implications of the League's failure

Why did the League fail?

- The organisation of the League contained weaknesses. For example, decisions had to be unanimous, which was impractical. The League met infrequently, and so there were delays.
- Important nations were absent. The USA never joined. Germany did not join until 1926 and left in 1933. Japan left in 1933 and Italy in 1937. The Soviet Union did not join until 1934 and was expelled in 1939 after going to war with Finland.
- Sanctions were not effective, especially without the USA as a member.
- The League did not have a ready army at its disposal. Individual countries were reluctant to commit troops.
- As part of its Covenant, the League had to uphold the peace treaties of 1919–20. These were increasingly seen as unfair and in need of amendment.
- Countries were often reluctant to act unless their own interests were at stake and sometimes even acted against League decisions. For example, rather than proposing sanctions against Mussolini, Britain and France were preparing to carve up Abyssinia.

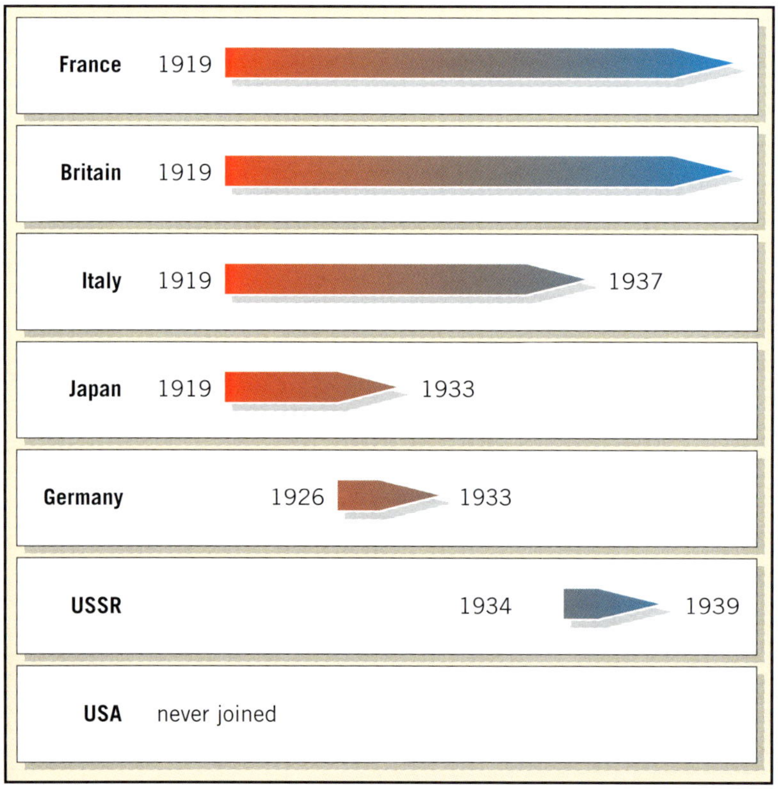

The most powerful members of the League of Nations, 1919–46.

What were the implications of the League's failure?

Violence and aggression were shown to pay. Mussolini and Hitler learnt from Japan's example. Aggressive countries kept the territory gained with no penalties, except for the strongly expressed disapproval of some other countries.

The victims suffered. Manchuria and Abyssinia were occupied by foreign powers and abandoned by the League. Other weak nations came to realise that they could not expect the League to protect them.

Britain and France saw that they could not achieve success against dictators through the League. They tried to pacify Hitler by agreeing to some of his demands (the policy of appeasement), but at the same time a programme of re-armament began.

The Manchurian and Abyssinian crises showed that the League's notion of collective security did not work. The members of the League were not capable of acting firmly in the face of determined aggression. The League lost its credibility as a peace-keeping organisation.

QUESTION

1. Did the League of Nations have any chance of long-term success? Explain your answer carefully.

German actions and expansion, 1933–9

The aims of German foreign policy

Hitler had become Chancellor of Germany in January 1933 (see Chapter 5). He had never kept his aims a secret . They were laid out in his book, Mein Kampf, written in 1924.

He called those Germans who had agreed to end fighting in 1918 'the November Criminals'. He also wanted, like many Germans, to abolish the Treaty of Versailles. Germany had already stopped making reparations payments. Now Hitler wanted other parts of the treaty changed as well.

He wanted to expand German territory and unite all the Germans in Europe into one country. He wanted boundaries changed so that Germans living in other countries could be part of Germany, and he wanted to unite with Austria. Moreover, he wanted to expand German territory in eastern Europe and Russia to create more **Lebensraum** (living space) for the German race. The Germans, of Aryan blood, were believed by the Nazis to be superior to the Slavs of the East, as well as to other races.

He wanted to defeat communism. He loathed its beliefs. He believed that the communists wanted to expand into other countries, with Germany as one of their first objectives. After all, there had been a lot of support for the Communist Party in Germany in the years when the Nazis were gaining support (see Chapter 5).

Violations of the Treaty of Versailles, 1934–8

Re-armament and conscription

Germany had left the League of Nations in 1933. Germany's excuse was that other countries had not disarmed and had kept their armaments at a high level. Germany thought that this was unfair. In fact, Hitler had been increasing the size of Germany's armed forces since he had become Chancellor, thereby reducing unemployment. His aim was an army of 600,000 men and he introduced conscription in 1935 in order to achieve this. New tanks, planes and submarines were built from 1934 onwards, all in defiance of the Treaty of Versailles. German military spending increased from 1 billion marks in 1932 to 13.5 billion marks in 1936.

Other countries had some sympathy with Germany. A strong Germany would be a barrier against the possible threat of the expansion of communism. Also, if Germany was allowed to ignore parts of the Treaty of Versailles, it might help to reduce German resentment at how the country had been treated in 1919.

The Anglo-German Naval Treaty was signed in 1935, allowing Germany to have a navy up to 35 per cent of the size of the British navy. This clearly broke the Treaty of Versailles. Britain had consulted neither France nor Italy before signing this treaty.

Hitler and Mussolini could see that even the victorious countries, such as Britain, were ignoring the League of Nations. In October 1936, Hitler and Mussolini signed a formal alliance called the Rome–Berlin Axis. Britain and France's attempt to keep Mussolini as an ally against Hitler had failed. In November, the Axis was widened with the formation of the Anti-Comintern Pact between Germany and Japan, to protect themselves against communism. Italy joined this pact in 1937.

Reoccupation of the Rhineland, March 1936

In the Treaty of Versailles it was stated that the Rhineland, an area of Germany on the French border, should be demilitarised. This was to make France feel more secure from further attacks by Germany. Hitler argued that, while the Rhineland remained demilitarised, Germany could easily be attacked from the west.

In March 1936 he decided to send troops into the Rhineland. This was a gamble because it might lead to France and Britain invading Germany. But Hitler sent in only a small force, so that it would look less threatening to the French and British. He rightly calculated that they were preoccupied with the Italian invasion of Abyssinia, and that they could say to themselves that Hitler was only putting troops in his own backyard for self-protection. Britain and France protested, but they took no action.

QUESTIONS

1. Why did Hitler choose to send troops into the Rhineland at this time?

2. What would he have learnt from the response of other countries and of the League of Nations?

In fact, Hitler was very nervous when he sent German infantry into the Rhineland, and told his generals to withdraw if there was any opposition. As it was, the Rhineland incident increased Hitler's confidence and led him to consider taking other steps to fulfil his aims.

SOURCE A

More than once, even during the war, I heard Hitler say, 'The 48 hours after the march into the Rhineland were the most nerve-wracking of my life.' He always added, 'If the French had then marched into the Rhineland, we would have had to withdraw with our tails between our legs, for the military resources at our disposal would have been completely inadequate for even moderate resistance.'

From the writings in 1951 of Paul Schmidt, Hitler's interpreter.

SOURCE B

THE GOOSE-STEP.

"GOOSEY GOOSEY GANDER,
WHITHER DOST THOU WANDER?"
"ONLY THROUGH THE RHINELAND—
PRAY EXCUSE MY BLUNDER!"

A British cartoon of 1936 about the remilitarisation of the Rhineland. The 'goose-step' was the style of marching used by the German army.

Austria, March 1938

As early as 1934, Hitler had had ambitions to take over Austria. Austria shared the same language as Germany, and Hitler was born and brought up in Austria. His wish to unite Germany and Austria (*Anschluss*) was well known, even though it was forbidden by the Treaty of Versailles.

There was already a Nazi Party in Austria, and Hitler used this to campaign for union with Germany. However, the Austrian Chancellor, Englebert Dollfuss, was determined to keep his country independent of Germany. In an effort to stop the campaign, he outlawed the Austrian Nazi Party.

In July 1934 the Austrian Nazi Party struck back by assassinating Dollfuss and trying to seize power. But the rising was not successful. At that time, Mussolini had no alliance with Hitler and was suspicious of his actions. Mussolini regarded Austria as an important territory next to northern Italy; he thought he could have influence there. Mussolini sent 100,000 troops to the Austrian frontier in case Hitler decided to invade. Hitler was surprised by this, and was forced to abandon hopes of a takeover at that time.

By early 1938 the situation had changed. Hitler was more sure of his position. He had already achieved successes in the Rhineland and in re-armament. He had also seen the weakness of the League of Nations and its reluctance to support the Treaty of Versailles. More important, Mussolini was now his ally.

Anschluss

The new Austrian Chancellor, Schuschnigg, had appointed Nazis to his government, and Germany had agreed to respect Austria's independence. However, in January 1938 Austrian police raided Nazi headquarters in Vienna and found plans to take over the government. The Nazis were also holding parades and causing chaos by bombing buildings. Schuschnigg was worried about a possible Nazi takeover of Austria.

In February 1938 he met Hitler and agreed to the Nazis having a larger role in his government. Schuschnigg was hoping to satisfy Hitler and prevent the takeover of his government by the Nazis. He also announced that a plebiscite (referendum) would be held for Austrians to decide whether or not they wanted to join with Germany. Hitler was now worried about the consequences if the vote was not favourable to his plans.

Hitler demanded that Schuschnigg should resign and threatened invasion if he did not. As Schuschnigg had no offer of help from Britain and France, he reluctantly agreed. A Nazi supporter, Seyss-Inquart, took over as Chancellor. The next day, 12 March 1938, German Nazi troops crossed over the border. There was no resistance, and many Austrians welcomed them. *Anschluss*, forbidden in the Treaty of Versailles, had been realised. The plebiscite was held and over 99 per cent voted in favour of the union with Germany.

SOURCE C

Herr Hitler returned here yesterday, a conquering hero ... His triumphant welcome was shared by the Army he sent into Austria. Flowers were strewn in the path of their armoured cars. If any Austrians were against him on Friday, they either hid their faces or were completely converted yesterday and today.

Dr Seyss-Inquart told Hitler, 'In spite of a dictated peace treaty, Germans have found their way to each other. Today the entire German people stand united and indivisible. You, my Führer, are the leader of the German nation in its struggle for honour, freedom and right.'

A report from Germany published in The Times *on Monday, 14 March 1938.*

QUESTIONS

1. Why did Hitler take over Austria in March 1938?
2. What would he have learnt from the reactions of other countries to the take-over?

The Sudetenland, September–October 1938

It was clear that Czechoslovakia would be the next country to attract Hitler's attention. It consisted of various different ethnic groups, including 3.5 million Germans living near the German–Czech border. Moreover, its geographical position meant that it was encircled on three sides by Nazi-controlled territory.

Hitler used the German-speaking people of the Sudetenland to stir up trouble. Henlein, the leader of the Nazis in the Sudetenland, demanded the right of Germans in Czechoslovakia to self-determination – that is, to be ruled by Germany. The Czech leader, Eduard Benes, was determined not to give in, and he gained promises of support from Britain, France and the Soviet Union. Hitler knew that taking over the Sudetenland would not be easy.

Neville Chamberlain, the British Prime Minister, was sure that a peaceful solution could be found to the crisis. He met Hitler three times during September 1938.

- At Berchtesgaden on 15 September, Hitler told Chamberlain that the crisis could only be ended by the transfer of the Sudetenland to Germany. After the meeting, Britain and France persuaded the Czechs that areas of the Sudetenland where the German population was more than half should be transferred to Germany.

- At Bad Godesberg on 22 September, Hitler demanded the whole of the Sudetenland by 1 October. In addition, claims by Hungary and Poland on parts of Czech territory must be met. Chamberlain returned to Britain and began preparations for war.

- A third meeting was held at Munich on 29 September, with Chamberlain (Britain), Daladier (France), Mussolini (Italy) and Hitler present. The Soviet Union was not invited; nor were the Czechs. Neither would have agreed to give in to Hitler's demands. At the meeting, the four leaders signed an agreement that allowed Germany to take over the Sudetenland. It was also agreed that the four countries that signed would guarantee the new frontiers of Czechoslovakia. This enabled Britain and France to argue that they had saved Czechoslovakia. The next day Hitler and Chamberlain met and agreed never to go to war with each other. They would settle any further disputes peacefully. It was a copy of this agreement that Chamberlain waved to the cheering crowds on his return to Britain. He claimed it was 'peace for our time'.

The position of Czechoslovakia.

On 1 October 1938, German troops entered the Sudetenland. Crowds of German-speaking Sudetens greeted them as they passed. By 10 October the occupation was complete. The Czechs on their own did not have the power to resist.

What are the verdicts on the Munich Agreement?

SOURCE D

The Sudetenland is the last problem that must be solved and it will be solved. It is the last territorial claim that I have to make in Europe. The aims of our foreign policy are limited. Ten million Germans found themselves beyond the frontiers of the Reich – Germans who wished to return to the Reich as their homeland.

Hitler speaking in Berlin in 1938.

SOURCE E

How horrible, fantastic, incredible it is that we should be digging trenches and trying on gas masks here, because of a quarrel in a far-off country between people of whom we know nothing.

From a radio broadcast by Neville Chamberlain, 22 September 1938.

SOURCE F

Be glad in your hearts. Give thanks to your God. People of Britain, your children are safe.
Your husbands and sons will not march into battle. If we must have a victor, let us choose Chamberlain. For the Prime Minister's conquests are mighty and enduring – millions of happy homes and hearts relieved of their burden.

Daily Express, *30 September 1938.*

SOURCE G

I believe that it is peace for our time ... peace with honour.

Neville Chamberlain speaking about the Munich Agreement in a radio broadcast, 1 October 1938.

SOURCE H

We have suffered a total defeat. I think you will find that in a period of time Czechoslovakia will be engulfed in the Nazi regime. This is only the beginning.

Winston Churchill speaking in the House of Commons in October 1938.

SOURCE I

By repeatedly surrendering to force, Chamberlain has encouraged aggression. Chamberlain's policy has always been based on a fatal misunderstanding of the psychology of dictatorship.

Yorkshire Post, *December 1938.*

SOURCE J

The final settlement forced Czechoslovakia to give Germany 11,000 square miles of territory. Within this area lay all the vast Czech fortifications.

Czechoslovakia's entire system of rail, road, telephone and telegraph communications was disrupted. It lost 66% of its coal, 86% of its chemicals, 80% of its textiles, 70% of its electrical power, and 40% of its timber. A prosperous industrial nation was split up and bankrupted overnight.

An American historian, William Shirer, writing in 1959.

SOURCE K

A cartoon from the *London Evening Standard*, 30 September 1938.

QUESTIONS

1. Using Sources D to J, what arguments are made (a) in favour and (b) against the Munich Agreement?
2. What do you think the cartoonist in Source K was trying to say about the Munich Agreement?
3. Did Hitler get what he wanted in the Munich Agreement simply because he was cunning?

Appeasement and the role of Chamberlain

From 1935 until 1938 Britain followed a policy of appeasement – that is, giving into demands made by Hitler when they were thought to be reasonable. Neville Chamberlain is the man most associated with the policy, although he did not become Prime Minister until 1937. Some historians believe that the British (and the French) should have stood up to Hitler before he became too powerful; the leaders of western Europe should have protected the smaller nations much more from Nazi aggression.

More recently, there have been attempts to defend Chamberlain's policies by explaining why he was forced to act as he did. It is true that, at the time, the policy of appeasement seemed to many people to be right, and in 1938 Chamberlain was considered a hero in Britain for avoiding war.

- Many British and French leaders remembered the horrors of the First World War, in which nearly 1.5 million French and over 900,000 British people had been killed. The French and British governments wished to avoid another similar conflict at almost any cost.
- Many had come to believe that Germany had been treated too harshly in the Treaty of Versailles. Some of the terms were simply unfair. Britain had already agreed to some changes (for example, by the Anglo-German Naval Treaty of 1935) and had not protested about others (such as the takeover of Austria, which could be seen as the Austrians achieving the self-determination denied to them at Versailles). When Hitler had gained his reasonable demands, they believed Germany would become a peaceful nation again.
- Many people in western Europe saw communism as the greatest threat. They thought that a strong Germany would act as a buffer.
- Britain and France were not ready for a war. A programme of re-armament had only started in 1936 and was not planned to be complete until 1940. Giving into Hitler (as at Munich in autumn 1938) allowed Britain and France to be better prepared when the war did start in September 1939.
- The events of the Spanish Civil War, which started in 1936, showed Britain and France how powerful Germany was; and how horrific another world war would be.

SOURCE L

A cartoon from the *London Evening Standard*, 1938.

SOURCE M

German troops entering Prague in March 1939.

The invasion of Czechoslovakia, March 1939

Chamberlain's claim that he had secured 'peace for our time' was soon shown to be misplaced. In March 1939, Hitler ordered his armies to occupy Bohemia and Moravia, two parts of Czechoslovakia that had been protected by the Munich Agreement. Then Slovakia was forced to take its orders from Germany, and Hungary took Ruthenia. Czechoslovakia ceased to exist.

This time the advancing German soldiers were not greeted by cheering crowds. As the soldiers entered the Czech capital, Prague, people lined the streets in silent disbelief. There had been growing hostility between the Czech and Slovak peoples inside Czechoslovakia. But although Hitler claimed he was acting to restore order, it was clear to the rest of the world that this was an invasion. Hitler could not be trusted.

The Munich Agreement of September 1938 had merely given Britain and France six months in order to step up their programme of re-armament. Now it was obvious that Hitler had unlimited ambition, and that Poland was likely to be his next target.

The changing attitudes of Britain, France and the Soviet Union

Chamberlain's government had come to realise that Hitler could not be trusted. In France, there had been a series of weak governments. In 1938 the right-wing Daladier had become Prime Minister, but he was hampered in foreign policy by military leaders who were committed to a defensive strategy based on the Maginot Line, an extensive line of defences on the French–German border.

Hitler had already started speaking in 1938 about the return to Germany of the areas in Poland where German minorities lived. In particular, he wanted the return of the port of Danzig and hated the very existence of the so-called Polish corridor, as it split his country in two. He also wanted Polish territory as *Lebensraum* (living space).

Britain and France decided on a show of strength. On 31 March 1939 they jointly declared that if Poland were threatened, they would come to its support. This guarantee was rash; it would be physically very difficult to help a country in eastern Europe. It would have been wiser if they had first secured an agreement with the Soviet Union about a possible joint defence of Poland. As it was, Britain and France approached the Soviet Union afterwards, and Stalin was suspicious of entering into an agreement that might drag his country into a war for the benefit of western Europe.

Negotiations to form an anti-Nazi alliance dragged on until early August. The Poles were suspicious of Stalin's intentions, and Stalin thought that Britain and France would be happy to see the Soviet Union doing all the fighting if war broke out with Germany.

Although it was clear that Poland would be Hitler's next target, he was worried about the Soviet Union. He could not afford to risk a war on two fronts.

The Nazi–Soviet Pact, August 1939

The world was amazed when, on 23 August 1939, Germany and the Soviet Union signed the Nazi–Soviet Pact. Everyone had thought that fascist Germany and the communist Soviet Union were bitter political enemies. But now the foreign ministers of the two countries, Ribbentrop of Germany and Molotov of the Soviet Union, had reached an agreement. Both countries agreed not to attack each other, and in a series of secret clauses they divided Poland between them. Germany would attack from the west, the Soviet Union from the east.

Hitler was sure that Britain and France would not carry out their promise to defend Poland. They hadn't defended the Sudetenland and, even if they meant to defend Poland, its defeat would be secured before they could act. With the signing of the pact, Hitler no longer had to worry about the Soviet Union's reaction.

Understanding Stalin's support for the Nazi–Soviet Pact is slightly more difficult. He was frustrated by the failure to reach agreement with Britain and France. He had been angry at his omission from the discussions that led to the Munich Agreement. He was suspicious that the western countries were trying to encourage Hitler to attack the Soviet Union while they re-armed. This pact meant that Stalin need not fear an attack from Germany until he had built up his armed forces.

SOURCE N

A Soviet cartoon from 1939. The British (Chamberlain) and the French (Daladier) are directing Hitler away from western Europe and towards the Soviet Union.

Poland, September 1939

Once Hitler had reached agreement with Stalin, Poland's fate was sealed. Chamberlain re-affirmed his support for Poland on 25 August 1939, but this did not deter Hitler. On 1 September 1939, Hitler unleashed his *blitzkrieg* attack on Poland.

He was not deterred when Britain and France issued an ultimatum for Germany to withdraw from Poland. When this ultimatum expired at 11 a.m. on 3 September 1939 Britain and France were at war with Germany.

The Soviet Union invaded eastern Poland on 17 September. Within weeks Poland had been defeated.

SOURCE O

Unless not later than 11 a.m., British summer time, today September 3rd, satisfactory assurances have been given by the German government and have reached His Majesty's Government in London, a state of war will exist between the two countries from that hour.

The ultimatum from the British to the German government.

The role of Hitler

It used to be taken for granted that Hitler caused the Second World War. More recently, historians have begun to consider to what extent he was really responsible.

Of course, Hitler planned for war, although there is a debate about exactly when he became totally committed to war. He always moved one step at a time, and always tried to ensure that he did not face a powerful coalition of enemies.

He also took advantage of Germany's genuine dissatisfactions with the Treaty of Versailles – and the countries of western Europe were willing to admit these. Once the principle of agreeing to changes in the treaty was accepted, Hitler could exploit this and demand the complete overturn of the treaty's details.

Hitler was helped by the weakness of Britain and France, made worse by the consequences of the Wall Street Crash and by their fear of communism. They often saw a strong Germany as their best defence against the spread of communism. Hitler saw that Britain and France had effectively stopped working through the League of Nations, and that this organisation was in practice useless long before 1939.

Hitler was greatly helped by the isolationist policies of the USA. He knew that he could do what he liked in Europe without the USA intervening. The USA did not join the war until December 1941. Hitler was also reassured by his ally Mussolini and by the success of the fascists under General Franco in the Spanish Civil War.

The Second World War started because of Hitler's ambitions; but he was greatly assisted by circumstances.

SOURCE P

This is a sad day for all of us, and to none is it sadder than to me. Everything that I have worked for, everything that I have believed in during my public life, has crashed into ruins.

Chamberlain speaking in the House of Commons, 3 September 1939.

QUESTIONS

1. Why did the signing of the Nazi–Soviet Pact cause such surprise in 1939?
2. How much should Hitler be blamed for the outbreak of the Second World War?

Exam-style questions

These questions follow the pattern of questions set by AQA/SEG for Paper 2 of its current Modern World History syllabus.

1. The peace settlements of 1919–20

Study Source A and then answer **all** parts of Question 1.

Source A: Lloyd George's attitude during the peace negotiations

> Lloyd George means business this week. He will stand no more nonsense either from the French or the Americans. He is taking the long view about the Peace, and insists that it should be one that will not leave bitterness for years to come, and probably lead to another war.

From the diary (March 1919) of Frances Stevenson, Lloyd George's secretary.

Question 1

(a) What does **Source A** suggest about Lloyd George's hopes and fears during the negotiations in the months before the signing of the Treaty of Versailles? *(4 marks)*

(b) Describe the main terms of the Treaty of Versailles. *(8 marks)*

(c) There were four other peace treaties signed in 1919–20, dealing with the other four defeated countries – Austria, Hungary, Bulgaria and Turkey.
Explain how far these four treaties changed territorial boundaries. *(8 marks)*

2. Failures of the League of Nations

Study Source A and then answer **all** parts of Question 2.

Source A: The League of Nations

> Of the fifty-seven states in the League of Nations, half are unfit for membership. They cannot usefully assist in its discussions and cannot take any responsibilities. Having twenty South and Central American republics is not a source of strength. It does not make up for the absence of Japan, Germany and the USA.

From the writings of a British MP in March 1936.

Question 2

(a) In 1931 a crisis in Manchuria started. Describe what happened in the years 1931–3, including how the League of Nations responded. *(8 marks)*

(b) Does **Source A** show that the League of Nations by 1936 had only less powerful countries as members? *(4 marks)*

(c) 'Mussolini was able to succeed in Abyssinia, 1935–6, because the League of Nations was a weak organisation.' Do you agree? Explain your answer. *(8 marks)*

3. German actions and expansion

Study Source A and then answer **all** parts of Question 3.

Source A: Stalin and Hitler after the signing of the Nazi–Soviet Pact, August 1939

A cartoon by Low, published in a London newspaper soon after the signing of the Nazi–Soviet Pact.

Question 3

(a) Did Britain and France follow a policy of appeasement in the 1930s simply out of fear of Hitler? Explain your answer. *(8 marks)*

(b) Describe the events in Europe that led to the Second World War, from the beginning of the Munich Crisis (September 1938) to the beginning of the German invasion of Poland (September 1939). *(8 marks)*

(c) What is the attitude of the cartoonist in **Source A** to the Nazi–Soviet Pact of August 1939? *(4 marks)*

Chapter 2

The USA and the Soviet Union as world superpowers, 1945–63

Introduction

With the ending of the Second World War, the uneasy alliance between the western allies and the Soviet Union began to disintegrate. The old suspicions between capitalists and communists resurfaced. The result of this was the development of a Cold War in Europe between two superpowers, the USA and the Soviet Union. This was gradually to spread worldwide, starting with the Korean War in 1950 and ending with the Cuban Missile Crisis in 1962 when, for a short time, nuclear war seemed very likely. Yet direct fighting never broke out between the superpowers. However, the Cold War was to be characterised by tension, provocation, propaganda and a nuclear arms and space race as each side tried to outdo the other.

The conflict first became obvious with the wide-ranging disagreements at the Yalta and Potsdam Conferences. They were heightened by the Soviet takeover of eastern Europe and by the establishment of the Iron Curtain in 1946. The USA tried to prevent the spread of communism through the Truman Doctrine, by providing aid to Europe through the Marshall Plan and by setting up NATO. It also stood up to Stalin when he tried to force the western powers out of Berlin in 1948. The Soviet Union saw these as examples of interference and reacted by setting up Cominform and the Warsaw Pact. Despite its move away from the policies of Stalin, the Soviet Union clearly demonstrated that it intended to remain in eastern Europe by its response to the revolt in Hungary in 1956 and by the building of the Berlin Wall in 1961.

In 1963 the Cold War was far from over. Indeed, it had been complicated by the emergence of communist China and growing difficulties in Indo-China. Yet at the very moment of greatest tension, the two superpowers chose to stand back from nuclear war and to co-operate. Co-operation would be an increasingly important feature of the Cold War after 1963.

1945 End of Second World War
Yalta and Potsdam Conferences

1946 Winston Churchill's Iron Curtain speech

1947 Truman Doctrine, Marshall Plan formulated

1948 Berlin blockade and airlift

1949 Formation of West Germany
Establishment of NATO

1950 Start of the Korean War

1953 End of the Korean War
Death of Stalin

1955 Warsaw Pact established

1956 The Hungarian Rising

1957 Soviet Union launches Sputnik

1959 Castro seizes power in Cuba

1960 U2 spy plane incident

1961 Building of the Berlin Wall
Bay of Pigs

1962 Cuban Missile Crisis

1963 Nuclear Test Ban Treaty

The beginning of the Cold War

Why did the wartime alliance break down?

From 1941, the Allies – the USA, Britain and the Soviet Union – were united in the common aim of defeating the Axis powers – Germany, Italy and Japan. They achieved this by closely co-operating with and helping each other. By 1945 they had succeeded in their aim, but the war had exhausted Britain economically and militarily, and its role as a leading world power was almost over.

The Allied friendship did not last long. When it became clear that Germany would be defeated, the co-operation between the USA and the Soviet Union began to break down and they started to quarrel. They became very suspicious of each other. Disagreements developed about the best way to win the war and how to keep the peace once the war had ended.

Some historians believe that the co-operation of the war years was not the natural state of affairs. After 1945, the capitalist powers and the communist Soviet Union simply returned to the conflict and mistrust that had characterised their relations earlier in the century.

Main Allied powers	Main Axis powers
USA	Italy
Britain	Germany
Soviet Union	Japan

The alliances of the Second World War.

What was the Cold War?

The increasing tensions that developed between the superpowers created a frosty atmosphere that became known as the 'Cold War'. It started in 1945–6 and lasted for well over 40 years. At first it was confined to Europe, but during the 1950s and 1960s it gradually spread worldwide, as both superpowers tried to bring newly independent states within their own sphere of influence – that is, under their control.

The Cold War had all the characteristics of a war. It had a number of quite clear causes and consequences and there were two sides: the western allies led by the USA in conflict with the Soviet Union and its supporters. Each side tried to extend its influence and win diplomatic victories over the other. Yet there was to be no direct fighting between the superpowers. This is why it was a cold rather than a hot war. The main features of the Cold War are shown in the diagram below.

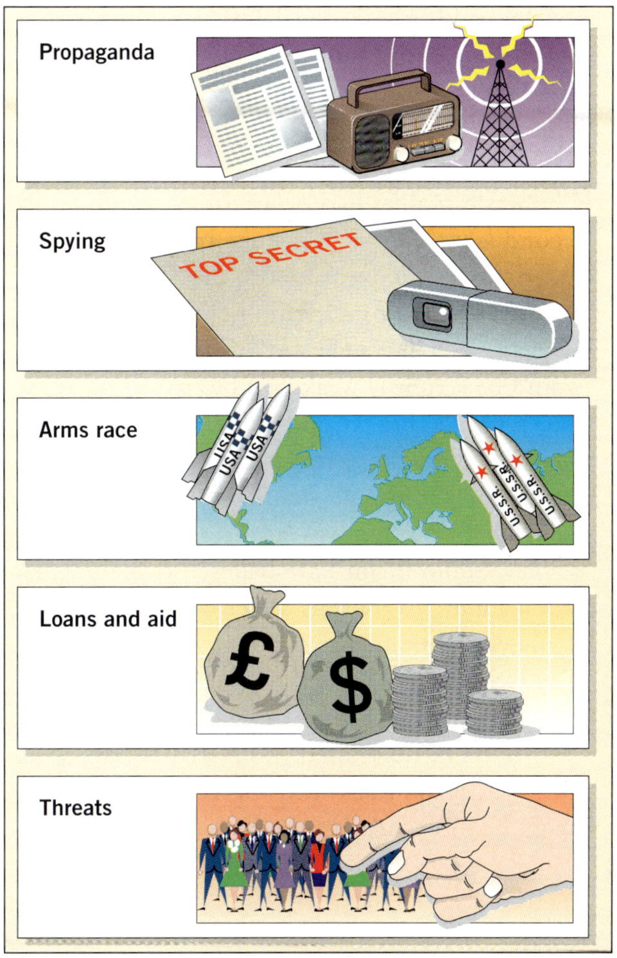

Key characteristics of the Cold War.

Communism versus capitalism

The superpower tensions that were to develop during the Cold War had their origins in the conflicting ideas of communism and capitalism. Stalin, the Soviet leader, believed in communism. This ideology was based on the ideas of Karl Marx, who had suggested that the good of society as a whole should come before individual interests. Marx had denounced the democracies of the West and particularly their belief in capitalism, by which individuals would be encouraged to make a profit. They were the enemies of communism. Stalin saw a threat from the West and feared that the capitalist countries were intent on wiping out communism. He believed that they had already tried to do so in the recent past:

- The West had sent troops to fight the communists in the Russian Civil War in 1918. Stalin also suspected that the western allies had encouraged Hitler in the 1930s by following a policy of appeasement. He had been angered by the western rejection of his offer of alliance with them in 1938.
- Germany had invaded the Soviet Union in 1941.
- The western allies had delayed the opening of a second front until 1944. This was needed in order to take the pressure off the Soviet Union on the Eastern Front. Stalin believed it had been postponed deliberately so that the Soviet Union would be seriously weakened by having to fight the Germans directly and alone.
- The USA had dropped atomic bombs on Japan, but had not informed the Soviet Union of its development. Stalin was suspicious of the USA's secrecy. Stalin might have believed that the USA was planning to use this secret weapon against the Soviet Union.
- The USA was seen as a threat because it was the greatest economic power. In 1945 over half of all the world's manufactured goods were produced in the USA. Stalin feared that this economic power might be turned against the Soviet Union and used to extend western influence. The USA was already promising financial aid to help countries to recover after the war.
- The USA had the world's largest navy and airforce. Stalin saw them as a threat.

Western countries were fearful of communism. They disapproved of the lack of democracy in communist countries. They had fought the Germans for six years to prevent them dominating Europe and did not want to see the Soviet Union take Germany's place. They were concerned by the threat from Soviet expansion and the possible triumph of communism over capitalism. Soviet support for the communist side against the royalists in the Greek Civil War of 1946–9 merely confirmed their suspicions.

SOURCE A

The Soviet government is alarmed by the attitude of the United States government. The American attitude cooled once it became clear that Germany was defeated. It was as though the Americans were saying that the USSR was no longer needed.

Stalin's views on the attitude of the US government in May 1945.

SOURCE B

There is not much comfort in looking into a future where you and the countries you dominate are all drawn on one side and those who rallied to the English-speaking nations are on the other. It is quite obvious that their quarrel would tear the world to pieces.

An extract from a letter from Churchill to Stalin on 29 April 1945.

The Yalta Conference

In early 1945, the western allies were about to cross the river Rhine and invade Germany. Soviet troops were preparing to invade in the east. Both were aware that the war against Germany was nearing its end. In February, therefore, Winston Churchill, the British Prime Minister, Franklin D. Roosevelt, the President of the USA, and Joseph Stalin met at Yalta in the Soviet Union to plan the final stages of the Second World War and to consider what should happen once there was peace.

Decisions reached at Yalta

The Allies were all still fearful of Germany and were therefore prepared to work together. This is why there was considerable agreement at Yalta. The Allies agreed the following:

- Germany would be temporarily divided into four zones of Allied occupation.
- Since Berlin, the German capital, would be in the Soviet zone, it too would be divided up into four Allied sectors.
- Stalin agreed to allow France to have its own zone. The USA agreed that this would be created from part of its zone.
- The Soviet Union should have influence in eastern Europe and would join in the war against Japan within three months of Germany's defeat.
- Stalin promised to allow free elections in those eastern European countries occupied by Soviet forces.
- Plans to set up a United Nations Organisation (UNO) to keep world peace would be completed at a special conference in San Francisco in April 1945.

Only a framework settlement was agreed at Yalta. The details would be added later at another conference to be held at Potsdam.

Disagreement at Yalta

Despite reaching agreements on most issues, the Allies were divided on others. They disagreed over how much Germany was to pay in reparations. Stalin wanted to fix a sum that the West thought was far too large. So the decision was postponed. The greatest source of conflict, however, was Poland. Stalin wanted to set the Polish–German border much further to the west than the western allies wished. His troops had already liberated much of Poland and a communist government had been established in Lublin. Meanwhile a non-communist government in exile already existed in London – the 'London Poles'.

Stalin insisted on the need for a 'friendly' government in Poland, so that his country would have some protection from Germany. The western allies took this to mean a Soviet-dominated government and were not prepared to allow Stalin to get his own way in Poland. They persuaded him to agree that the London Poles would be included in the new Polish government and that free elections would be held as soon as possible. In fact, the London Poles were ignored and Stalin refused to allow democratic elections to take place.

QUESTIONS

1. What do you understand by the term 'Axis powers'?
2. Explain what is meant by the phrase 'Cold War'.
3. Read Source B. What development had Churchill already seen as a problem for the future?
4. Why do you think the wartime co-operation between the Allies was already breaking down in 1945?

The Potsdam Conference

The Allies met again at Potsdam in July 1945. Roosevelt had died suddenly in April, so the USA was represented by Harry S. Truman. He was much less willing to trust the Soviet Union than Roosevelt had been. He believed that the West had been too soft with the Soviet Union. He was highly suspicious of Stalin's intentions for a number of reasons:

- The Red Army was the biggest in the world, but Stalin refused to cut down his armed forces after the war. While there was demobilisation in the west, the Soviet Union continued to expand its armed forces rapidly.
- The Soviet Union was also trying to catch up with the USA by developing its own atomic bomb. The USA had exploded its first nuclear weapon in 1945 and the prospect of the Soviet Union developing nuclear weapons was seen as threatening by Truman.
- The Soviets gained large amounts of territory at the end of the war in Europe, but were not satisfied. The Red Army had liberated the countries of eastern Europe from the Nazis, but then they did not leave. Instead they refused to hold free elections and set up communist satellite states in eastern Europe under Soviet control. These were countries dominated by communist parties that were subject to the control of the Soviet Union. The West saw this expansion as aggressive and dangerous. Stalin argued that a buffer zone of 'friendly' countries was necessary to give the Soviet Union security. In this way, any conflict would be fought in eastern Europe and not on Soviet soil. To Stalin it was purely a defensive move.

SOURCE C

Attlee, Truman and Stalin at the Potsdam Conference in July 1945.

Decisions reached at Potsdam

Churchill attended the early stages of the conference, but Clement Attlee replaced him after the Labour victory in the 1945 general election. Both Roosevelt and Attlee lacked the experience of the men they had replaced and Stalin tried to take advantage of this. However, many of the decisions reached at Yalta were confirmed at Potsdam:

- Germany and Berlin were divided as previously agreed. Each of the four zones of Germany and the four sectors in Berlin was occupied and administered by one of the Allies.
- Germany was to be demilitarised.
- Democracy would be re-established in Germany. Free elections would be held and there would be a free press and freedom of speech.
- Germany was to pay reparations to the Allies to compensate them for their war losses. This compensation would be in the form of equipment and materials. Most of it would go to the Soviet Union, which had suffered particularly badly. The Allies agreed that the Soviet Union should be given a quarter of the industrial goods made in the western zones in return for food and coal from the Soviet zone. Stalin wanted even more severe reparations, but Truman blocked them.
- The Nazi Party was banned. Nazis were removed from important positions and 21 leading Nazis were put on trial for war crimes at Nuremberg in 1946.
- Poland, with Soviet backing, moved its frontier westwards to the rivers Oder and Neisse (see map on page 44). The Poles had lost their eastern territories to the Soviet Union and were compensated with former German lands in the west. The western allies disliked this, but were unable to do anything about it because of the presence of the Soviet troops there.
- The Allies agreed to participate fully in the UNO.

Growing divisions between East and West

Despite these agreements it soon became clear that the divisions between east and west were growing. At first the Allies had agreed that Germany was to be kept weak, but the western allies soon realised that this was an error – a weak Germany would be prey to communist westward expansion. They began to realise that a stronger, reunified Germany would be a buffer against the spread of Soviet influence. So they decided that the German economy should be strengthened. Stalin viewed this with suspicion. He continued to weaken the Soviet zone in Germany by stripping it of all useful equipment and machinery. The West sent industrial goods to the Soviet Union as agreed at Potsdam, but Stalin failed to send back the promised food and coal. This angered the West.

SOURCE D

In order to destroy Germany's war potential, the production of arms, ammunition and weapons of war shall be prohibited.

In organising the German economy, emphasis shall be given to the development of agricultural and peaceful domestic industries.

An extract from the Potsdam Declaration printed in the New York Times on 3 August 1945.

QUESTIONS

1. What actions were agreed upon at the Yalta Conference with regard to Germany?
2. Why did the Polish problem become a focus of dispute at both Yalta and Potsdam?
3. Read Source D. What was decided at Potsdam about the future economic and military strength of Germany?

The division of Germany in 1945.

The division of Berlin into sectors in 1945.

Truman tried to force the Soviet Union to allow free elections in eastern Europe. He wanted to weaken Soviet control in the region. But Stalin refused to allow free elections. He believed that at Yalta and Potsdam, Europe had been divided up into spheres of influence. He expected that Britain and the USA would do as they wished in the west, but the Soviet Union would have a free hand to do as it liked in eastern Europe. He would not submit to US pressure, which he viewed as unwelcome interference.

Potsdam was to be the last of the conferences between the wartime Allied leaders. Divisions about the future of Germany became a major feature of the Cold War. Allied disagreements prevented any form of German peace treaty being made.

The nuclear arms race, 1945–63

After 1945, when it exploded its first atomic bomb, the USA had a huge advantage in the developing Cold War. At first, it was the only country with nuclear weapons, and it could use this to put pressure on the Soviet Union. This situation changed in 1949 when the Soviet Union successfully exploded its own atomic device. Both sides began to develop more powerful atomic weapons and long-range bombers that could deliver them to a target. The USA successfully tested its first hydrogen bomb in 1952, but the Russians exploded their own H bomb just one year later.

The launch of Sputnik in 1957 led to the Soviet development of missiles with atomic warheads that could be fired at targets thousands of kilometres away. These inter-continental ballistic missiles were also developed and stockpiled by the USA. They were land-based and stored in large underground silos.

In 1960, a US nuclear submarine fired its first Polaris missile from beneath the sea. The Soviets soon followed. It was possible to fire a missile that had a range greater than 1500 kilometres from anywhere under the sea.

Other countries also joined the nuclear club. Britain exploded an atomic bomb in 1952 and a hydrogen bomb in 1957. France too was a nuclear power by 1963. So the number of nuclear weapons increased dramatically as each side in the Cold War tried to outdo the other. Although they became more powerful, they were also more easily targeted. By 1960 the superpowers had enough nuclear weapons to kill everyone on the earth (see page 59). The nuclear arms race had become an important and frightening characteristic of Cold War.

The deepening of the Cold War, 1945–53

Soviet expansion into eastern Europe

Having freed much of eastern Europe from the Nazis, the Red Army remained in occupation and the Soviet Union established communist governments that were closely controlled from Moscow. The following countries became satellite states of the Soviet Union:

- Bulgaria
- Romania
- Hungary
- Poland
- Czechoslovakia
- East Germany
- Albania (until 1958)

The same pattern of domination was followed in each country. At first, coalition governments were set up in which the communists shared power with other political parties. Backed by Soviet power, the communists then infiltrated the civil service and took control of the media, security and defence. They then set about discrediting the other parties. Opposition politicians were arrested, or forced to resign or flee. Where elections were held, the results were fixed, or voters were threatened and intimidated into supporting the communists. 'People's democracies' were set up. These were communist dictatorships controlled by Moscow.

Stalin claimed that this action was necessary to give the Soviet Union security. He feared a possible attack from the West, and the satellites would be a useful buffer against such a threat. The West saw it as the blatant extension of communism, planned and carried out by the Soviet Union. Such expansionism was a clear and worrying threat to the capitalist democracies.

SOURCE A

This anti-communist cartoon, published in France, shows Stalin spreading communism throughout eastern Europe after 1945.

Soviet expansion into eastern Europe.

Poland

At the end of the Second World War, Poland had two possible governments. One was the non-communist government in exile in London. The other was the pro-Soviet government set up by the Soviets in Lublin. Representatives from both made up the Polish Government of National Unity in late 1945 and although the communists held just six seats in the coalition, they made sure they controlled security and the media. By January 1947, however, elections saw the return of a totally communist government. The non-communists had been intimidated and many of their supporters imprisoned during the election campaign by pro-communists who were backed by Soviet forces. A Soviet-style dictatorship was set up. Any political opposition was destroyed and only the Catholic Church was able to offer some quiet resistance.

Romania

Romania was occupied by Soviet troops in 1944 and a coalition government dominated by the communists was established. The monarchy was abolished in 1947 after the elections were fixed, and a people's republic was proclaimed under communist control.

Bulgaria

The Red Army forced the Nazis out in 1944 and a communist-dominated coalition government was founded, which abolished the monarchy in 1946. The communists steadily gained total political power.

Hungary

In 1945 free elections were held and the non-communist Smallholders' Party won the most seats. In August 1947 the elections were fixed and the communists won total control. All other political parties were banned.

East Germany

The communists, who firmly followed the Soviet line, ran the new German Democratic Republic established in 1949. All 'pro-fascist' parties were banned and the communists controlled every aspect of people's lives.

Czechoslovakia

A coalition, the National Front, governed until 1948. The communists gained control of the media, the trade unions and security. They used the army to seize control. The elections were fixed to produce an overwhelming victory for the communists. All other political parties were banned and leading members of the opposition were imprisoned. The non-communist President, Benes, was forced to resign and Jan Mazaryk, the popular Foreign Minister, was murdered.

Yugoslavia

The Nazis were removed without the need for any Soviet intervention. This was achieved largely by the communist resistance movement under Marshal Tito. In 1945 he became President of a one-party communist state after the abolition of the monarchy. But Tito refused to be dominated by Moscow and was expelled from the Communist Information Bureau (see page 51) in 1948. When Stalin refused to give Yugoslavia aid, Tito obtained it from the West.

Albania

Enver Hoxha, a communist resistance leader, freed his country from fascist control and set up a communist dictatorship in October 1944. This was done without any help from Stalin. Hoxha's harsh government partly followed the Soviet line and joined the Warsaw Pact (see page 53), but it retained considerable independence from Soviet control.

The Iron Curtain

SOURCE B

Armed East German guards in a watch tower scan the Iron Curtain.

From 1946, Stalin ordered that communist eastern Europe should be sealed off from capitalist western Europe. He wished to keep out capitalist influences that might undermine communism. He believed that western spying and espionage could be more easily controlled, and the growth of US influence could be prevented, by cutting off the countries under his control from the West.

The communists were also concerned by the number of people in eastern Europe trying to flee to the West. If this continued, the economies of eastern Europe would suffer. The construction of a physical barrier would stop this movement to the West.

This was to be achieved by wiring and mining the frontiers. But what started as a simple fence gradually developed into a complex barrier with lookout posts, minefields, armed patrols and tank traps. It stretched for over 1600 kilometres from the north to the south of Europe.

No one could pass without official permission. Road, rail and canal links were controlled by the communists at the border. Cars, trains and boats were all carefully searched before being allowed to proceed. Westerners could not visit the East without permission from the communist authorities. Families on each side of the border remained permanently separated. Sometimes villages, even houses, were literally cut in half.

SOURCE C

> From Stettin in the Baltic to Trieste in the Adriatic, an iron curtain has descended across the continent. Behind that line lie all the capitals of the ancient states of central and eastern Europe – Warsaw, Berlin, Prague, Vienna, Budapest, Bucharest and Sofia. All these famous cities and the populations around them lie in the Soviet sphere and all are subject to a very high and increasing measure of control from Moscow.
>
> *An extract from Churchill's speech at Fulton, Missouri, on 5 March 1946.*

SOURCE D

A cartoon from the *Daily Mail*, March 1946.

QUESTIONS

1. What is the meaning of the following terms:
   a Iron Curtain
   b satellite state?

2. Does Source D provide a fair view of the Iron Curtain?

3. Explain how Yugoslavia became a communist state but not under Soviet control.

SOURCE E

I believe that it must be the policy of the United States to support people who are resisting attempted subjugation by armed minorities or by any outside pressures. I believe that we must help free peoples to work out their own destiny in their own way.

An extract from President Truman's speech on 12 March 1947.

Winston Churchill visited the USA in 1946. It was in a speech given at Westminister College in Fulton, Missouri that he first referred to this barrier as the Iron Curtain. The building of the Iron Curtain was seen as a provocative move by the western powers. It clearly increased tension between East and West and made the Cold War worse.

The Truman Doctrine

Since October 1944 the British government had been sending troops to support the Greek government in its civil war against the communists. But in 1947 it informed Truman that it could no longer afford to do this. So Truman agreed to accept the responsibility by providing $400 million in aid. In March 1947, he made a speech setting out US policy towards governments under threat. He was careful not to refer to the Soviet Union directly, but it was clear that he was not going to allow any further Soviet expansion in Europe.

This statement, known as the Truman Doctrine, in effect said that the USA would support governments trying to resist Soviet influence. It had two main strands: containment and co-existence. Containment was a positive attempt by the USA to prevent any further spread of communism by offering aid to any government under threat. Co-existence was the recognition that the West would have to live with those states that were already communist because any attempt to interfere in the affairs of the Soviet satellites could easily result in war.

With US aid, communism was defeated in Greece. Stalin blamed the Americans for interfering and denounced the Truman Doctrine as anti-communist. Relations in the Cold War deteriorated further.

SOURCE F

An American cartoon depicts the effects of the Truman Doctrine on the Soviet Union.

The Marshall Plan

General George Marshall introduced the European Recovery Programme in June 1947 to offer aid to the countries of Europe to help them recover after the war. $13,150 million were to be made available. All countries in Europe were invited to participate, but Stalin refused to allow the Soviet Union or its satellite states to take part. He believed that it was just a trick to stop the spread of communism into western Europe. He may well have been right because in France, Germany and Italy in particular, the communists were gaining support. Communism prospered in the economic hardship that Europe suffered after the end of the war. To contain communism, therefore, the Americans were willing to offer aid. In this sense, the Marshall Plan can be seen as part of the Truman Doctrine.

There were other reasons for the USA offering aid to Europe. The USA needed to sell its goods to Europe, but this would not be possible until Europe had recovered enough to be able to afford them. So the USA needed to help Europe for what could be seen as selfish economic reasons. Aid to Europe would also make the USA more popular and therefore increase its standing and influence.

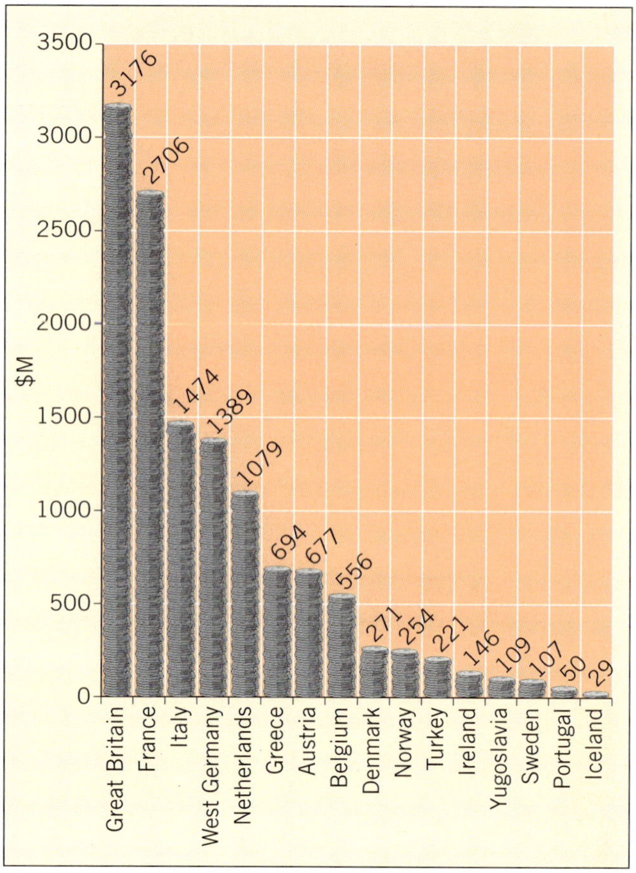

Countries receiving Marshall Aid.

SOURCE G

A West German poster welcomes the Marshall Plan.

Sixteen nations asked the USA for help. These included wartime allies like Britain and former enemies such as West Germany. The aid often arrived in the form of products, such as machinery and fertilisers. Between 1948 and 1950, industrial production in western Europe had increased by 25 per cent. By 1952, most west European economies were on their way to recovery. Industrial unrest in France and Italy came to an end and communist influence decreased.

Stalin was unhappy at this development. He had insisted that the Soviet satellites withdraw their applications for Marshall Aid, so he was forced to offer assistance to them himself. The Molotov Plan was introduced, which established the Council for Mutual Economic Assistance. Comecon, as it became known, was intended to offer Soviet aid to the satellite states, but since the Soviet Union lacked the necessary resources, it was never effective. Stalin saw the Marshall Plan as a crude attempt by the USA to dominate Europe. His fear and suspicion intensified the Cold War and further increased the divisions within Europe.

The Cominform

In 1947 communist leaders from all over the world were summoned to a conference in Warsaw, where the Communist Information Bureau (Cominform) was created. This was designed to spread communism and protect communist states from US aggression. In 1948, Stalin ordered Cominform to expel Tito, the communist leader of Yugoslavia, because he would not give in to Stalin's wishes. This shows that Stalin wanted total control of the communist world and would allow no opposition at all. The USA saw Cominform as a serious challenge to the West. Relations between the superpowers deteriorated further.

QUESTIONS

1. Why did the Soviet Union mistrust the Truman Doctrine?
2. The Marshall Plan set up a fund of $13,150 million for Europe. Why did the USA offer Europe so much aid?
3. Why did Stalin refuse to allow the satellite states to accept Marshall Aid?

The post-war division of Germany

After the Second World War, the growth of tension between the superpowers encouraged the western allies to modify their policy towards Germany. They had initially agreed with the Soviet Union that Germany was a threat and should be kept weak. However, they now saw that the Soviet Union was a greater threat. A weak Germany might be taken over by the communists, but a strong Germany would act as a buffer against communism. In addition, only with a strong German economy could the economic situation in Europe generally improve.

The West now favoured strengthening Germany through industrialisation and reunification. This process had already started with the setting up of Bizonia in January 1947, by which the British and US zones were united to strengthen Germany economically. Reparations payments, which were weakening Germany, would be ended and there would be a speedy return to full democracy. A new German currency, the Deutschmark, would be introduced. The Soviet Union saw this as a betrayal of the earlier agreements at Yalta and Potsdam, whereby the Allies would take decisions about Germany jointly. It had not been consulted and became increasingly suspicious of western motives.

The Berlin Crisis, 1948–9

Specific difficulties arose over Berlin, which became a centre of Cold War conflict. The communists saw Berlin as a capitalist base in eastern Europe. It provided an escape route to the West for people in the East. It was a hotbed of western spies operating in eastern Europe. It could be used as a western forward position for an attack on the satellites. Soviet policy was to remove the West from Berlin as soon as possible, preferably legally and peaceably.

The western view was very different. Berlin was seen as the first line of defence against communism and therefore it had to be protected. It was a strategically important city and its people in the western sectors had already rejected communism in elections. It would be necessary for the western powers to remain in Berlin whatever the cost, and the introduction of the Deutschmark into Berlin and their own zones was an indication that they intended to do so. The Soviet Union saw this as an attempt to unify Germany.

The Berlin blockade

Stalin decided to force the West out of Berlin. This he hoped to do by cutting off communications between the western zones and West Berlin. He intended to starve Berlin, and therefore the West, into submission. Starting in June 1948, railway, road and canal links were all cut. Gas pressure was reduced and electricity cut off.

However, Stalin could not cut off the air corridors to West Berlin without causing a war. So the western powers decided to use their air forces to supply West Berlin by air. They certainly had no intention of handing Berlin over to the Soviets. That would have made a mockery of the Truman Doctrine, which stated that the West would support people trying to resist communism.

SOURCE I

When Berlin falls, western Germany will be next. If we withdraw our position in Berlin, Europe is threatened. Communism will run rampant.

General Clay, the US commander in Berlin, commenting on the dangers of the blockade.

The Berlin airlift

Supplying 2.5 million people by air was an enormous undertaking, as the city would need 4000 tons of food, fuel and other essentials just to keep everyone alive. The largest plane could manage only 11 tons per flight. Over the next eleven months, a flight landed in Berlin from bases in West Germany every 90 seconds. By March 1949, western pilots were bringing in 8000 tons every day. Crisis point was in January when Berlin was down to just one week's supply of coal. Despite Soviet provocation, long delays and the death of 79 pilots in accidents, the airlift continued. Stalin tried to tempt West Berliners with promises of food if they moved to East Berlin, but few took up the offer.

SOURCE H

A *Punch* cartoon from July 1948.

In May 1949, Stalin backed down and called off the blockade. The western powers saw this as a victory. Tensions had run high and the Cold War had worsened, but the West had survived and stood up to Stalin. Within a few days, the western allies announced that their zones would join together to form the Federal German Republic or West Germany. Stalin's response was to turn the Soviet zone into the German Democratic Republic. These moves amounted to the division of Germany and a worsening of relations between the Soviet bloc and the West.

SOURCE J

A painting by a US artist, Bob Lavin, entitled *Approach to Templehof*. Templehof was an airport in West Berlin where US planes delivered supplies.

QUESTIONS

1. Explain the meaning of the following:
   a Cominform
   b Comecon
   c Bizonia.

2. Why did Stalin blockade Berlin in June 1948?

3. a Who is the 'bird watcher' in Source H and what is he considering doing?
   b What did the 'bird watcher' actually do? Why?

NATO and the Warsaw Pact

In 1949 the western allies formed the North Atlantic Treaty Organisation (NATO). The aim of the twelve founder members was to act together to protect democracy and freedom. They would contain communism by encircling the Soviet satellites with a ring of capitalist allies. In 1955 the communists set up the Warsaw Pact. This military alliance of eight nations headed by the Soviet Union was designed to counter the threat from NATO. Clearly these military alliances made the Cold War worse, especially when both sides began to build up their nuclear arsenals and point missiles at each other.

North Atlantic Treaty Organisation			
1949	1952	1955	1982
Belgium	Greece	West Germany	Spain
Britain	Turkey		
Canada			
Denmark			
France			
Iceland			
Italy			
Luxembourg			
Netherlands			
Norway			
Portugal			
USA			

Warsaw Pact
Albania (Expelled 1968)
Bulgaria
Czechoslavakia
East Germany
Hungary
Poland
Romania
USSR

Membership of NATO and the Warsaw Pact.

Soviet and US involvement in Korea

From 1910 to 1945 the Japanese had occupied Korea. Japan was defeated in the Second World War and had to pull out of Korea. Soviet forces in the north and American forces in the south replaced Japanese troops. At this point, both promised to leave once free elections had been held under the control of the United Nations, as had been agreed at the Yalta Conference. However, the Soviets changed their minds and when the UNO tried to organise free elections in the northern part of Korea, they would not allow UNO officials entry.

Instead, a communist satellite was established under Kim Il Sung in the North Korean capital, Pyongyang. Free elections were never held. In South Korea, elections were held and an anti-communist, military government was set up under Syngman Rhee, based in the South Korean capital of Seoul.

Korea is divided

It had proved impossible to unite the country. The setting up of separate governments after the 1948 elections encouraged the USA and Soviet Union to withdraw their troops. So Korea became permanently divided along the 38 °N parallel. It still remains divided today. Each side claimed to be the rightful government of all Korea. Frequent border clashes occurred along the demilitarised zone into 1950.

In 1949, all of China except Taiwan became communist. South Korea felt very isolated because communist North Korea, China and the Soviet Union surrounded it. The Americans were frightened of the spread of communism and the threat to Japan and other non-communist counties in the Far East. They believed in the so-called domino theory that once one state became communist, others would also fall.

Stalin and the Chinese encouraged Kim Il Sung to attack South Korea. They saw a perfect opportunity to spread communist influence by taking over South Korea. They provided aid and military equipment, but the Soviets never involved themselves directly. In June 1950, North Korea attacked the South and the Korean War began.

The Korean War

North Korea was very successful at first. Most of South Korea fell, except the Pusan Pocket in the south-east. In desperation, South Korea asked the UNO for help. It had the power to support South Korea if all the permanent members of its Security Council – Britain, France, the USA, nationalist China (the West failed to recognise the communist government in mainland China) and the Soviet Union – agreed to do so. Normally the Soviet Union would have vetoed any attempts to send aid, but in 1950 it was boycotting UNO meetings in protest at the refusal to admit communist China. So the Security Council declared North Korea to be the aggressor and promised to send help to the South.

Sixteen nations, headed by the USA, took part immediately and later 32 countries participated. The commander-in-chief was the American war hero, General Douglas MacArthur. He organised a successful seaborne landing at Inchon that surprised the communists and forced them to retreat. North Korean resistance collapsed and UN troops advanced into North Korea and approached China.

Communist China feared for its security and warned UN troops not to approach the Yalu River. MacArthur disobeyed Truman's orders and did so. He wished to invade China and was prepared to use nuclear weapons. Truman dismissed him in April 1951 and appointed General Ridgeway as his replacement. Meanwhile, in November 1950, China sent 200,000 'volunteers' to help North Korea, and UN forces were pushed back to the 38 °N parallel.

The rest of the war was a stalemate in which neither side made gains and many lives were lost. Finally, both sides agreed on a cease-fire at Panmunjom in 1953. Stalin had died and the Soviets now had their own internal problems to deal with. They wanted the war to end as quickly as possible.

SOURCE K

General MacArthur.

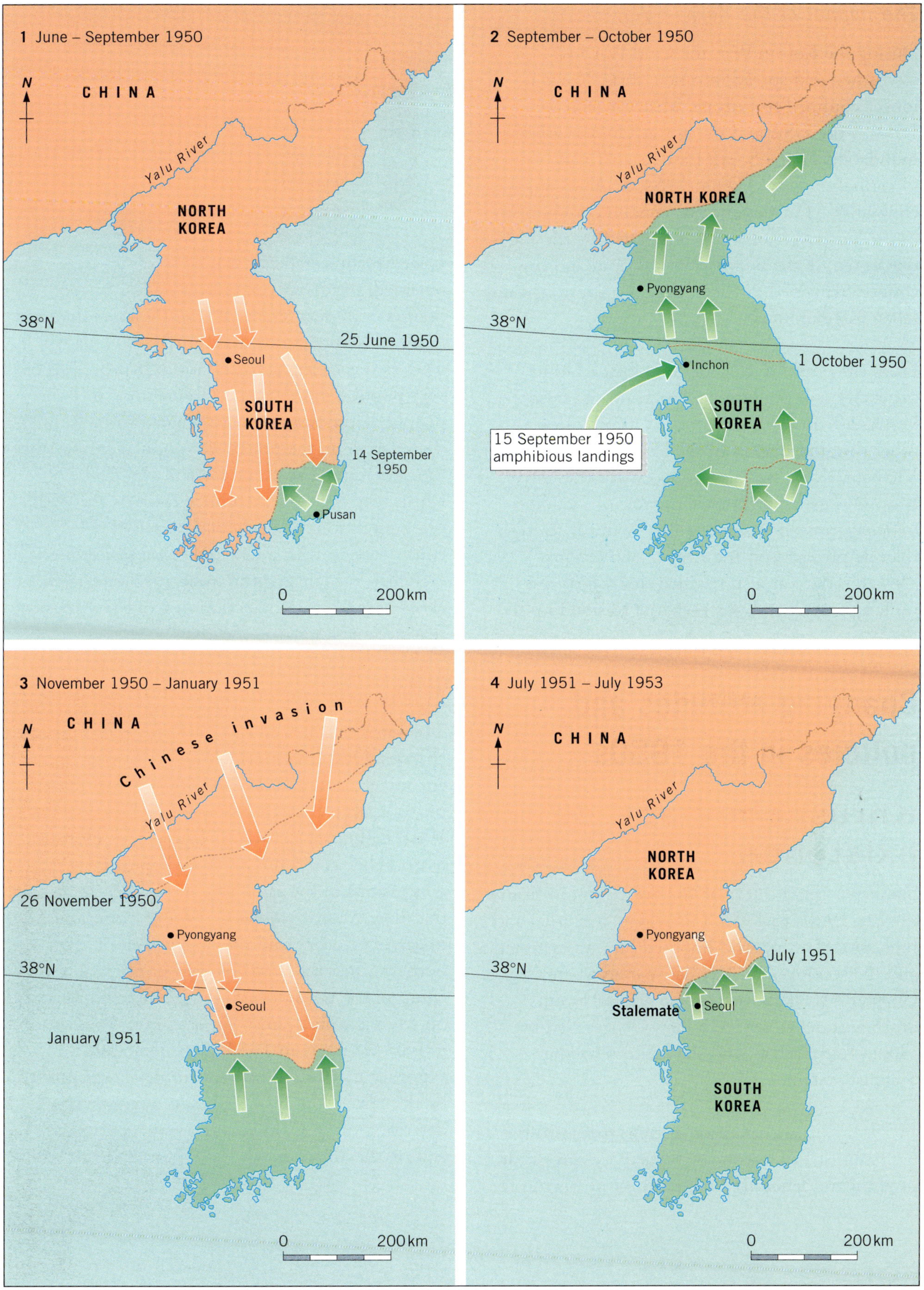

The Korean War, 1950–3.

The impact of the Korean War

During the Korean War, the Cold War had intensified and spread into new areas. It was no longer confined to Europe. Mistrust increased between the USA and the Soviet Union with the foundation of the South East Asian Treaty Organisation (SEATO) in 1954. SEATO was a copy of NATO, designed to contain communism in the Far East. Korea was devastated by the war – one in ten of the population was dead and the country remained divided – but the South had not fallen to communism.

From the point of view of the USA, a bid to break through the Truman Doctrine had been beaten off, and the USA turned its attention to other threatened areas in the Far East, particularly Vietnam. Korea was also a success for the UNO because it had shown itself capable of standing up to aggression and seemed to be much stronger than its predecessor, the League of Nations. However, the war also revealed that China was no longer weak and was prepared to stand up to the West.

QUESTIONS

1. Why did the UNO become involved in Korea?
2. What were the consequences of the Korean War?

Changing attitudes and policies in the 1950s

Khrushchev and co-existence

Stalin was the dictator of the Soviet Union from the late 1920s to 1953. His regime was cruel and repressive. Anyone who opposed him was arrested, and the secret police were active everywhere (see Chapter 4). The Soviet people greeted Stalin's death with relief. In 1955 he was succeeded by Nikita Khrushchev, who started to relax the Stalinist system.

In 1956 Khrushchev made a secret speech to the Communist Party at its 20th Party Congress. He used this to denounce Stalin as part of his bid for power. Stalin's statues came down, cities were renamed, the secret police became less active, Stalin's body was removed from the Kremlin and more consumer goods were produced. This whole process was called destalinisation. It proved to be very popular in the Soviet Union, and since the people of the Soviet Union seemed to be gaining more freedom, the policy was popular in the West too. The capitalist states particularly liked Khrushchev's change of policy towards the West. He wanted to replace the old policy of confrontation with a new policy of peaceful co-existence, recognising the western powers' right to exist. This led to a reduction in Cold War tensions that became known as the 'thaw'.

Raised expectations in eastern Europe

The satellite states of eastern Europe also expected changes. Destalinisation within the Soviet Union encouraged them to demand concessions and to try to weaken Soviet influence. But they, like the West, had misunderstood Khrushchev's motives. Khrushchev could not grant widespread concessions in the satellite states because he feared that they could result in the end of communism in eastern Europe and the destruction of the buffer against the West. He was not prepared to compromise the security of the Soviet Union. So when revolts against Soviet control took place in East Germany in 1953 and Poland and Hungary in 1956, they were ruthlessly suppressed by the Soviet Union. This led to a renewed deterioration in Cold War relationships and the end of the 'thaw'.

Challenging the West

It soon became clear to the capitalist states that, despite co-existence, Khrushchev was determined to show that communism could compete with, and beat, the West. This was demonstrated in a number of differing areas:

- The Soviet Union set out to challenge the domination of the USA in sport. The Olympic games became particularly important.
- Khrushchev undertook high-profile visits across the globe to meet foreign leaders and offered aid to newly independent Third World states. In this way, he deliberately raised the political profile of the Soviet Union.
- The Soviet Union challenged the West's lead in nuclear weapons. It exploded its first atomic bomb in 1949, four years behind the Americans. It exploded its first hydrogen bomb less than a year after the Americans had done so. The nuclear race that developed clearly increased tensions and aggravated the Cold War situation.
- Khrushchev engaged in a space race with the USA in order to demonstrate technological superiority. The Soviets launched the first satellite, Sputnik, in 1957. In the same year they put a dog into space, and in 1961 they put the first man into orbit. They took an early lead in the space race (see page 60).

The Hungarian Rising, 1956

The Hungarians were inspired by the death of Stalin and by the emergence of Khrushchev. They believed that destalinisation and the 'thaw' had created a new atmosphere in which the country could undergo reform. The revolt in Poland in June 1956 had resulted in the Soviet Union granting concessions to the Poles, and this seemed to be confirmation that changes could be achieved. The Hungarians wanted an end to Soviet control in Hungary. This would lead to more political freedom and economic improvement through greater contact with the West. Some even hoped for the withdrawal of Soviet troops from Hungary.

SOURCE A

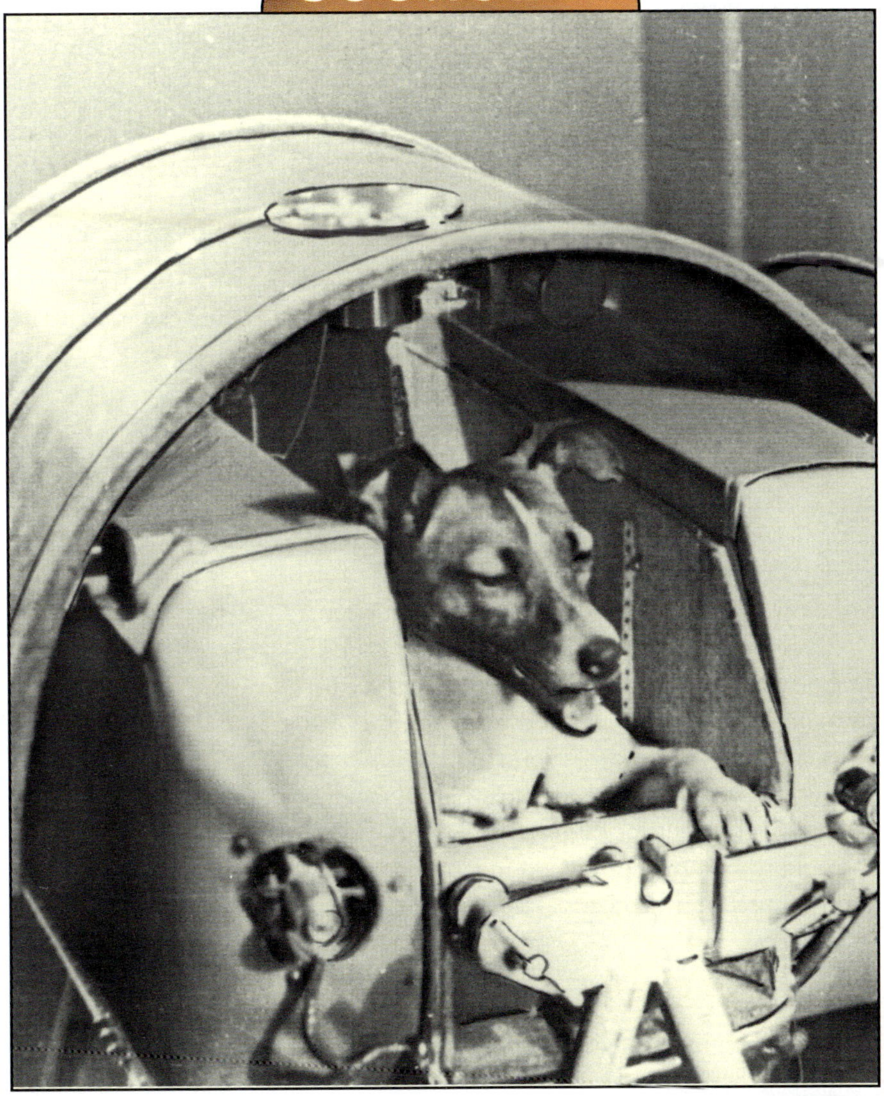

Laika, the first dog in space.

SOURCE B

A photograph taken in Budapest in November 1956.

Reform in Hungary

Demonstrations and protests in the capital of Hungary, Budapest, led to the election of Imre Nagy as Prime Minister in October 1956. He had been Prime Minister from 1953 to 1955 and was known to be a moderniser. In the demonstrations, the Soviet Union was caught off guard by the strength of opposition and retreated. However, its retreat was not a defeat but a tactical move to regroup and strengthen its forces. Khrushchev also hoped that the withdrawal would calm down a difficult situation.

The new Hungarian leadership began to implement a programme of reform. Government control of the press and radio was ended. Non-communists were allowed to participate in government and Nagy demanded the right for Hungary to leave the Warsaw Pact and to become neutral and independent. He also promised free democratic elections.

The rising is crushed

These developments were completely unacceptable to Khrushchev. On 4 November 1956, the Soviets returned in strength and crushed the revolt. In the bitter fighting that followed, 30,000 Hungarians were killed and 200,000 fled to the West.

Nagy took refuge in the Yugoslavian embassy. He emerged later when promised safe passage, but was arrested and later executed. Protesters were imprisoned and the reform programme was reversed. A hard-line communist government was re-established in Hungary under Janos Kadar.

SOURCE C

There is no stopping the wild onslaught of communism. Your turn will come, once we perish. Save our souls! Save our souls! We implore you to help us in the name of justice and freedom.

A broadcast to the West from Hungarian fighters on 4 November 1956.

The West ignored the pleas for help from Hungary. The British and French were too heavily involved in the Suez Crisis in Egypt and the Americans had no wish to get involved in a conflict that could result in a nuclear war.

The 'thaw' was now clearly over. Khrushchev was not prepared to allow change to threaten the Soviet Union's own security. The optimism of 1953–4 had started to disappear when it became clear that Khrushchev was intent on taking on, and beating, the USA at its own game. The Cold War was again starting to hot up.

QUESTIONS

1. What was destalinisation?
2. How similar were the policies of Stalin and Khrushchev towards the satellite states?
3. Why was the Hungarian Rising so easily put down in November 1956?
4. Does Source C throw any light on the Hungarian Rising?

The beginnings of the space race, 1957–62

The launch of the satellite Sputnik in 1957 upset US pride and was the start of a race that was to continue well into the 1980s. The rocket that blasted Sputnik into space was a more immediate threat. A rocket powerful enough to do this could also carry a nuclear weapon to its target. Advances in space technology therefore encouraged the development of nuclear missiles, particularly inter-continental ballistic missiles (ICBMs), by both sides. By 1960, each had enough nuclear missiles to destroy the Earth. This balance of terror stabilised the Cold War because both superpowers realised that a nuclear war would be mutually destructive. The policy of peaceful co-existence came to be increasingly important in the politics of the Cold War.

At the end of the 1950s, Khrushchev could argue that the Soviet lead in space proved that communism could outdo capitalism. However, the vast amount of money spent on the space race would later lead to superpower scientific co-operation in space. Money spent on both the space race and the arms race would also help to put so much strain on the Soviet economy that the country faced bankruptcy in the 1980s.

SOURCE D

The Sputniks prove that communism has won the competition between the communist and the capitalist countries. The economy, science, culture and the creative genius of people in all spheres of life develop better and faster under communism.

Khrushchev comments on the successes of communism.

QUESTIONS

1. Why did the Soviet Union take part in the space race against the USA?
2. 'Source D is of no use because it is just exaggerated opinion.' Do you agree?

Date	Country	Event
4 October 1957	Soviet Union	Sputnik 1 first artificial Earth-orbiting satellite
3 November 1957	Soviet Union	Sputnik 2 first animal in space, a dog called Laika
31 January 1958	USA	First US satellite in space
12 September 1959	Soviet Union	Luna 2 hits the surface of the Moon
4 October 1959	Soviet Union	Luna 3 takes pictures of the far side of the Moon
12 April 1961	Soviet Union	First man, Yuri Gagarin, put into orbit in Vostock 1
5 May 1961	USA	Alan Shepherd becomes first American in space
20 February 1962	USA	Colonel John Glenn becomes the first American to orbit the Earth
16 June 1963	Soviet Union	Valentina Tereshkova becomes the first woman in space

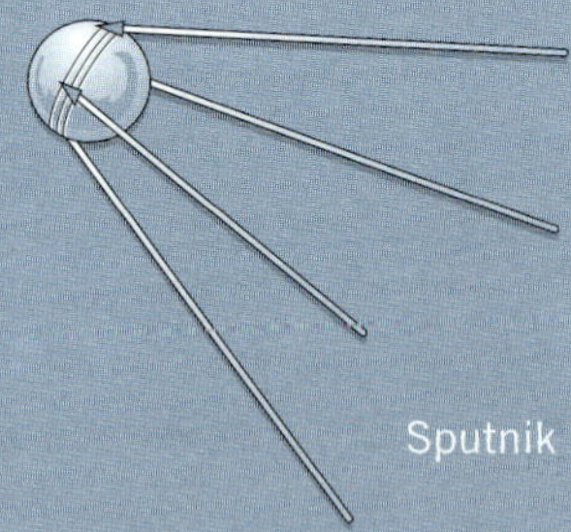

Sputnik 1

Luna 3

Key events in the space race, 1957–63.

Crises in the early 1960s and their causes and results

The U2 Crisis

Although the West had hoped that the succession of Khrushchev to power in the Soviet Union might lead to better relations with the West, events in Hungary in 1956 had shown that the Cold War was still very much in operation. In 1960 that Cold War intensified.

The year had begun with great hope. A summit meeting of the 'Big Four', Eisenhower of the USA, Khrushchev of the Soviet Union, De Gaulle of France and Macmillan of Britain, had been arranged for Paris in May. Perhaps the time had come for East and West to patch up their differences and begin a new period of friendly relations? Yet before the leaders even arrived in Paris, those hopes had been dashed.

The 'Spy in the Sky'

By the 1950s the Americans had developed a lightweight spy plane that could fly at 75,000 feet. This meant that even if it was picked up on Soviet radar it was too high for Soviet planes to intercept. Hi-tech cameras meant that even at that height it could take pictures of military sites in the Soviet Union.

On 1 May 1960, just two days before the summit conference, a U2 plane, piloted by Gary Powers, took off from a US base in Peshawar, Pakistan. The flight went well and Powers was able to take photographs deep inside the Soviet Union. Then came disaster. As Powers crossed the Ural mountains near the Soviet town of Sverdlovsk, his plane was hit by a Soviet SAM-2 missile. Powers ejected from the plane and parachuted to the ground, where he was captured by the Soviet forces. The U2 crashed near Sverdlovsk and was recovered by Soviet scientists for study.

The intended route of Powers' U2.

The American response

As soon as the Americans discovered that the spy plane had been shot down, they began an elaborate campaign to cover up what had happened. If they admitted to spying on the Soviet Union, the summit talks would be ruined. At first the Americans announced that a U2 research plane studying weather conditions at high altitude had disappeared somewhere over Turkey.

What the Americans did not know was that the Soviet Union had captured Powers alive and that he had admitted to spying. They also had the remains of the U2 with thousands of photographs. The Americans had been caught spying and there seemed no way it could be denied. On 7 May Khrushchev announced that he had both Powers and the U2. He demanded a full apology from the USA.

The end of hopes for peace

Khrushchev accused the USA of being 'unable to call a halt to their war effort', but offered to attend the summit meeting as long as the Americans apologised. Eisenhower refused to apologise and said that it was the responsibility of the USA to protect itself from the possibility of a surprise attack. The U2 flights were an important part of US defence strategy. Not surprisingly, Khrushchev was not satisfied with this answer and stormed out of the summit meeting. He then cancelled an invitation for Eisenhower to visit the Soviet Union. The Cold War had just got colder.

SOURCE A

A cartoon from a British newspaper in 1960.

SOURCE B

Instructions to Mr Powers and other pilots on similar missions is to feel free to tell the full truth about their mission. We think this is a firmly American way of behaviour – we can leave the bald-faced lying to the Soviets. We have to do this work, but we can be manly about it.

An extract from the Washington Daily News *after Gary Powers' release from the Soviet Union.*

Postscript: Gary Powers

Powers was tried in Moscow on charges of spying. He was found guilty and sentenced to ten years imprisonment. After serving seventeen months of his sentence he was sent back to the USA in return for the release of a top Soviet spy from a US prison.

QUESTIONS

1. Why do you think the Americans sent U2 planes across Soviet air space?
2. Why did the Americans feel the need to pretend that Powers' plane was lost whilst researching weather conditions?
3. What do you think the cartoonist was trying to say in Source A?
4. What does Source B tell us about attitudes towards the Cold War in the USA in the 1960s?

The building of the Berlin Wall, 1961

The Iron Curtain was an attempt to prevent western ideas from entering communist eastern Europe and to stop people escaping to the West, but there was a hole in the Iron Curtain. This hole was in Berlin. There was freedom of movement between East and West Berlin, and many East Germans decided that life was better in the West. So between 1945 and 1960, people moved to the West at an average rate of about 500 each day. Most were well-qualified, young people and this had a bad effect on the East German economy. It was also embarrassing for the communist governments of eastern Europe because people were voting with their feet against communism.

SOURCE C

The Berlin Wall.

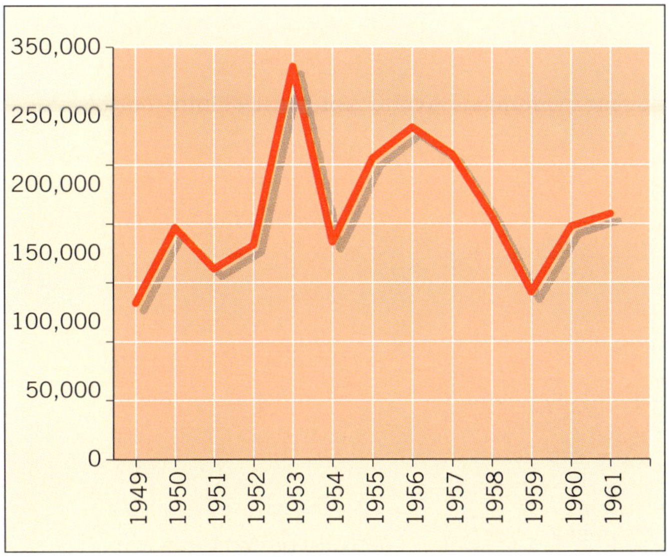

Refugees from East to West Berlin, 1949–61.

On 13 August 1961, the communists began to build a 160-kilometre barrier around West Berlin. At first, it was just a simple wall and barbed wire, but it soon became very complicated. It completely sealed off West Berlin from East Germany. Fewer people tried to escape. Many of those who did were killed in the attempt. Between 1961 and 1989, 86 people are known to have died attempting to cross the Berlin Wall.

SOURCE D

In no part of the world are so many spies of foreign states to be found as in West Berlin. Nowhere else can they act with such freedom. These spies are smuggling agents into East Germany, causing sabotage and riot.

The view of the East German government, 1961.

Propaganda

Relations between the superpowers, already strained by the U2 spying incident, got much worse. The Americans used the Berlin Wall for propaganda purposes, asking why, if communism was such an ideal system, it was necessary to build a barrier to cage people in. In 1963, President Kennedy visited West Berlin. The people turned out to hear him and applauded him warmly when, in his speech to them, he said, 'Ich bin ein Berliner' (I am a Berliner). He was using the opportunity to show the USA's commitment to the people of West Berlin by suggesting that the USA would never desert the city. This angered the communists, who saw the visit as a deliberate attempt to cause trouble.

SOURCE E

Democracy may not be perfect but we never had to put up walls to keep our people in.

The view of John F. Kennedy, 1962.

QUESTIONS

1. Look at Source D. Why was the Berlin Wall necessary, according to the communists?
2. Do you accept the viewpoint of the communists in Source D?
3. Why did J. F. Kennedy say 'I am a Berliner' in his speech of 1963 when in fact he was American?
4. What impact did the building of the Berlin Wall have on the Cold War?

The Cuban Missile Crisis

The background

Cuba, a large island in the Caribbean Sea, is part of the West Indies. Its capital city is Havana and the nearest important island to it is Jamaica. Cuba's main industries are concerned with agriculture. It produces both tobacco and sugar cane for export. The USA is only 150 kilometres away, the state of Florida being the nearest point.

Cuba was discovered by the Spanish in the fifteenth century and became a Spanish colony. It was freed from Spanish control, with the help of the USA, after the Spanish–American War of 1898. From then, Cuba was dominated by the USA, which provided aid and bought Cuban goods.

The government of Batista

During the 1950s, the Cuban government was very corrupt. Its leader was Fulgencio Batista, who had taken power in 1934 with US backing. He misused US aid by spending it on his family and friends, and he finally bankrupted his country, but the Americans would not criticise him because he was a strong supporter of the USA. He used his secret police to destroy any opposition. A reign of terror dealt with people who got in his way.

A few young men were prepared to stand up to Batista, but they had to flee inland to the mountains and jungle. They were led by Fidel Castro, who promised the people reform and gained considerable support. Batista was unable to destroy this guerrilla group which, in January 1959, overthrew him and took over the government of Cuba.

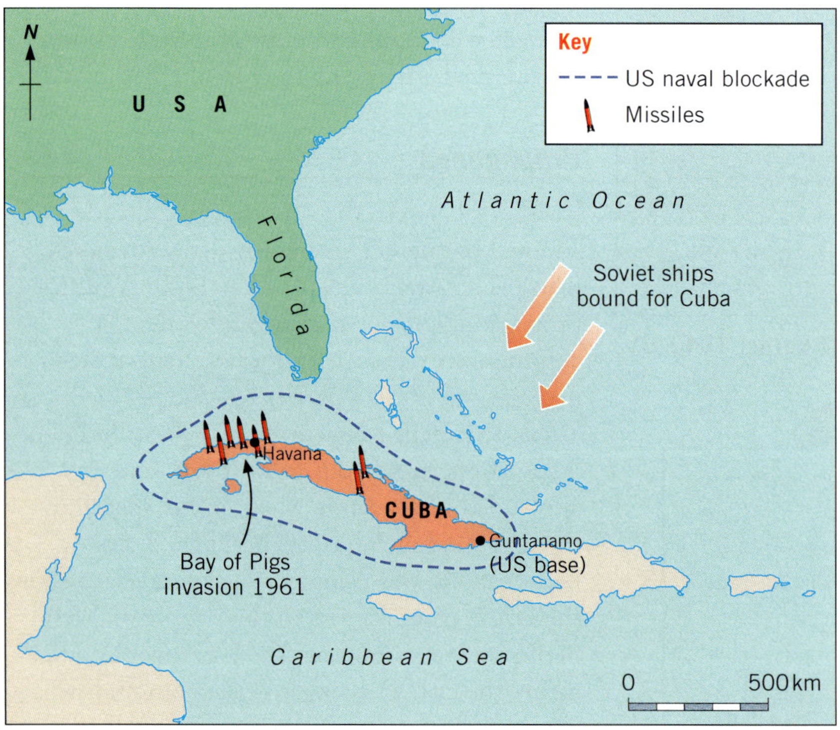

Cuba.

The communist government of Cuba

Following the rebellion, Castro became Cuban President and his government seemed to be very pro-communist. The USA disliked having what appeared to be a communist government so close because it feared that communism could spread to other Central and South American countries. The US government wanted to destroy the new Cuban government so that communism in the region could be contained. Eisenhower therefore allowed supporters of Batista to train for an invasion of Cuba, and the US Central Intelligence Agency (CIA) was encouraged to try to get rid of Castro.

The USA cut off aid to Cuba in the hope that Castro would be overthrown. It no longer bought Cuba's sugar and tobacco. Castro retaliated by approaching the communist states of eastern Europe for help. They offered aid and bought the sugar and tobacco. He went further by taking all industries and businesses in Cuba under state control. Most of these had been owned by the Americans, who reacted angrily.

The Bay of Pigs invasion

In April 1961, President Kennedy allowed 1400 Batista supporters to invade Cuba. So as not to arouse world anger, this force set off from US bases in Guatemala rather than from the USA. It failed to gain any local support and was ruthlessly destroyed by Castro as it landed in the Bay of Pigs. Castro now realised that the USA would not rest until he had been destroyed. He felt vulnerable and sought military aid from the Soviet Union.

Khrushchev was determined to exploit the USA's difficulties. The Soviet Union responded to Castro's requests by sending inter-continental missiles secretly to Castro, and these were installed in Cuba. However, U2 spy planes from the USA located and photographed the missile sites. They also spotted twenty Soviet ships, possibly carrying missiles, bound for Cuba. The USA realised that virtually all its cities were in direct danger in the event of nuclear attack. Kennedy knew that he must act. He summoned the US National Security Council, which considered what action to take. It insisted that the missiles be removed and suggested a military response, but Kennedy was not prepared to risk nuclear war by attacking Cuba.

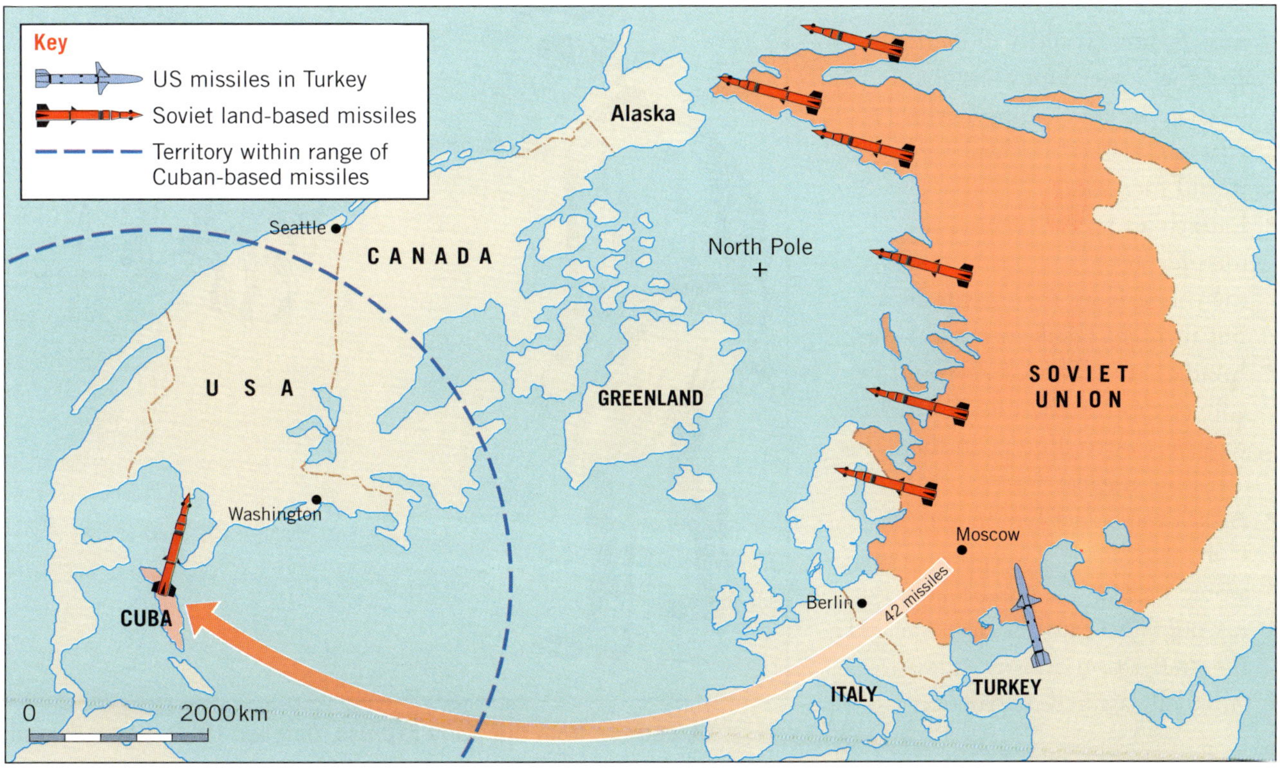

The threat from nuclear missiles based on Cuba.

SOURCE F

A photograph of missile sites on Cuba with labels added by the US government.

Kennedy's options

- Do nothing. This would provide a breathing space to respond. But it would be unpopular in the USA because it would be seen as a Soviet success. The threat to the USA would remain.
- Blockade Cuba using the US navy. This was a measured response that would leave the Soviet Union to decide the next move. But the missile sites would still be intact, and the Soviet Union might retaliate by blockading Berlin. Also the risk of nuclear war would increase.
- Launch air strikes against the missile sites. This would destroy the threat from the missile sites. But it might result in nuclear war.
- Invade Cuba. The USA would be able to destroy the missile sites and remove Castro. But again there was a risk of nuclear war.
- Attack the Soviet Union and/or Cuba with nuclear weapons. This would destroy the missile sites. But it would also cause nuclear war and the destruction of both sides (mutually assured destruction).

Kennedy's response

On 22 October 1962, the USA ordered a naval blockade of Cuba. Kennedy went on national television to explain his response.

SOURCE G

A cartoon from the *Daily Express*, October 1962. Kennedy and Khrushchev are shown as gunslingers waiting to see who will draw first. Castro is riding on a donkey.

The world watched nervously as the threat of nuclear war increased. Luckily, Khrushchev was unwilling to risk war. On 24 October he backed down and ordered his ships to stop and turn away. This action created a breathing space, which allowed both sides to reach an agreement.

The main results of the crisis

Much of the credit for avoiding conflict must go to the two leaders. Kennedy realised that he must make a stand, but refused to be pushed into a war. Khrushchev saw that he had pushed too far and relented so as to prevent any risk of war. Both saw that there was a need for the other to save some face. So the Soviet Union publicly agreed to remove all its nuclear missiles from Cuba, while the USA publicly promised not to invade Cuba.

The real threat of nuclear war in 1962 encouraged a more positive atmosphere. While the Cuban Missile Crisis was going on, the Cold War reached an all-time low, but its ending helped to reduce tensions and improve the atmosphere between the superpowers. Both sides now tried to co-operate. A test ban treaty was signed in 1963, which stopped all Soviet, US and British nuclear testing in the atmosphere. A direct 'hot line' telephone link was established between the White House and the Kremlin to ease discussion in times of crisis.

The Cuban problem led to divisions within the communist world. The Chinese criticised the Soviet Union for backing down. Many Soviet politicians also took this view and blamed Khrushchev personally. This hastened his fall from power in 1964.

SOURCE H

This secret, swift and extraordinary build-up of communist missiles is a deliberately provocative and unjustified change in the state of affairs which cannot be accepted by this country. To halt this offensive build-up, a strict quarantine on all offensive military equipment under shipment to Cuba is being set up.

From President Kennedy's television broadcast on 22 October 1962.

SOURCE I

Our aim was only to defend Cuba. Everybody saw how the Americans were sharpening their knives and threatening Cuba with attack. The Americans were threatening war. By placing rockets on Cuba we made the Americans realise that this war would start at their own borders.

Some people pretend that the rockets were for an attack on the United States. Why should we place rockets on Cuba for that purpose? We were and are able to strike from our own territory.

From a speech made by Khrushchev to the Soviet parliament in December 1962.

QUESTIONS

1. What is the cartoonist's message in Source G?
2. Both Sources H and I were public speeches. Does this make them reliable as evidence of the Cuban Missile Crisis?
3. Both Kennedy and Khrushchev claimed to have won in October 1962. Explain why both were able to do so.

Exam-style questions

These questions follow the pattern of questions set by AQA/SEG for Paper 2 of its current Modern World History syllabus.

1. The deepening of the Cold War, 1945–53

Study Source A and then answer **all** parts of Question 1.

Source A: The Marshall Plan

> The Americans said the Marshall Plan was 'a plan to save peace'. This was not true. It was really intended to unite countries against the Soviet Union. The Marshall Plan led to a reduction in the trade of the Soviet Union and the other communist countries with the rest of the world. The USA hoped that this would lead to a split among the communist states and bring them under American influence. It was also clear that much of the Marshall Plan was aimed at rebuilding the military power of West Germany.

A Soviet historian writing in 1968.

Question 1

(a) What can you learn about the Marshall Plan from **Source A**? *(4 marks)*

(b) Describe how the Marshall Plan was implemented from 1948 to 1952. *(8 marks)*

(c) 'The Marshall Plan was largely responsible for the rapid increase in Cold War tensions between 1948 and 1952.' Do you agree or disagree with this interpretation? Explain your answer. *(8 marks)*

2. Changing attitudes and policies in the 1950s

Study Source A and then answer **all** parts of Question 2.

Source A: The space race

A US cartoon commenting on the launch of Sputnik 1 by the Soviet Union.

Question 2

(a) Describe the relationship between the Soviet Union and its satellites from the death of Stalin in 1953 to the crushing of the Hungarian rising in November 1956. *(8 marks)*

(b) What is the message of the cartoonist in **Source A**? *(4 marks)*

(c) What were the consequences of the failure of the Hungarian Rising of November 1956 for superpower relationships to 1960? *(8 marks)*

3. Crises in the early 1960s

Study Source A and then answer the **all** parts of Question 3.

Source A: The Cuban Missile Crisis

A cartoon from the New Statesman about the Cuban Missile Crisis.

Question 3

(a) What is the attitude of the cartoonist in **Source A** to the Cuban Missile Crisis? *(4 marks)*

(b) In May 1960 the U2 Crisis occurred. Describe what happened and how the superpowers responded. *(8 marks)*

(c) 'It was the Cuban problem that made the period 1961 to 1963 so dangerous for relations between the superpowers.' Do you agree or disagree with this interpretation? Explain your answer. *(8 marks)*

Chapter 3

The USA and the Soviet Union as world superpowers, 1963–91

Introduction

The Cuban Missile Crisis marked the height of Cold War tension. From 1963 the superpowers tended to try to work together. The first indications of this were the setting up of the 'hot line', a direct telephone link between them, and the signing of the Test Ban Treaty. From the late 1960s onwards, this easing of superpower tensions could be seen in the development of détente, meaning 'relaxation'. Attempts were made to control the arms race through SALT 1 (Strategic Arms Limitation Talks) in 1972, which reduced the number of nuclear missiles on each side. The Soviet Union and USA also tried to normalise relations through the Helsinki Agreement of 1975. Superpower leaders visited each other and there was co-operation in space, in culture and in sport.

Such improvements in relations between the superpowers were often short-lived. US involvement in the Vietnam War strained relations, as did Soviet intervention in Czechoslovakia in 1968 to destroy the 'Prague Spring' uprising. A 'second Cold War' broke out after the Soviets invaded Afghanistan in 1979. All the effort of preparing for SALT 2 was frustrated because the USA did not allow this agreement to come into effect. The Soviet Union disliked the West's insistence that it allow more human rights to Soviet citizens. It was also wary of President Reagan's increase in defence spending and his wish to establish a 'Star Wars' project, which would create an anti-missile shield in space and so prevent Soviet missiles reaching their targets in the USA.

However, this hotting up of the Cold War was short-lived. By the mid-1980s, the cost of the arms race had become too much for both superpowers. The Soviet Union was virtually bankrupt and its confidence had been shattered by its failures in Afghanistan. The West used Soviet difficulties to pressure Mikhail Gorbachev, after 1985, into agreeing to further arms reductions. Gorbachev's introduction of reforms into the Soviet Union stimulated opposition movements and protests throughout Soviet-controlled eastern Europe. The communist governments there were overthrown and the Iron Curtain was torn down. The Soviet Empire disintegrated in 1989 and the Cold War came to an end.

1963	Overthrow of President Diem
1964	Tonkin Resolution
1968	Prague Spring and the invasion of Czechoslovakia My Lai massacre
1969	Death of Ho Chi Minh
1970	Demonstration at Kent State University Policy of vietnamisation introduced
1972	SALT 1
1973	USA pulls out of Vietnam, ceasefire agreed
1975	Fall of South Vietnam, Laos and Cambodia to communism Helsinki Agreement
1979	Soviet invasion of Afghanistan
1981	Russia imposes martial law in Poland
1989	Disintegration of the Soviet Empire
1991	End of communist rule in Russia under Yeltsin

Vietnam, 1963–75

Background to the situation in 1963

Indo-China to 1945

Before the Second World War, the region between India and China, which now includes Vietnam, Laos and Kampuchea (Cambodia), belonged to France. France had taken control of the whole region and called it Indo-China, but French rule was unpopular and harsh, and so the different people in the region were seeking independence. Many Indo-Chinese fought in the First World War and brought back to Vietnam new ideas of democracy and communism from Europe. As French rule became more unpopular, there were uprisings like that in 1930 led by the Nationalist Party of Vietnam. However, such attempts to resist the French were brutally crushed.

Indo-China today.

Japan invaded and occupied Indo-China in 1940. A secret guerrilla organisation in Vietnam, the Vietminh or League for the Independence of Vietnam, was set up to resist Japanese rule. This organisation was led by a communist revolutionary called Ho Chi Minh. The Vietminh co-operated with the Allies to get rid of the Japanese, and in September 1945, after the defeat of Japan, Ho Chi Minh was able to declare Vietnam independent. However, this situation lasted for only three weeks because, in 1946, the French returned and fought the Vietminh. Although the USA supported France, the French underestimated the Vietminh, who were supplied with weapons by communist China and the Soviet Union. In May 1954, the French suffered a crushing defeat at Dien Bien Phu when they surrendered after a siege lasting 55 days. This broke the French will to fight on. A small nation had defeated an important European power. This was humiliating enough for France, but also 74,000 French troops had been killed by 1953 and the war was costing France 435 million francs per year. The struggle was just too costly and, in 1954, the French decided to pull out.

Ho Chi Minh

Born as Nguyen That Thanh in 1890, he left Vietnam in 1911 to live in the Soviet Union and Europe. He was a revolutionary, who in 1920 helped to set up the French Communist Party. He spent time in the Soviet Union and in China, learning the techniques of revolution and guerrilla warfare. In 1930 he established the Indo-Chinese Communist Party, and he later organised Vietminh resistance to the Japanese in the Second World War. Ho Chi Minh became the President of North Vietnam and started to build up a communist society there. He successfully led its fight against South Vietnam until his death in 1969. Recognised as the founder of Vietnamese communism, Ho Chi Minh became the very soul of the Vietnamese revolution and the struggle for freedom and unity.

SOURCE A

Ho Chi Minh.

US interest in south-east Asia

The USA feared the growing strength of China after it became communist in 1949. The US government suspected that the Chinese would try to spread communism and feared that the whole of south-east Asia might fall to the communists, country by country. This was known as the domino theory. The Americans wanted to contain communism, which is why they had supported France. The region was important strategically because it occupied a dominant geographical position on the trade routes between Europe and the Far East and was rich in raw materials. The Americans believed they could not allow communism to triumph.

The domino theory.

The Geneva Conference

In 1954, a conference was held in Geneva to try to establish a settlement for the whole of Indo-China. North Vietnam, South Vietnam, Cambodia and Laos were all represented at this conference. Also attending were the USA, the United Kingdom, communist China, the Soviet Union and France. Together they were able to agree on the withdrawal of French troops, the creation of a cease-fire and a new territorial settlement. Indo-China was split up and Laos, Cambodia, North Vietnam (communist) and South Vietnam (non-communist) were formed. Vietnam was divided in two along the 17th parallel, a demilitarised zone between North and South Vietnam. It was intended that Vietnam would be reunited after elections but the USA refused to allow free elections throughout Vietnam because these might have resulted in a communist victory. President Eisenhower offered aid to South Vietnam and sent military advisers to train the South Vietnamese army.

The Vietminh now started fighting against the South Vietnamese government and its backer, the US government. North Vietnam indicated that it intended to wage war on South Vietnam in order to reunify Vietnam. The Americans provided aid to President Diem, the leader of South Vietnam, while the Soviet Union and China helped North Vietnam and the Vietminh by providing weapons, equipment and food. These supplies arrived in South Vietnam down the Ho Chi Minh Trail, a series of supply lines through the jungle, which were vital to the communists and had to be kept open despite constant attacks. About 40,000 people were needed to do this.

South Vietnam

The non-communist government of President Diem was very harsh and corrupt. It crushed all opposition and imprisoned its enemies. Little money was spent on social reform; most went on weapons. Diem was intensely unpopular because he was a Catholic in a largely Buddhist country. The South Vietnamese government persecuted the Buddhist majority. Monks protested against the lack of religious toleration in the country. Some even demonstrated their discontent by burning themselves to death. Despite Diem's widespread unpopularity, the USA backed him because he was anti-communist. But many South Vietnamese favoured the Vietminh.

SOURCE B

A photograph taken in 1963 of a Buddhist monk who had set fire to himself.

The Vietcong

The National Liberation Front or Vietcong was formed in 1960 with the specific task of reunifying the country. The Vietminh had succeeded in beating the Japanese and the French. Its successor, the Vietcong, set out to beat the government of South Vietnam and its allies. It was a guerrilla movement supported by North Vietnam and many people in the South. Its recruits were trained in the art of ambush and secret war, which the US soldiers would find difficult to combat. Rather than using open, face-to-face confrontation, the Vietcong chose to wage a war using surprise tactics, laying traps and using the cover of the jungle to hit their enemy hard before quickly disappearing.

SOURCE C

A Vietnamese poster showing the communist forces attacking US troops.

The Vietcong took advantage of South Vietnam's increasing problems and became popular in rural areas because it gave land to the peasants and provided schools, postal and banking systems. The Vietcong set out to treat the local people well and so win their respect. It therefore carefully established itself in the villages before starting to wage guerrilla war.

The situation in 1963

The situation was quite desperate by November 1963 because the South Vietnamese government was close to collapse. President Diem was overthrown and killed by his own troops, but there seemed little prospect of creating a more stable political situation. South Vietnamese governments did not last long. The country had ten different governments within two years of Diem's removal and looked to be very weak. The Vietcong appeared to have the upper hand. With its 100,000 fighters active, it already controlled large areas of rural South Vietnam. The very survival of South Vietnam was now at stake and the expansion of communism throughout south-east Asia appeared to be a distinct possibility.

QUESTIONS

1. Why did the French choose to withdraw from Indo-China in 1954?
2. Why were there dramatic protests, such as that shown in Source B, against the government of South Vietnam in the early 1960s?
3. What does Source C tell you about the method of warfare used in Vietnam?

Increasing US involvement in Vietnam

President Eisenhower had offered aid and advisers to South Vietnam in 1954 and US support continued to grow. In December 1961 President Kennedy pledged further help, and by December 1962 he had sent over 11,000 US troops to Vietnam.

Lyndon Johnson became the new US President after the assassination of John F. Kennedy in November 1963. He decided that US involvement in Vietnam must be greatly increased. He believed the situation was desperate because of the weakness of the South Vietnamese government. If the USA was to succeed in defeating the Vietcong, it would need to win the war as quickly as possible. He therefore made use of a rather insignificant naval incident in the Gulf of Tonkin in August 1964 to carry out this policy. Three North Vietnamese ships had attacked the USS Maddox, a naval destroyer, which suffered minor damage. This event provided an excuse for the US Congress to pass a resolution giving Johnson the wide military powers he needed to wage war in Vietnam. Despite the fact that the USA was not officially at war with North Vietnam, Johnson now sent in more US troops. By the end of 1965, 180,000 US soldiers were fighting in Vietnam. Other countries, including Australia, New Zealand, Thailand and the Philippines, gave them help.

Johnson had already ordered the start of 'Operation Rolling Thunder', by which US aircraft started to bomb strategically important targets in North Vietnam. Such precise bombing was later replaced by saturation bombing, particularly upon the cities of Hanoi and Haiphong and along the Ho Chi Minh Trail. Bombs were not carefully targeted, but were just dropped indiscriminately in order to cause maximum damage. Johnson hoped that this would starve the Vietcong of vital supplies and so reduce the need to use so many US troops in the war. But these tactics did not work. The bombing continued for many years and the USA dropped more bombs on North Vietnam than had been dropped by both sides during the whole of the Second World War. However, the war did not end. The many civilian casualties gradually turned much of world opinion against the USA. US involvement was seen as superpower interference in Vietnam. Many saw the Vietcong as a heroic resistance group attempting to expel a foreign invader.

SOURCE D

> If we quit in Vietnam, tomorrow we'll be fighting in Hawaii and next week we'll have to fight in San Francisco.
>
> *From a speech made by President Johnson in 1964.*

By 1968, Johnson had been forced to increase the number of US troops involved to 500,000 and yet the Vietcong still continued to pose a serious threat. In January 1968, it launched the Tet Offensive on the cities and military bases of South Vietnam, including the capital, Saigon. Although the communists were beaten back because they were still not strong enough to engage in open, conventional fighting, the Americans were embarrassed by the attacks. It seemed unbelievable to the US public that even their own embassy in Saigon could come under attack from a Vietcong suicide squad.

The effects of US involvement in the Vietnam War

The Vietnam War was the first televised war because it received so much media coverage. Every day the US public witnessed its horrors in their own living rooms. The war became increasingly unpopular inside the USA because of its high cost both financially and in terms of casualties. Over 50,000 US troops were eventually to lose their lives, and, by 1968, 300 soldiers were dying weekly. Most Americans knew of a relative or friend who had died.

There were also stories of widespread drug addiction and indiscipline within the armed forces. US atrocities against the Vietnamese people received widespread media coverage and turned many against the war. One example that particularly shocked the US people when they saw it on television was the massacre at the village of My Lai in March 1968 when about 300 people were massacred. The villagers, largely women and children, were suspected of having sheltered communist fighters and were gunned down by US troops. But there was no evidence that the villagers had any connections with the Vietcong. Lieutenant William Calley was charged with responsibility for their deaths and found guilty, but he was released after serving only three years of a life sentence.

The economic cost of the war was high. President Johnson had offered the USA an ambitious programme of sweeping social and welfare reform to bring about his promise of a 'great society'. He had hoped that this would increase his popularity and improve his chances of re-election. However, many of these projects for improving education, health and civil rights, and for reducing crime, had to be postponed in order to pay for the war, which was costing $30,000 million annually by 1968. Such cutbacks turned more Americans against President Johnson.

US tactics

The use of new horrific weapons, such as napalm, caused more opposition to the war. This burning petroleum jelly was often used against civilians when villages were bombed. It stuck to the skin of its victims and burned them badly. The Americans also chose to spray the land with chemical defoliants such as agent orange. This destroyed the vegetation and so prevented Vietcong fighters from hiding in the jungle. However, these chemicals polluted the land and also continued to poison human beings well after the end of the war.

SOURCE E

The Train Robbery

A *Punch* cartoon from 1967.

QUESTIONS

1. What does Source D tell us about US foreign policy in Vietnam?
2. What do you understand by the following terms:
   - **a** napalm
   - **b** defoliants
   - **c** Tet Offensive
   - **d** Operation Rolling Thunder
   - **e** Vietcong
   - **f** Ho Chi Minh Trail?
3. What is the message of Source E?

The Vietnam War.

Increasing opposition to the war

Widespread anti-war demonstrations began to occur regularly in US cities. Thousands of young men burnt their 'draft' cards, which called them up to fight, or fled abroad rather than take part in the war. Many students organised sit-ins and demonstrations at their colleges. Others, horrified by what was happening in Vietnam, turned against war and rejected the society that had allowed it to happen. They demonstrated their anti-war attitudes by joining hippie groups, who were preaching love and peace. Considerable criticism was levelled at President Johnson for having stepped up the war.

President Johnson realised that the cost of continuing to fight was too great for him and for the US people. He sought a political rather than a military solution. He had already chosen to stop the bombing of North Vietnam in 1968, which allowed the start of peace talks in Paris, but little progress was made. Johnson knew that his unpopularity would prevent him standing for president for a second term, and so he chose to retire.

SOURCE F

Hey! Hey! LBJ, LBJ, how many kids have you killed today?

A popular chant used against President Johnson during the Vietnam War.

Death at Kent State University

The election of a new president did not stop the anti-war demonstrations. One of the worst incidents took place at Kent State University in Ohio in May 1970. A peaceful student demonstration had been organised, but the Governor of Ohio sent in the National Guard to stop the protest because it was against state law. Tear gas canisters were tossed among the students, who reacted by throwing them back and by throwing stones at the Guards. The Guards responded by firing into the crowd. Four students were killed and others were injured. An investigation showed that the victims had not even been part of the protest, but had simply been going about their daily business. Such incidents demonstrated the depth of feeling against the war, and showed the deep divisions that it had created within US society. Many people still supported the war and denounced the anti-war protesters as 'cowards' or 'communists'.

SOURCE G

A US anti-war poster from the Vietnam War.

SOURCE H

Today the brutal struggle still goes on. Victory is far from won. But the light of Vietnam's victory over America can already be seen. Therefore we must still help to bring the struggle of the Vietnamese people to a successful end. They are shedding their blood and laying down their lives for the sake of the world communist movement.

Khrushchev's comments on Vietnam, during the late 1960s.

Vietnamisation

Johnson's successor was President Nixon, who wanted to end the war but without losing face. He did not want the USA to be humiliated, which would destroy his own political credibility and his chances of re-election. So in 1970 he introduced a policy of Vietnamisation, by which the USA was able to begin to withdraw its troops, replacing them with trained South Vietnamese soldiers. The South Vietnamese army was to be strengthened with US training and equipment so that it could defend itself. Nixon's foreign affairs adviser, Henry Kissinger, held secret talks with the communists, but the North Vietnamese seemed reluctant to agree to a cease-fire. President Nixon therefore took a tough line with them by renewing the full-scale bombing of North Vietnam. The war was also extended into Cambodia and Laos during 1970 and 1971 when the Americans attacked the Ho Chi Minh Trail in these countries to try to cut off the flow of supplies from North to South Vietnam. All this pressure forced the communists into a cease-fire agreement, which was signed in Paris in January 1973.

The USA is defeated

At first, Nixon's policy seemed to work. As the table shows, by 1972 the number of US troops in Vietnam had fallen to about 40,000. This reduction helped Nixon to be re-elected in 1973, by which time the last US troops had left Vietnam. The cease-fire did not last, however, and the war broke out again in 1974. By this time Nixon had been weakened by the Watergate Scandal. This scandal arose as he was associated with an illegal attempt to bug the offices of the Democratic Party and was threatened with being put on trial. He chose to resign as US President in August 1974.

Year	Military aid to South Vietnam ($ million)	US armed forces in South Vietnam
1966	6,100	280,000
1968	21,000	545,000
1970	16,700	330,000
1972	9,300	40,000

US aid to South Vietnam, 1966–72

The USA had promised military support if the cease-fire ended and South Vietnam was attacked. But when this happened, Nixon's successor, President Ford, only sent supplies, not soldiers. There was no longer any real political desire to become directly involved in such an unpopular war again. Without direct US support the South Vietnamese army gave up the struggle and the Vietcong was able to overrun South Vietnam. In April 1975 Saigon itself was captured and the non-communist government was overthrown. Vietnam became a united country under communist control. Saigon was renamed Ho Chi Minh City.

SOURCE I

A British cartoon from 1969 about Nixon's policy of Vietnamisation.

Causes of the US defeat

One of the main problems for the USA was that the Vietnam War was far more than a military struggle. It was also a political one, in which the USA failed to win the hearts and the minds of the peasants of South Vietnam. They generally viewed the Americans as invaders and chose to support the Vietcong, which offered to improve their lives, rather than the South Vietnamese government, which seemed to offer them nothing. Indeed, under the 'safe villages' policy, the Americans and their allies had forcibly removed South Vietnamese peasants from the areas where the Vietcong was strong and placed them in fortified zones. This angered the peasants, who did not wish to leave their homes.

The Americans also lost support at home when it became clear that the USA could not win the war, and that the cost of continuing to fight was unacceptably high, both politically and economically. This problem stemmed from the fact that the communists were able to dictate the nature of the war. The Vietcong fighters were skilled in guerrilla warfare. They would launch a surprise attack and then disappear into the jungle, protected and supported by the local inhabitants. The young US soldiers, with an average age of just nineteen, often had no enemy to strike back at, and they were frightened in such a hostile environment. This led to anger and frustration, which destroyed their confidence and sometimes resulted in terrible atrocities like the one at My Lai.

By contrast, the morale of the communists was high. They passionately believed in their cause and displayed real determination to succeed. They were careful in most situations to avoid open conventional warfare, which they could not win because of the superiority of US military equipment.

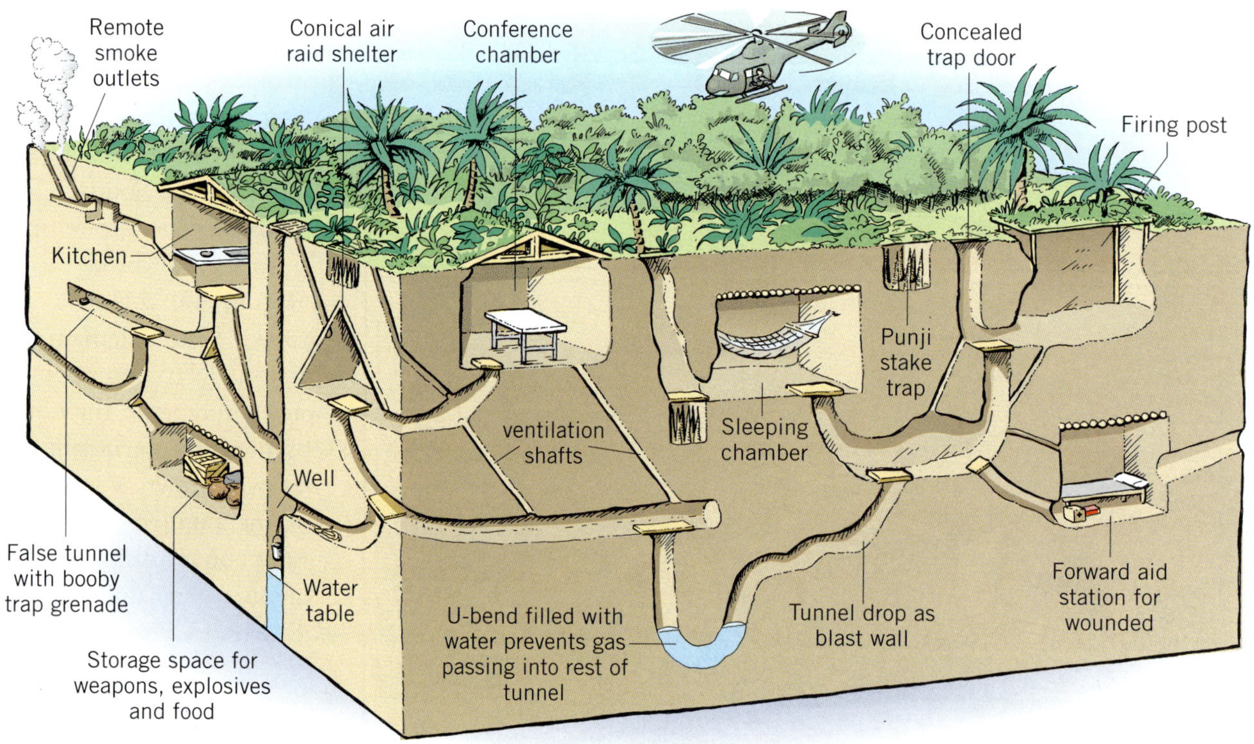

The tunnel system used by the Vietcong in Vietnam.

The Vietcong was backed by communist China and the Soviet Union, and used the Ho Chi Minh Trail to bring supplies to their bases in South Vietnam. These were well hidden, as the diagram opposite shows. The Vietcong were frightened of the US bombing so they built extensive underground bunkers, containing workshops, kitchens, hospitals and storehouses, all connected by networks of narrow tunnels that were carefully booby-trapped to kill US soldiers who might discover them. This meant that they could only be destroyed by direct hits from US bombers. It is estimated that over 300 kilometres of tunnels were built under South Vietnam.

So the USA never gained the backing of most of the people in South Vietnam and gradually lost support both at home and internationally. The war then proved to be too costly both politically and economically. The USA was ultimately left with no choice but to withdraw its troops. When this point was reached, South Vietnam was left isolated and open to defeat.

Consequences of the Vietnam War

The consequences for the USA

The ending of the Vietnam War had seen the USA defeated. The war caused considerable social conflict in the USA and even a feeling of self-doubt. After all, it was the first time that the country had been beaten in war. Its foreign policy seemed to be in tatters because of its failure to contain communism in the region. The communists took not only South Vietnam, but also neighbouring countries such as Laos and Cambodia. However, the Vietnam War had soured the international atmosphere for many years, so when it ended there was an improvement in superpower relations. Cold War tensions began to ease (see page 86).

The consequences for Indo-China

The cost to the Vietnamese people was horrific. It has been estimated that one million North Vietnamese were killed and 600,000 soldiers and civilians in the South. It seemed a high price to pay in order to be saved from communism. No wonder, then, that so many people in Vietnam hated the Americans and supported the Vietcong.

Of the 12 million people who lost their homes and relatives in Indo-China, many fled abroad. Bombing and defoliation had destroyed much of Vietnam. The war ruined over 5 million acres of forest, and much of the land was left so heavily polluted that the country was unable to grow enough rice to feed the people. Economic problems plagued Vietnam and many starved because of poor harvests and the US embargo on trade. This prevented any trade between Vietnam and the USA. Half a million 'boat people' tried to flee from Vietnam by sea, and many of those died or ended up in camps until they were forced to return to Vietnam. Relations between communist Vietnam and the USA remained hostile for a long time, but in 1993 the US embargo was ended and diplomatic relations were restored.

QUESTIONS

1. Why might the communists in South Vietnam have been a more effective fighting force than the non-communists?
2. Explain why the Americans stopped the bombing of North Vietnam in 1968, but started it up again in 1970.
3. Why did the USA choose to pull its troops out of Vietnam in the early 1970s?
4. Does the diagram of the tunnel system on page 80 show that the Vietcong was forced underground by US bombing?

Czechoslovakia, 1968

Czechoslovakia had been a Soviet satellite since 1948, with its government taking orders from Moscow. However, the Czech people felt bitter about the loss of their political and economic independence. They remembered that Czechoslovakia had been a democracy in the period before the Second World War. They resented the fact that Czech industry produced very few consumer goods and seemed to be run entirely for the benefit of the Soviet Union.

Dubcek and the Prague Spring

Protests began to grow in the 1960s and the demand for changes brought someone new to power. In January 1968, Alexander Dubcek took over as the new Czech leader. Although he led the Communist Party, he saw a need for some limited democratic reforms and began to introduce changes.

SOURCE A

Alexander Dubcek.

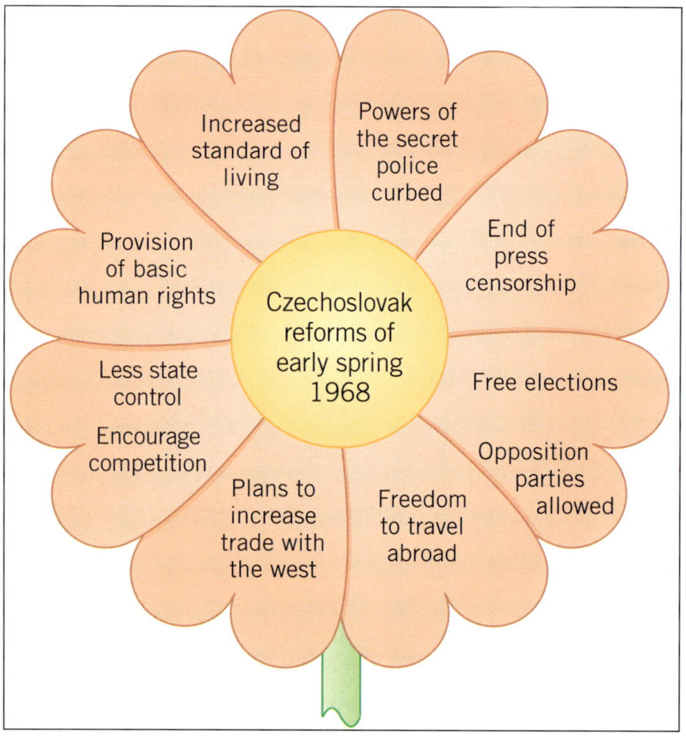

The Prague Spring.

These changes were known as the 'Prague Spring' because they seemed to reveal a thawing of the old harsh system of communism. Dubcek promised the people 'socialism with a human face'. He hoped to increase people's standard of living and make the political system more democratic. He allowed competition between different factories. This was unheard of in the communist world. He wanted to increase trade with the West and to borrow funds from the USA to restructure and rebuild Czech industry. He proposed to abolish censorship and allow free travel abroad. He did, however, try to reassure Brezhnev, the Soviet leader, that his changes would not threaten the security of the Soviet Union, and he promised that Czechoslovakia would not leave the Warsaw Pact.

SOURCE B

The effects of the change in leadership in January were felt almost within days. Books that had been held up for months or years were suddenly freed for publication. Banned films that had been gathering dust were distributed.

The Times, *23 February 1968.*

The Soviet response

Brezhnev remained unconvinced by Dubcek's reassurance. To allow reform in Czechoslovakia would weaken communism and encourage the growth of capitalism and increased contact with the West. He felt that if these changes continued they would also be demanded elsewhere in eastern Europe. The Iron Curtain might well disappear and the Warsaw Pact might collapse. The very existence of the Soviet Bloc would be threatened and, if Soviet influence were removed from eastern Europe, the security of the Soviet Union would be undermined.

Dubcek's reform programme was highly popular in Czechoslovakia because it offered the possibility of free, democratic government, human rights and an improved standard of living. However, the other Warsaw Pact countries disapproved and asked Dubcek to stop. They were concerned that the dominant position of the Communist Party was being weakened, and this could undermine Soviet-style socialism in eastern Europe and turn Czechoslovakia against its communist neighbours. The whole system of 'people's democracies' could be threatened.

Dubcek reacted by promising even more changes, particularly the setting up of opposition parties and the holding of free elections. Faced by what they saw as defiance, the neighbouring Soviet satellites and the Soviet Union decided to use force. On 20 August 1968, 500,000 troops from the Warsaw Pact countries invaded Czechoslovakia.

SOURCE C

A drawing on a wall in a Prague street in 1968.

In Hungary in 1956, the Soviet Union had sent in troops to prevent a similar move away from communism, and the people had actively resisted this intervention with considerable loss of life (see pages 57–9). As a result the Czechs did not resist in the same way. They wanted to avoid the bloodshed of Budapest. At the same time they were clearly outnumbered by the military might of the invading forces, and the Czech army could not act independently because many Soviet officers occupied important positions within it. Yet although there was no armed resistance, there was passive resistance from the population. This was largely non-violent in nature and took the form of demonstrations, sit-ins and peaceful protest.

Organised violent protest against the Soviet troops was discouraged. However, violent acts did occur. Soviet tanks were attacked with home-made petrol bombs called molotov cocktails, and one student, Jan Palach, set himself alight in Prague in January 1969 as a protest against the Soviet occupation of his country. Secret radio and TV stations kept the outside world informed of events until they were discovered and silenced.

SOURCE D

Youths with flaming rags and newspapers set fire to Russian tanks encircling the Prague radio building. Others threw wooden crates, rubbish bins and mattresses at the occupying forces who had moved swiftly into the city. Snipers kept up fire much of the day. Scores of people were injured and several killed when the Russians answered back and when munitions lorries exploded. I saw four young Czechs killed, minutes after a machine gun from a Russian tank had opened fire upon their vehicle.

The Times, *22 August 1968.*

SOURCE E

Czech youths attacking a Soviet tank on the streets of Prague in August 1968.

The Brezhnev Doctrine

Eventually, the Soviets forces crushed all resistance in Czechoslovakia. Many supporters of Dubcek were imprisoned. He was taken to Moscow and made to abandon his reform programme. At first, he was sent abroad as ambassador to Turkey. Later he was forced to resign this post and was expelled from the Communist Party.

The new leader who replaced Dubcek, Gustav Husak, returned to the old ways. The reforms of the Prague Spring were reversed. The Soviet grip on Czechoslovakia was once again secure. Brezhnev set out Soviet policy in what became known as the Brezhnev Doctrine. He stressed that a threat to one socialist country was a threat to all. He indicated that force would be used whenever necessary to keep the satellite states firmly under Soviet influence. He was determined that there would be no repeat performance of the Prague Spring.

SOURCE F

Go to your places of work. Carry out passive resistance. Do not resist. We are incapable of defending these frontiers.

Radio Prague, 21 August 1968.

SOURCE G

When forces that are hostile to socialism try to turn the development of some socialist country towards capitalism, the suppression of these counter-revolutionary forces becomes not only a problem of the country concerned, but a common problem and concern of all socialist countries.

The Brezhnev Doctrine, August 1968

East–West relations

The invasion of Czechoslovakia did nothing to help improve East–West relations. Western states had welcomed Dubcek's relaxation of communism in Czechoslovakia. The Soviet invasion of Czechoslovakia showed the West that the Soviet Union would not allow reform, or permit any opposition of which it disapproved. East–West relations remained very frosty. The West had watched the invasion with horror, but it was not prepared to intervene and so risk the outbreak of a war. In September 1938, western countries had left Czechoslovakia to its fate to avoid war. They did so again in August 1968.

For 20 years, Alexander Dubcek worked in a lowly position in the Forestry Department, but during the anti-communist revolutions of late 1989 (see pages 95–6), he was able to appear in public once more. He spoke of the need for reform and received warm and enthusiastic praise from the Czechoslovak people. He was able to see many of his policies of 1968 come to fruition at last.

QUESTIONS

1. Explain the meaning of the following terms:
   - **a** Prague Spring
   - **b** molotov cocktail
   - **c** passive resistance.
2. Why did the Warsaw Pact disapprove of Alexander Dubcek's reforms?
3. What point was the person who drew Source C trying to make?
4. 'The new leaders of Czechoslovakia returned to the old ways after 1968.' What does this mean?

Détente

In the late 1960s and through most of the 1970s, the word 'détente' was used to mean a relaxing of tension between East and West. The USA and the Soviet Union became less hostile towards each other. People talked of a thaw in the Cold War. It was really an extension of Khrushchev's policy of peaceful co-existence (see pages 56–7).

SOURCE A

> In the Cold War, everything moved on the level of a cheap western. You have an enemy who is the source of all evil. The policy of détente is more difficult to grasp. You have to be able to see the possibility and desirability of co-existence and co-operation between nations that are vastly different in their social systems and political values. You have to realise that despite all differences and difficulties, they still might have overwhelming mutual interests.
>
> *Georgi Arbatov, a member of the Soviet Central Committee, looking back in 1983 at the period of détente.*

Reasons for détente

The Cuban Missile Crisis of 1962 (see pages 64–7) had shown how dangerous the Cold War was. Attempts to improve relations between the superpowers had started in the 1960s. But relations had been difficult because of continuing fears and suspicions, both generally and over specific issues. Increasing US involvement in the war in Vietnam had not helped. Events in Czechoslovakia in 1968 seemed to put an end to all hope of better relations.

However, both the USA and the Soviet Union had come to accept each other's areas of influence in the world, and both felt the need to improve relations with their 'enemies' for a variety of reasons:

- Events in Vietnam were denting the confidence of the USA.
- Both the USA and the Soviet Union had economic problems during the 1970s. In the USA there was rising inflation. This, together with expenditure on the war in Vietnam, was crippling the US economy. The Soviet Union had low living standards and poor industrial efficiency, and needed to trade more with the West.
- Both sides were spending vast sums of money on defence. In the case of the Soviet Union, it was 20 per cent of total spending by the government. Both sides had stockpiles of weapons with a capacity to destroy the earth many times over.
- Both the USA and the Soviet Union were worried about conflict over the Middle East. Oil supplies from that area were vital for both countries, and the Suez Canal was important for sea routes. Communist and non-communist countries had become involved in the conflicts there between Arabs and Israelis.
- Both the USA and the Soviet Union were worried about the growing power of China. Although China and the Soviet Union were co-operating over Vietnam, they quarrelled about other issues. The USA, on the other hand, was afraid of the possibility of the two communist giants, China and the Soviet Union, reaching agreements that threatened the USA.

In the USA, President Nixon and his Secretary of State, Henry Kissinger, were keen to establish better working relations with Moscow (and also Peking (Beijing)). In the Soviet Union, President Brezhnev was keen to extend Khrushchev's policy of peaceful co-existence. He wanted to persuade the West to accept Soviet control in eastern Europe. He also wanted to increase the Soviet Union's trade with the West in order to improve Soviet living standards.

Therefore, throughout the late 1960s and 1970s, US and Soviet leaders tried hard to reduce tension.

Attempts at arms control and improving human rights

During the 1960s, there had already been agreements between the Soviet Union, the USA and Britain over nuclear weapons. For example, the Test Ban Treaty of 1963 had banned nuclear tests in the atmosphere, in outer space and under water. Then, in 1968, the same countries had signed the Nuclear Non-Proliferation Treaty with the aim of stopping the spread of nuclear weapons. When Richard Nixon became US President in 1969, both he and President Brezhnev of the Soviet Union began talking about ways in which to slow down the arms race.

SOURCE B

A cartoon about the reasons for the SALT talks. It was published in the USA in 1970.

SALT 1 (1972)

The Strategic Arms Limitation Talks (SALT) started in 1969 and led to the SALT I agreement in 1972. This agreement, which ran for five years, limited the number of inter-continental ballistic missiles (ICBMs) and anti-ballistic missiles (ABMs) on both sides. Each side was allowed to use spy satellites to check that the other was not breaking the agreed limits. The signing of the agreement in Moscow was seen as a huge achievement at the time. However, it did not reduce existing stocks of weapons.

Helsinki Agreement (1975)

In August 1975, at Helsinki in Finland, 35 countries, including the USA and the Soviet Union, signed the Helsinki Agreement. This marked the high point of détente.

- The West recognised the frontiers of eastern Europe and Soviet influence in that area.
- West Germany officially recognised East Germany.
- The Soviets agreed to buy US grain and to export oil to the West.
- All countries agreed to improve human rights – freedom of speech, of religion and of movement.

SOURCE C

Presidents Brezhnev and Nixon meeting in 1974.

Union began to meet each other. For example, in 1972 President Nixon visited Moscow, the first US President to go to the Soviet Union since F. D. Roosevelt went to the wartime conference at Yalta. In return, Brezhnev visited Washington in 1974.

Relations between the USA and the Soviet Union were helped by events in Germany. The Chancellor of West Germany, Willy Brandt, worked hard to form closer ties with communist East Germany, in spite of the Berlin Wall. In 1972 agreements were signed between East and West Germany recognising each other's frontiers and developing trade links. This removed one of the areas of tension for the leaders of the superpowers. It also helped the USA and the Soviet Union to develop trade links. For example, the USA sold its surplus wheat cheaply to the Soviet Union.

All this pleased the Soviet Union. It had gained definite statements from the West about Soviet boundaries and spheres of influence. In return the Soviet Union had made promises about human rights issues.

In fact, abuses of human rights continued in the Soviet Union, and President Carter of the USA complained about this in a follow-up conference at Belgrade in 1977. Within the Soviet Union itself, leading opponents of the communist government criticised travel restrictions and prison conditions. These dissidents (those who disagreed with the government) included the scientist Andrei Sakharov, who wanted a worldwide ban on nuclear weapons, an end to the Cold War and the introduction of democracy in the Soviet Union. He was eventually put under house arrest by the Soviet government.

Other contacts between the superpowers in the 1970s

In the 1970s there were many aspects to détente – political, cultural, sporting, economic and scientific. The leaders of the USA and the Soviet

At the same time, relations between the USA and communist China improved. In 1971 the USA agreed that communist China should be allowed to join the United Nations. (Previously the USA had insisted that the Chinese people of the island of Taiwan should have the Chinese seat in the United Nations, to avoid another large communist country being there.) The US table tennis team visited and played matches in Peking (now Beijing). This 'ping pong diplomacy' went on side by side with meetings between government officials. In 1972 President Nixon visited Peking and met the elderly Chinese leader, Mao Zedong. Meanwhile, relations between the Soviet Union and China remained poor, mostly because of border conflicts and suspicion of each other, and this helped the USA during the period of détente.

SOURCE D

STARS AND STRIPES FLIES OVER THE KREMLIN

Mr Nixon began his visit to the Soviet Union today, becoming the first American President to visit Moscow.

The Times, *23 March 1972.*

There was also co-operation in space. In July 1975 three US astronauts and two Soviet cosmonauts docked their Apollo and Soyuz spacecraft together in orbit round the world. It was a very visible sign of détente.

The failings of détente in the later 1970s

The mid-1970s marked the high point of détente. The USA was pleased that the Soviet Union and China were still quarrelling; yet as we saw on pages 71–81, communism triumphed in Vietnam, and support for communism was growing in parts of Africa.

The West was becoming frustrated by the low priority given by the Soviet Union to improving human rights. There were also suspicions about whether the Soviet Union was keeping to the terms of the SALT I agreement. In fact, both the Soviet Union and the USA were positioning more missiles against each other.

The SALT I agreement had been due to last for five years, so it ended in 1977. The new US President, Jimmy Carter, attempted to achieve more arms reductions through the SALT 2 talks. However, he annoyed Brezhnev by trying to link cuts in weapons to discussions on human rights in communist countries. The talks went on and on, until an agreement was finally reached in 1979. But before the agreement came into effect, an event happened in the last days of 1979 that shattered any hopes of détente continuing in its present form. The Soviet Union invaded Afghanistan.

QUESTIONS

1. What was détente?
2. Why did it come about?
3. What were its most important consequences:
   a for the USA
   b for the Soviet Union?

SOURCE E

This cartoon was published in a British newspaper in 1976. It shows Kissinger of the USA on the left and Brezhnev of the Soviet Union on the right.

A 'second Cold War': the 1980s

Soviet involvement in Afghanistan

Background

The strategic importance of Afghanistan.

Although Afghanistan was poor and mostly barren, it occupied an important position in East–West land routes. It also provided the Soviet Union with a land route to the oil-rich Middle East. The two superpowers had been competing for influence in Afghanistan for some time. Ever since Afghanistan had become a fully independent state in 1921, it had held strong ties with the Soviet Union. These were strengthened in 1955 when Khrushchev visited the capital, Kabul, and promised the Afghanistan government aid and armaments. The USA was increasingly worried about Soviet influence there and tried to compete by also offering aid, but it never gave more than one-third of the Soviet total.

Meanwhile to the west of Afghanistan in neighbouring Iran, the Shah (King) was overthrown in a Muslim revolution in January 1979. As the USA had supported the Shah, the revolution was very anti-American. In November 1979, 53 US hostages were seized at the US Embassy in Tehran and were held for over a year. The USA and its leader, President Carter, felt humiliated. To the east of Afghanistan, the Chinese government was worried about its borders and was seeking to extend its influence in neighbouring countries such as Pakistan.

Afghanistan itself had an unstable government. In 1979 Hafizullah Amin seized power as president. He was a communist, but was not friendly with the Soviet Union, and large Muslim groups in the country also opposed him. The Soviet Union feared that these Muslim groups were planning to take control of the country and set up a Muslim state in the style of Iran. The Soviet Union was also aware that it, too, had a large Muslim population in its areas near the Afghanistan border. This Muslim population might try to break away from the Soviet Union and support the Afghans.

Soviet invasion

On 25 December 1979, Soviet troops invaded Afghanistan. The airport at Kabul was quickly captured and in the next few days 350 Russian aircraft landed there with troops and equipment. Within a week about 50,000 Soviet troops were in Afghanistan. The president's palace at Kabul was captured and President Amin was killed. On New Year's Day 1980 a new government was set up in Kabul, led by Babrak Karmal. He was a previous Afghan leader who had been in exile in the Soviet Union and had been specially flown back to take over the government.

Reactions from the other world powers

President Brezhnev announced to the world that the airlift of Soviet troops and equipment was justified to restore order. He told the US President, Jimmy Carter, that Soviet troops had been invited in by the Afghan government to protect it, and that troops would be withdrawn from Afghanistan as soon as the situation stabilised. However, the Americans were furious. Carter described the Soviet invasion as a threat to world peace. China also reacted angrily – it promised to support the Mujaheddin, who were Islamic Afghan fighters carrying out guerrilla warfare against the Soviet troops to seize back control of their country.

SOURCE A

In the next few days the leaders of the world must make it clear to the Soviets that they cannot upset world peace without paying severe consequences.

President Carter's response to the Soviet invasion of Afghanistan.

SOURCE C

Russia's actions are a stepping-stone for a southward thrust towards Pakistan and the Indian sub-continent. There will be no peace in southern Asia with Soviet soldiers in Afghanistan.

Peking People's Daily, *1 January 1980.*

The Soviet Union retaliated by accusing the USA and China of interference. But President Carter had decided to take steps to show the USA's disapproval of what had happened in Afghanistan. In late January 1980, he pulled the USA out of the forthcoming Moscow Olympic Games. He also advised the US Senate not to ratify (agree to) the SALT 2 treaty. He sent a US Navy Task Force of 1800 marines to the Arabian Sea to protect oil routes. To damage the Soviets economically, he cut trade between the USA and the Soviet Union. For example, he stopped the export of 17 million tons of grain and the sale of technological goods such as computers and oil drilling equipment to the Soviet Union.

SOURCE B

In this cartoon from the *Guardian* in 1980, President Carter views the Soviet invasion of Afghanistan.

The war continues

After the first few months of 1980, Soviet troops controlled the towns where they were based, but the Afghan rebels, the Mujaheddin, controlled the countryside. The Mujaheddin were not just fighting to get rid of Soviet troops. They were fighting to turn Afghanistan into a Muslim country. They were well equipped because both China and the USA gave them weapons.

The war was similar to the Vietnam War in that a superpower had difficulty defeating a less powerful enemy – but this time it was the Soviets rather than the Americans who were on the receiving end. The Mujaheddin attacked Soviet supply routes and shot at Soviet planes. The Soviets suffered increasing casualties, but succeeded only in propping up the unpopular communist government in Kabul. Although there were 125,000 Soviet troops in Afghanistan by the early 1980s, they found it impossible to defeat the Afghan rebels. In 1982 a massive attack against the Mujaheddin in the Panjahir Valley failed.

QUESTIONS

1. Why did the Soviet Union invade Afghanistan in December 1979?
2. Why could the Soviet Union, a superpower, not defeat the rebel forces of Afghanistan?
3. What were the consequences of the Soviet invasion of Afghanistan?

SOURCE D

Some boys who fought for the Mujaheddin against the Soviet Union.

The Soviet Union faced hostility from Muslim nations such as Pakistan. Indeed, the Soviet Union increasingly became worried that some of the 30 million Muslims within the Soviet Union might revolt in support of the Mujaheddin.

In 1985 a new Soviet leader, Mikhail Gorbachev, realised that the war could never be won. He started talks in 1987 with the USA and agreement was reached at Geneva in 1988 between himself and the US President, Ronald Reagan. The last Soviet troops left Afghanistan in February 1989.

The consequences of the war were disastrous for Afghanistan. Over 3 million refugees fled to Pakistan or Iran. About a million people died – and the fighting continued between rival Afghan groups after the Soviet departure. Afghans who remained suffered from food shortages because the war had destroyed so much farmland.

The Soviet Union had lost about 20,000 soldiers in the war against the Mujaheddin. The war also caused great damage to the Soviet economy, costing several billion dollars a year.

The Cold War renewed: Reagan and the Strategic Defence Initiative

Ronald Reagan became US President in January 1981 when criticism over Soviet involvement in Afghanistan was at its height. Reagan's tough anti-communist stance helped his election; he referred to the Soviet Union as 'that evil Empire'.

SOURCE E

A cartoon from the *Sunday Times*, 29 November 1981.

Development of new weapons

Reagan increased the USA's defence spending from $178 billion in 1981 to $367 billion in 1986. New weapons were developed, such as the Cruise missile, and NATO agreed that 464 US Cruise missiles should be positioned in western Europe. In 1981, Reagan announced that the USA had developed a new type of bomb – the neutron bomb. This could kill many people without destroying much property. The Americans were also developing the MX missile. This powerful missile could be transported underground and be launched from different underground launch sites.

The Soviet Union was afraid that these developments would upset the existing 'balance of terror'. This balance was based on the idea of mutually assured destruction (MAD), which meant that, as each side had the ability to destroy the other side totally many times over, neither side would be prepared to risk nuclear war.

The Strategic Defence Initiative (SDI)

In 1983, US scientists began work on the Strategic Defence Initiative. This came to be known as the 'Star Wars' project, after a popular film. It was a satellite anti-missile system that would orbit the earth. The aim was to make it impossible for Soviet missiles to reach US targets by creating a huge laser shield in space.

Arms talks between the USA and the Soviet Union nevertheless resumed in 1982, at Geneva in Switzerland. They were called START (Strategic Arms Reduction Talks) and their main aim was to limit nuclear weapons, initially in Europe. Reagan knew that the USA was vastly superior to the Soviet Union in its nuclear capacity, but the USA had huge debts and could not afford to continue spending at its current level.

The situation in Poland

Meanwhile the Soviet Union had its own problems. In 1980 there were protest movements in Poland, caused by high prices and food and fuel shortages. The shipyard workers at Gdansk went on strike. The Polish government was forced to allow the workers to form a trade union called Solidarity, which was led by Lech Walesa. However, in 1981 the Soviet government encouraged the Polish armed forces to seize control of the government, ban the trade union and imprison its leaders. The Soviet government knew that it had to keep control of Poland, otherwise other communist countries in eastern Europe might also claim their freedom. The USA provided secret support for those in the outlawed Solidarity movement.

Leadership of the Soviet Union

The Soviet Union's leadership was weak in the early 1980s. Brezhnev was ill for some time before he died in 1982. He was followed as leader by Yuri Andropov and then by Konstantin Chernenko. These men both suffered from ill health, and they died in 1984 and 1985 respectively.

There were a lot of petty squabbles at this time between the Soviet Union and the USA. For example, the Soviet Union condemned the US invasion of Grenada in 1983, which crushed a communist take-over there. In 1984, along with other communist countries, the Soviet Union boycotted the Los Angeles Olympics in protest.

Mikhail Gorbachev became President of the Soviet Union in 1985. This was to allow Reagan to complete his eight years as US President with some positive achievements.

Changing Soviet and US attitudes

Mikhail Gorbachev

Mikhail Gorbachev became a member of the Politburo, the most powerful group within the Communist Party, in 1980. When Chernenko died in 1985, Gorbachev was chosen as the leader. At the age of 54, he was the youngest man to hold supreme power in the Soviet Union since Joseph Stalin. He appeared to be open to new ideas and was keen to see progress, both within the Soviet Union and in world relations.

Gorbachev saw that the economy of the Soviet Union was on the edge of disaster. Too much money was being spent on the arms race and on the war in Afghanistan. Industry was being run in the same way as it had been under Stalin, but without the climate of fear that had kept workers trying to meet production targets. These factors, combined with growing corruption within the Communist Party and an increasing problem with alcoholism, meant that both industrial output and the quality of goods produced was falling. Many people believed that the system could not be changed. But Gorbachev knew that there had to be changes, even though introducing reforms would anger some members of the Communist Party.

SOURCE F

Mikhail Gorbachev.

New Soviet policies

Gorbachev introduced new policies. The two most famous were *perestroika* and *glasnost*:

- *Perestroika* means restructuring – that is, changing some economic policies to allow more competition and more incentives to produce goods. He believed that the Soviet Union could survive only if it changed from the command economy that had existed since the era of Stalin.
- *Glasnost* means openness – in this case, restoring faith in government and ending corruption. Gorbachev believed that people should not be punished for simply disagreeing with government policies. There should be a more open debate. This feeling of openness applied both within the Soviet Union and in its relations with the West.

In addition, Gorbachev believed that the Soviet Union would have to cut back on its world commitments and abandon the Brezhnev Doctrine by loosening control over its satellite states. This would mean cuts in arms expenditure and pulling out of Afghanistan.

US attitudes

President Reagan was naturally pleased to learn of Gorbachev's changing policies for the Soviet Union. The government of the USA had also come to realise that cuts in expenditure were essential. As the Soviet Union planned to cut its defence expenditure, Reagan felt that it was safe for the USA to do the same.

Arms reduction

Reagan and Gorbachev met several times in the 1980s. In Geneva in November 1985, they agreed in principle to cut offensive weapons by 50 per cent. A summit meeting in Iceland in 1986 was only partially successful as the USA refused to give up its SDI. However, the Soviet Union confirmed that its troops would be withdrawn from Afghanistan, and promised that the Soviet Union would not test any more nuclear weapons unless the USA did so.

In December 1987 the two leaders agreed to get rid of all medium- and short-range nuclear weapons. This was called the Intermediate Range Nuclear Forces Treaty (INF). This was an amazing turn-around for both countries, which had been building them up just a few years before. The dismantling of these weapons began at once.

Reforms in the Soviet Union

Gorbachev also introduced reforms in the Soviet Union. Many people who had been imprisoned for disagreeing with communist policies were released. Others, such as the physicist and human rights campaigner Andrei Sakharov, were allowed to return from exile. In 1987 changes in economic policy meant that people were allowed to buy and sell at a profit for the first time since Stalin had come to power over 60 years before.

However, hard-line communists were horrified at what Gorbachev was doing. They said that he was stirring up trouble and raising the expectations of the Soviet people too much. In some respects, they were right. For instance, once freedom of speech was allowed, Gorbachev could not control the media. Many people wanted to get rid of communism altogether. This was especially true in eastern Europe.

The end of Soviet control of eastern Europe

In 1989, Mikhail Gorbachev's popularity in the world was at its height. In October he was awarded the Nobel Peace Prize. Then, in December 1989, he and the new US President, George Bush, met to announce the end of the Cold War. Yet at the same time, Soviet control of eastern Europe was rapidly collapsing. Indeed, the speed of that collapse stunned the world.

The communist countries of eastern Europe had become more and more discontented with control from Moscow during the 1980s. In Poland, the trade union Solidarity campaigned against the government and received considerable support (see page 93). In Hungary in 1986, there were widespread demonstrations using the banned Hungarian flag. The police beat up the demonstrators. In particular, the economic problems of eastern Europe were becoming more severe than ever.

In March 1989, Gorbachev told the communist leaders of eastern Europe that the Red Army would no longer be able to defend them. It became clear to the people of those countries that Soviet tanks would not be used to put down demonstrations. Indeed, when there were troubles in Hungary in early 1989 and it was agreed that other political parties could be formed, Gorbachev began the withdrawal of Soviet troops.

Poland

In June 1989 free elections were held in Poland for the first time since the Second World War. Solidarity won nearly all the seats that it contested, and Lech Walesa became the first non-communist leader in eastern Europe since 1945. Gradually the Soviet Bloc began to disintegrate.

East Germany

By the autumn of 1989 thousands of people were fleeing East Germany through Austria. Massive demonstrations took place in East German cities when Gorbachev visited the country. Gorbachev told the unpopular East German leader, Erich Honecker, to allow reforms. He responded by telling his troops to fire on the demonstrators, but they refused. Honecker was forced to resign. On 10 November 1989 thousands of East Germans marched to the Berlin Wall, and the guards even joined the demonstrators in pulling it down. The symbolic barrier between East and West had disappeared nearly 30 years after it had been built.

Czechoslovakia

Thousands of people demonstrated in Prague, the capital city of Czechoslovakia, on 24 November 1989. The police tried to stop the demonstrations. However, Alexander Dubcek, the deposed communist leader, and the playwright Vaclav Havel appeared in public to encourage the demonstrators to continue. In December, the communist leader resigned and was replaced by Havel. Free elections were held in 1990.

Hungary

The communist government under Imre Pozsgay accepted the need for change and led the moves for reform in Hungary. Other political parties were allowed, and in November 1989 the Communist Party renamed itself as the Socialist Party, promising free elections in 1990.

Romania

In December 1989 there was a short and very bloody revolution in Romania. The hated communist dictator, Nicolae Ceausescu, and his wife, Elena, were executed.

SOURCE G

CITIZENS OF UNITED CITY OVERCOME THEIR DISBELIEF

Yesterday Berlin ceased to be a divided city. Tens of thousands of East Berliners streamed to the West, unhindered for the first time since the Wall was put up 28 years ago. Most crossed just for the experience of freedom they had been denied so long.

Huge crowds built up on the Western side of the Wall as West Berliners witnessed the historic developments, some even crossing over into the East for a walk. In front of the Brandenburg Gate and elsewhere, they perched precariously on top of the Wall, clapping and calling for it to go.

East Berliners have been offered free tickets for a football match today in West Berlin as well as to a number of concerts and the opera. It was unclear last night how many East Berliners planned to stay in the West. But as the West German cities of Bremen and Hanover said they could take no more refugees, Berlin was still offering a warm welcome.

'After all we are not just one people, we are also one city,' said one West Berliner, who described the last 24 hours as 'simply unbelievable'.

From The Guardian, *11 November 1989.*

Bulgaria

In November 1989 the communist leader resigned, and free elections were held the next year.

The Baltic States

In 1990 Latvia, Lithuania and Estonia declared themselves independent of the Soviet Union.

The fall of communist Europe, 1989.

The collapse of the Soviet Union

To many people, it seemed that Gorbachev had done very little to prevent the fall of communism in eastern Europe. Many Soviets saw this as weakness. They were also aware that economic reforms in the Soviet Union had produced no immediate effect. They still suffered from food shortages and rising prices. Many wanted to see the collapse of the communist system, not just reforms within communism.

SOURCE H

A cartoon from *The Guardian* in January 1990, showing the communist hammer and sickle in tears.

In February 1990, 250,000 people demonstrated in Moscow against communism. In the annual May Day parade in Moscow's Red Square, Gorbachev was booed. Although he was immensely popular in the West, among the Soviet people Gorbachev was increasingly criticised – both by those who believed he had gone too far, and by those who believed that more reforms were needed. The new President of the Russian republic, Boris Yeltsin, encouraged the break-up of the Soviet Union.

In August 1991, hardline communists led a coup against Gorbachev, who was made a prisoner in his own *dacha* (country home) in the Crimea. Yeltsin led a demonstration against the coup, insisting that the reform movement had to continue in order to save Russia. Yeltsin was seen as a hero, who would rescue Russia from a slide back into the days of communist repression. He was also seen increasingly as the man with the power.

Yeltsin went on to disband the Communist Party in Russia, and formally ended the Soviet Union in December 1991. Later in the same month, Gorbachev resigned as Soviet President, as there was no longer a Soviet state for him to preside over. The communist red flag was lowered for the last time over the Kremlin.

Implications for world affairs

The Cold War had ended. Communist eastern Europe had collapsed. The arms race was at an end. However, this did not, of course, mean the end of world problems. New ones arose in the former Soviet Bloc countries, as ethnic groups sought independence for their own nationalities. For example, in January 1993, Czechoslovakia split into two separate states, the Czech Republic and Slovakia.

The worst troubles were in the former Yugoslavia, as a number of areas tried to win independence after the collapse of communist control in 1990. The Serbs refused to accept a Croat as leader, and both Slovenia and Croatia declared independence in 1991. The resulting civil war, with all its horrors of so-called ethnic cleansing, continued on and off for years, as long-held national attitudes fuelled people's hatred for each other.

East and West Berlin were reunited in 1991, and East and West Germany became a single country. Since then, eastern Germany has undergone many reforms and received considerable aid from western Germany to reduce the gap in living standards between the two parts of Germany.

Although the Cold War was over, it could be argued that it had achieved something positive. Compared with the first half of the twentieth century, there had been no world war. It was an open question whether, in the absence of a Cold War, this relative peace could be continued into the next millennium.

QUESTIONS

1. Why did Gorbachev need to carry out reforms in the Soviet Union?
2. Why did the reforms lead to the collapse of the Soviet Union and the loss of its control of eastern Europe?
3. Read Source I carefully.
   According to the article, why has the USA become so powerful in the twentieth century?
   Using your own knowledge, what other reasons would you add?

SOURCE I

UNCLE SAM'S CENTURY

America's unique blend of confidence and self-doubt should guarantee another era of dominance

When the phrase 'the American century' was coined in 1941, it was used at a time when America was being told off for not fulfilling its duty as 'the elder brother of nations'. America then dominated the Second World War and the post-war world.

In the year 2000 America is more dominant in the world than ever before – its economy booming, its military power unmatched, its technology thriving, and its culture over all the globe. In science, art, war and business America has played the leading role in framing the modern world.

Yet only ten years ago in 1990 the USA appeared to have overstretched itself. Japan's economy was roaring, China was a rising power and a united Europe was coming to life. Meanwhile spiralling US debt, economic problems and government indecision seemed to be attacking America from inside.

However, at the end of the 1990s it is clear that the last decade of the twentieth century has been more America's than any decade before it. Japan is still struggling out of economic problems, the euro cannot compete over the world with the dollar, and the Cold War has been won. Next month, the US economy will be able to declare the longest period of sustained growth in its history. The astonishing success of the 1990s has been typical of American success in the twentieth century.

The Times, *3 January 2000.*

Exam-style questions

These questions follow the pattern of questions set by AQA/SEG for Paper 2 of its current Modern World History Syllabus.

1. Czechoslovakia, 1968

Study Source A and then answer **all** parts of Question 1.

Source A: Russian tanks in Wenceslas Square in Prague, August 1968

From a newspaper photograph of the time, 1968.

Question 1

(a) What can you learn from **Source A** about the Soviet invasion of Czechoslovakia in 1968? *(4 marks)*

(b) Describe the events of the 'Prague Spring' from Dubcek's reforms to his being forced from office early in 1969. *(8 marks)*

(c) In spite of episodes such as the Czech crisis of 1968, why did détente occur in the 1970s? *(8 marks)*

2. The war in Vietnam

Study Source A and then answer **all** parts of Question 2.

Source A: The massacre at My Lai

> My troops were being massacred by an enemy they could not see. But I remembered what I had been told. The enemy was communism: it didn't have a sex, race, or an age. Yet I knew it was out there, and that when I came face to face with it I had to put the lives of my troops first.

From a statement made by the officer in charge of the soldiers at My Lai, during his trial for the murder of the victims there.

Question 2

(a) How does **Source A** help you to understand why the massacre of My Lai happened during the Vietnam War? *(4 marks)*

(b) Describe the main events of the Vietnam War. *(8 marks)*

(c) 'The Vietnam War had shown that the USA could not stop the spread of communism.' Was this the main consequence of the Vietnam War for the USA?
Explain your answer by reference to the statement above and to other possible consequences. *(8 marks)*

3. Soviet involvement in Afghanistan

Study Source A and then answer **all** parts of Question 3.

Source A: The Soviet Union's invasion of Afghanistan, December 1979

> The Soviet Union was forced to make a choice: we had to bring in troops or let the Afghan revolution be defeated. We knew that the decision to bring in troops would not be popular. But we also knew that we would have ceased to be a great power if we did not take unpopular but necessary decisions.

Written by Alex Bovin in an article in a Soviet newspaper, *Izvestia*, in 1980.

Question 3

(a) What can you learn from **Source A** about the Soviet Union's reasons for invading Afghanistan? *(4 marks)*

(b) 'The Cold War got worse in the early 1980s simply because of the Soviet invasion of Afghanistan.' Is this true?
Explain your answer carefully. *(8 marks)*

(c) Describe the collapse of Soviet control in eastern Europe at the end of the Cold War. *(8 marks)*

Chapter 4

Russia, 1917–41

Introduction

At the beginning of 1917, Russia was ruled by Tsar Nicholas II. Despite some economic and political progress in the years after the turn of the century, Russia was still in desperate need of modernisation. The 1905 revolution provided a dress rehearsal for the first revolution of 1917. The Tsar survived the first revolution, but the chaos caused by Russia's involvement in the First World War led to his abdication in February 1917.

The Provisional Government, which succeeded Nicholas II, was short-lived. In November 1917 it was overthrown by the Bolsheviks (communists), a small, dedicated group of revolutionaries, led by Lenin. They defeated their opponents, the Whites, in a fiercely fought civil war and consolidated their control of what became known as the Soviet Union.

In 1924 Lenin died. Over the next few years Stalin outwitted several rivals, including Trotsky, to establish himself as leader. In the 1930s, through a series of purges, Stalin removed all potential rivals and made himself absolute dictator of the Soviet Union. By 1941, through ruthless economic policies, he had transformed the Soviet economy. He established total control of the countryside by a brutal policy of collectivisation, while modernising industry through a series of Five-Year Plans.

The Soviet Union of 1941 was not very different from the Russia of the Tsars. The dictatorship of Nicholas II had been replaced by that of Stalin.

1894	Nicholas II becomes Tsar
1904	Russo-Japanese War
1905	Revolution
1914	Russia enters the First World War
1917	Two revolutions in March and November
1918	Treaty of Brest-Litovsk with Germany
1921	New Economic Policy introduced
1924	Death of Lenin
1928	Stalin introduces collectivisation and first Five-Year Plan
1934	Assassination of Kirov
1936	New constitution introduced
1940	Assassination of Trotsky
1941	Germany invades the Soviet Union

Russia in 1914.

The nature and diversity of Russian society in 1917

Russia at the beginning of the twentieth century

Russia in 1900 was a huge country that spread across the continents of both Europe and Asia. It had a population of 125 million, of which only 55 million were Russian. The rest were made up of 25 other nationalities, including Finns, Poles, Ukrainians, Estonians, Lithuanians and Georgians. Many of these nationalities resented being part of Russia and wanted to be able to rule themselves. Communications were poor, with few railways by 1900. Most people did not travel beyond their immediate neighbourhood. The sheer size of Russia, the backward communications and the diverse nationalities meant that there was little sense of national identity.

The government of Russia

Russia was an autocracy. This means that it was ruled by one man, the Tsar, who had almost total power. He was assisted by ministers whom he chose and who were answerable to him. There was no parliament and the people had no right to vote in elections. Most Tsars ruled in a harsh and repressive manner, and crushed any opposition to their regime. Newspapers were censored and could only print what the government wanted them to say. The Tsar's secret police, the Okhrana, had agents in every town and village to report back on anyone who criticised the government.

Tsardom was a very personal system that depended almost totally on the character of the Tsar. A strong Tsar could just about make the system of government work, but it could well collapse under a weak ruler.

The countryside

Russia was a rural society. Over 90 per cent of the people were poor peasants who were barely able to scratch a living from the land, which they rarely owned for themselves. Agriculture was in desperate need of modernisation. Peasants farmed with old-fashioned tools on strips of land in fields as they had done for centuries. This was inefficient and made it difficult for new methods to be introduced.

Russia was a land of great contrasts. While the majority of peasants lived in abject poverty, at the other end of the scale was the aristocracy, or great landowners. They lived comfortably on huge estates. They controlled the local government, especially the local councils called zemstvos, and acted as a link between the people and the Tsar. Some ran their estates very inefficiently, although a minority saw the need for a more up-to-date agricultural system.

The towns

Compared to most western European countries in 1900, Russia was economically backward. This situation began to change with the onset of industrialisation. Large factories were springing up and industry grew faster in Russia than in any other European country. A whole range of industries, such as coal mining, iron and steel, and textiles, emerged. Large numbers of peasants flocked to the towns to work in the factories. This industrial working class was known as the proletariat. The number of workers grew rapidly as more factories were built, especially in the already large cities of Moscow and St Petersburg. Their living and working conditions were appalling. The proletariat often lived in slums or even in the factories where they worked. They earned very low wages and worked long hours. They were not allowed to form trade unions to fight for better conditions. The police or the army rapidly crushed any protests or strikes.

SOURCE A

Very often the peasants do not have enough allotment land. They cannot feed themselves, clothe themselves, heat their homes, keep their tools and livestock, secure seed for sowing and lastly pay their taxes.

From a police report on conditions in the countryside, 1905.

SOURCE B

The whole day we pour out our blood and sweat. Every minute we expose our life to danger. When there are accidents, they accuse us of carelessness. The greed of the bosses, the long working hours, the meagre wages - there is the cause of all the accidents.

A Russian trade union leaflet of 1898, describing the conditions of town workers.

QUESTIONS

1. Using the map on page 103 and your own knowledge, explain the difficulties in ruling Russia in the early twentieth century.
2. What does Source A tell us about conditions in the countryside?
3. How reliable is Source B as evidence of working conditions in Russia in 1900?

The two revolutions of 1917

Reasons for the collapse of the Tsarist monarchy

On 15 March 1917 the Tsar, Nicholas II, was forced to abdicate. This was due to a variety of circumstances, including the fundamental failure of the Tsarist regime to modernise itself and the weaknesses of Nicholas II himself. There were other long-term problems, especially the growth of discontent in the years before the First World War. The effects of Russian involvement in the First World War made these problems worse.

SOURCE A

Tsar Nicholas II and his family. This photograph was taken shortly before the First World War in 1913.

The weaknesses of Nicholas II

Nicholas II came to the throne in 1894. He was hard working, conscientious and devoted to his family. But he had several major weaknesses. He found it difficult to make decisions and listened only to advisers, whom he appointed, and to his German-born wife, Alexandra. He did not realise or respond to the growing demands for change in Russian society, or the need for rapid modernisation. On the contrary, he wanted to go back to the golden era when the Tsars had total power. He and his wife believed that God had chosen them to rule, and that no one had the right to challenge them.

SOURCE B

What is going to happen to me? I am not prepared to be the Tsar. I never wanted to become one. I know nothing of the business of ruling. I have no idea of even how to talk to ministers.

Nicholas made these comments on becoming Tsar in 1894.

The growth of opposition

Many Russian people were unhappy with the way in which their country was run. There was a tradition of revolutionary violence against the Tsars. In 1881 revolutionaries had assassinated Tsar Alexander II. The rapid industrial changes at the beginning of the twentieth century, together with the attitude of the Tsar, did much to foster the growth of opposition. The Liberals were the largest opposition group. They wanted to replace the government of the Tsar with a written constitution and an elected parliament or Duma.

The most important of Russia's revolutionaries were Marxists. They followed the teachings of Karl Marx (1818–83). He was a German socialist who, in his book *Das Kapital*, described how capitalism would collapse and be replaced by communism. He argued that in industrialised nations such as Britain and the USA, it was the capitalists – the owners of mills, factories and workshops – who had the power, but it was the proletariat who produced the wealth. The workers would soon resent this and rise up and take over the government. All the wealth in the country would then be owned by all the people.

In Russia many revolutionaries, mainly from the emerging middle class, joined the Marxist Social Democratic Party. They argued a lot among themselves. In 1903, at a conference in London, the party split into two groups. The Bolsheviks (meaning 'majority' in Russian) were led by Vladimir Lenin and believed in seizing power at the first opportunity. The other group, the Mensheviks ('minority'), believed in co-operating with other groups to make life better.

There was another opposition group called the Social Revolutionaries. They believed that revolution in Russia would have to be based not on industrial workers, but on the peasants and their struggle for land.

The 1905 revolution

The growth of opposition culminated in the revolution of 1905, which, in many respects, was a dress rehearsal for the events of March 1917. The 1905 revolution was caused by growing discontent due to bad harvests, high prices and poor living and working conditions. Nicholas II decided that a short, victorious war was one way to boost the prestige of the government and win the support of the people. In February 1904, war broke out between Russia and Japan over Manchuria. The Russo-Japanese War of 1904–5 was a disaster for Russia. Heavy defeats on land and at sea increased discontent. The Tsar was forced to ask the Japanese for peace. Defeat was a tremendous blow to the Russian government. When the soldiers returned home to Russia, they told people about shortages of food and guns and the incompetence of their commanders.

The immediate event that sparked off revolution was 'Bloody Sunday', on Sunday 22 January 1905. A huge but peaceful march of ordinary people, led by a priest, Father Gapon, who was well known for his trade union activities, took a petition to hand to the Tsar at his Winter Palace in St Petersburg. They were unarmed and trusted the Tsar. Troops guarding the palace panicked and opened fire on the marchers, killing and wounding hundreds. The trust between the Tsar and his people was broken.

SOURCE C

A German cartoon of 1905 about the events of Bloody Sunday.

Bloody Sunday sparked riots and strikes in towns throughout Russia, and peasants turned against landowners in the countryside. In June, there was a mutiny on board the Russian battleship *Potemkin*. The trade unions joined together and formed a central committee called the St Petersburg Soviet.

The Tsar was eventually persuaded by his Prime Minister, Count Witte, to publish a document called the *October Manifesto*. This promised a number of reforms, including a parliament (Duma). This split the Liberals. Some accepted it and became known as the Octobrists. Many other Liberals remained deeply suspicious about the powers of the Duma and did not trust the Tsar.

The failure of reform, 1905–14

The 1905 revolution had been a close-run thing. Would the Tsar learn his lesson and carry out the necessary reforms?

Although Nicholas II kept his promise and allowed free elections for a Duma in May 1906, the four Dumas that met between 1906 and 1914 were not a success. The Tsar was determined that they should have as little power as possible, and he dismissed them whenever they asked for reform. The Prime Minister from 1906 to 1911, Peter Stolypin, tried to get the peasants on the side of the Tsar by wiping out their debts and making it easier for them to buy the Tsar's land. But Stolypin's repressive policy against revolutionaries and strikers led to his assassination in 1911.

The effects of the First World War

Russia entered the First World War in alliance with Britain and France against Germany and Austria-Hungary.

At first, there was a wave of patriotism and enthusiasm for the war. The only opponents were the Bolsheviks, who thought the war was being fought in the interests of rich people and those ruling Russia. The Russian 'steamroller' (huge armies) was expected to defeat easily the Central Powers of Germany and Austria-Hungary. But the mood soon changed as Russia suffered defeat after defeat, and casualties mounted. The war proved to be an economic, political, social and military disaster, and was the short-term cause of the collapse of Tsarism.

In the autumn of 1914, Russia was heavily defeated at the battles of Tannenburg and Masurian Lakes by superior German forces. An offensive in 1916, organised by General Brusilov, made great advances against the Austrian army. However, with German help, the Austrians halted the Russian advance. The Russian war effort collapsed due to poor leadership and lack of supplies. The Russian government, hampered by a totally inadequate transport system, could not keep the army supplied with food and equipment. By 1916, thousands of Russian soldiers were deserting.

SOURCE D

Wounded Russian soldiers in 1916.

In 1915 the Tsar took over personal command of Russia's armies. This was to prove a costly mistake. He knew little of military affairs and was no more than a figurehead. He was held directly responsible for subsequent military defeats. This task took him away from the centre of government at Petrograd, formerly known as St Petersburg.

Russia's railway system was unable to keep the country and its armies supplied. Russian cities experienced food shortages almost from the start of the war, but these became more severe as the war continued. This was to be an important factor in the immediate events leading to the downfall of the Tsar.

Agriculture was badly affected by the war. Millions of Russian peasants fought in the army and could not work on the land. The number of horses on the land fell by one-third due to the needs of the armed forces. There were several bad harvests, which increased the problems of providing adequate food for the towns and cities.

Industry became geared towards the war effort, with increased production of heavy industries such as iron and steel and armaments. Other factories closed down, however, leading to job losses. The increased demands of the armed forces led to a severe shortage of fuel for the civilian population. This also badly affected the transport system. Among the working class, enthusiasm for the war quickly disappeared. It was replaced by discontent and a wave of strikes.

The war was very expensive for the government. As the government printed more money to pay for the war, the value of money fell and there was inflation – a rapid rise in prices. The price of basic food went up by 300 per cent. By the winter of 1916–17, millions of people were close to starvation.

Alexandra and Rasputin

These economic, military and social problems were worsened by political developments in Russia. Between 1915 and 1917 there were four Prime Ministers. Nicholas' absence at the front left the government in the hands of his wife, Alexandra, who was already unpopular due to her German background. Alexandra was greatly under the influence of Rasputin, a peasant from Siberia who claimed to be a holy man. The Tsar's son, Alexis, suffered from haemophilia, a blood disease that meant his blood would not clot. If he cut himself, he could bleed to death. Rasputin seemed to be able to control Alexis' blood disease and became a close adviser to the Tsar and Tsarina.

SOURCE E

A Russian cartoon showing Rasputin with the Tsar and Tsarina.

Rasputin and Alexandra sacked ministers and replaced them with Rasputin's friends. The government became even more inefficient and unable to cope with the demands of war. The Tsarina and Rasputin's unpopularity increased as stories spread of Rasputin's heavy drinking bouts and womanising, and there were rumours of an affair between Alexandra and Rasputin. The Duma and important members of the court begged Alexandra to remove him, but she refused.

Finally, in December 1916, a group of noblemen assassinated Rasputin. But it was too late. The winter of 1916–17 provided the final 'trigger' for revolution. It was the coldest that Russia had known for many years. In Petrograd the temperature was –35 °C. The largest factory in the city, the Putilov Engineering Works, was closed due to lack of fuel. In the countryside, the ground was frozen solid for weeks. Animals died from cold and starvation. Fuel froze. If there were spare goods, goods trains could not move them into the towns. Hungry and cold women queued for hours to buy basic necessities, such as food, which was in short supply. Many starved.

The events of the March revolution, 1917

By early 1917 Russia seemed ripe for revolution due to military defeats, incompetent government, chaotic transport, rising food prices and severe food and fuel shortages. When the March revolution occurred, however, it came as a surprise and was a spontaneous reaction to people's suffering, worsened by the effects of the war. It was totally unplanned.

The revolution began in Petrograd. Strikes broke out and factory workers poured on to the streets, chanting slogans like 'Land and freedom' and 'Down with the Tsar'. By 9 March 1917, there were 200,000 people on strike. Women and factory workers rioted and bakeries were looted. Police and soldiers were sent to restore order.

On 11 March troops fired on the protestors. On the following day, however, some troops mutinied and refused to fire on the demonstrators. The mutineers included the famous Volynsky Regiment. Within a few hours Petrograd was in the hands of the rioting mob.

SOURCE F

The tips of the bayonets were touching the breasts of the first row of demonstrators. Women, with tears in their eyes, were crying out to the soldiers, 'Comrades, take away your bayonets, join us!' The soldiers moved. They threw swift glances at their comrades. The next moment one bayonet is slowly raised. There is thunderous applause. The soldiers then mixed freely with the demonstrators.

An eyewitness account of the soldiers' mutiny in March 1917.

In desperation, Rodzianko, President of the Duma, telegraphed the Tsar to inform him of the seriousness of the situation. The Tsar, marooned at army headquarters near the front, ignored this warning, insisting that the demonstrations were the work of a 'hooligan movement'. He made matters worse by ordering the dissolution (break-up) of the Duma. This upset the middle classes, many of whom now supported the revolution.

Because of the breakdown of law and order, the Duma reluctantly decided to take over the government. Meanwhile, on 12 March, the workers organised themselves into a soviet (workers' council) in Petrograd based on the 1905 St Petersburg Soviet. Many of the soviet's members were soldiers who had mutinied against their officers. The soviet asserted its authority over the armed forces and issued Order Number One. This stated that soldiers need not obey any orders from the Duma that went against the soviet.

The Tsar did not want to give up power. He wanted to return to the capital to take control, but the railway was blocked. Finally, on 15 March, Russian army commanders persuaded the Tsar to abdicate (give up the throne) when he realised he had little support and had lost the loyalty of the armed forces. He chose to give the throne to his brother Michael, but the Russian people had had enough of Tsardom.

The problems facing the Provisional Government and its failures

The Provisional Government was set up after the abdication of the Tsar. It faced many problems that eventually contributed to its downfall after only eight months.

After the Tsar's abdication, someone had to run the country. Members of the Duma formed themselves into a Provisional Government. This government had not been elected and was only a temporary arrangement until elections could be held for another parliament. However, the elections were postponed because the war was going on.

The Provisional Government had a mixture of views. The new Prime Minister, Prince Lvov, was a noble. Alexander Kerensky, the Minister of Justice, was a Social Revolutionary. He soon became Minister of War and then Prime Minister, in July 1917.

Many people were enthusiastic about the Provisional Government at first. Indeed, initially, the government made popular decisions. It released all political prisoners, legalised political parties, and introduced the right to strike and an eight-hour working day. It also called for the election of a Constituent Assembly to decide Russia's new constitution.

The enthusiasm did not last long. The government soon ran into serious difficulties. The government itself caused some of them. Others were due to unfortunate circumstances.

SOURCE G

In response to the call of the Bolsheviks, the workers of Petrograd factories went on strike ...
The Bolshevik Committee met late at night in a small house on the outskirts.

'We can no longer wait and do nothing. The time has come to act openly. We shall begin tomorrow.
We must seize the arms stores and disarm the police', the Committee decided.

From a children's textbook written in the communist Soviet Union in 1976.

SOURCE H

When other people say that they foresaw the revolution, they are telling a complete lie. Everybody expected some political reform that would paralyse the influence of the Tsarina and set up a new administration.

Written after the March revolution by a Tsarist minister, Kokovtsov.

QUESTIONS

1. Why was Tsar Nicholas II able to survive the 1905 revolution?
2. How useful is Source E as evidence of attitudes towards the Tsar and his wife during the First World War?
3. Do you think it was the First World War that caused the downfall of Nicholas II?
4. Why do Sources G and H give different interpretations of the March revolution of 1917?

The Petrograd Soviet

During March 1917, workers in Petrograd had formed a soviet similar to the one set up during the 1905 revolution. The soviet had 3000 members. Each member represented up to 1000 workers or soldiers. The soviet became even more powerful than the Provisional Government as it controlled Petrograd, especially the army, factories and railways. This was a period of dual authority. At first, the soviet gave its support to the government, due partly to the influence of Kerensky, who was a member of both. But this support was short-lived.

Government weaknesses

The Provisional Government was handicapped by a variety of weaknesses. Under Kerensky the government became divided and did little to solve the problems faced by Russia.

Most members had little experience of government and were reluctant to make important decisions because they felt they should wait until the election of the Constituent Assembly. The government seemed weak and indecisive. This encouraged instability, strikes and eventually mutinies.

Attitude towards the war

The First World War had already caused great discontent and it continued to cause problems for the Provisional Government. Most Russians wanted an end to the war, but Kerensky, in order to maintain supplies from the Allies, decided to continue the war effort. He hoped that victories would strengthen his own position and that of the government. But a Russian offensive against the Germans in the summer of 1917 failed.

SOURCE I

It inherited nothing from the Tsar, but a terrible war, a shortage of food, a paralysed transport system, no money, and a population in a state of furious discontent.

Alexander Kerensky commenting on the position of the Provisional Government in 1917.

SOURCE J

The Provisional Government has no real force at its disposal. Its orders are carried out only to the extent that is permitted by the Soviet of Workers and Soldiers' Deputies which has in its hands the most important elements of real power – the army, the railways, the post and telegraphs.

Guchkov, the Minister of War, writing in March 1917.

SOURCE K

A poster issued by the Provisional Government to try to increase support for the war. Workers and soldiers are backing a Russian soldier.

The attack of 1917 put another strain on the government. They neglected vital social and economic issues within Russia due to their preoccupation with the war. They failed to provide food for the starving population of the towns and cities, and for the soldiers at the front.

They also failed to understand the level of discontent created by the land question. Although they initially confiscated Tsarist land, this was not given to the peasants. The Provisional Government wanted to keep the support of the landowners.

Lenin's influence

Lenin returned to Russia from exile in Switzerland in April 1917. The German government arranged a special train to take him to Russia via Sweden and Finland. The Germans hoped that Lenin would cause trouble in Russia and disrupt the Russian war effort.

On his arrival at Finland Station in Petrograd, Lenin caused some surprise, even to his own followers, by reading out the April Theses. This was his programme for the Bolsheviks. He declared his opposition to the Provisional Government and called for its overthrow.

Lenin's programme was summed up by the slogans 'Peace, Bread, Land' and 'All power to the soviets'. This brought increasing support for the Bolsheviks.

SOURCE L

A Soviet painting of Lenin addressing a crowd.

Weak and indecisive government

In July 1917 massive demonstrations took place against the government. Many of the 500,000 demonstrators were armed sailors. They marched on the government, but Kerensky had enough support to crush them and 400 were killed. He seized this opportunity to arrest the leading Bolsheviks, including Trotsky. Lenin went into exile in Finland.

There was support from the middle classes for the new commander-in-chief of the army, General Kornilov. He wanted to restore discipline to the army and to destroy the Petrograd Soviet and the Provisional Government. To seize power, he ordered his troops to march on Petrograd. Kerensky, in desperation, was forced to release the Bolshevik prisoners and rely upon the 'Red Guards' to block the advance. The Bolsheviks persuaded many of Kornilov's men to desert.

The rebellion collapsed and the Bolsheviks boosted their image as 'Defenders of the Revolution'. Kerensky's government was seen as weak and indecisive. In the countryside, peasants were increasingly seizing land for themselves. More and more soldiers were deserting from the army.

The Russian calendar

Until February 1918, Russia used the old calendar, which was thirteen days behind the rest of Europe. Then the new Bolshevik government decided to bring Russia into line. This means that alternative dates exist for events before the changeover. This book uses the new dates, but you might come across alternatives elsewhere. This makes a particular difference with the second revolution of 1917, which is known as either the October or the November revolution.

The causes and nature of the Bolshevik revolution

In November 1917 the Bolsheviks, led by Lenin and Trotsky, successfully overthrew the Provisional Government and set up their own government. The November revolution was partly caused by the failures of the Provisional Government. It was also due to the appeal and planning of the Bolshevik Party.

The Bolsheviks

Lenin had spent many years preparing the Bolsheviks for revolution. From the start he had criticised the First World War. He thought it was a capitalist war. Lenin soon became aware of the discontent among both soldiers and civilians. By 1917 he had a small group of dedicated revolutionaries ready and able to seize power. Leon Trotsky, a leading Menshevik, only joined the Bolsheviks in the summer of 1917, but he became a close colleague of Lenin and was given the task of organising the seizure of power.

Support for the Bolsheviks increased due to Lenin's slogans, the mistakes and failures of the Provisional Government and the part played by the Red Guards in the defeat of the Kornilov Rebellion. Lenin ensured that he gained the support of the influential Petrograd Soviet, which began to work against Kerensky and the Provisional Government. By late September, the Bolsheviks had won majorities in the Moscow and Petrograd Soviets for the first time.

Lenin still had to persuade the other leading Bolsheviks that the time was right to seize power. He returned secretly from Finland in October to attend a Central Committee of the Bolshevik Party. The Committee voted 10–2 in favour of carrying out a second revolution.

The events of the Bolshevik revolution

The Bolshevik revolution, contrary to later communist propaganda, was quite a small-scale affair. Although Lenin was in charge, Trotsky did most of the planning. The plan was for the Bolsheviks to strike at the same time as the All-Russian Congress of Soviets was meeting in Petrograd. The armed Bolshevik Red Guards were to seize the important buildings and bridges in Petrograd. They had already won over some of the troops in the Petrograd garrison. The cruiser *Aurora*, with a Bolshevik crew, was to sail up the River Neva and fire its guns as a signal for the Red Guards to capture their targets.

Trotsky was Chairman of the Military Revolutionary Committee. From his office in Room 10 of the Smolni Institute, he issued arms to the Red Guards and drew up the plans for the seizure of the key places in Petrograd. Kerensky knew of the Bolshevik plans and had closed down the Bolshevik newspaper offices. He did not, however, have enough loyal troops to protect his government.

There was little fighting during the November revolution, much less than in March. The Red Guards took control of the capital, seizing the Telephone Exchange, the Telegraph Agency, the State Bank and the bridges over the river. The *Aurora* sailed up the river ready to bombard the Winter Palace.

Kerensky went to the front line to try to find loyal troops who would save his government. He failed and went into hiding. The Red Guards took the Winter Palace the same night (7/8 November). The All-Russian Congress of Soviets was meeting while these events took place. The Mensheviks and most of the Social Revolutionaries walked out of the meeting in protest at the Bolshevik revolution. This left the Bolsheviks in control.

The ministers of the Provisional Government were arrested in the Winter Palace, apart from Kerensky, who managed to flee abroad. The following day, Lenin set up a new government called the Council of the People's Commissars. He issued a decree declaring that power had been taken over by the Congress in the name of the soviets of all Russia.

A few days later, on 15 November, the Bolsheviks seized control of Moscow. They now had control of the two largest cities, but little else.

Reasons for the Bolshevik success

Later Bolshevik propaganda portrayed these events as a 'popular revolution' brought about by mass support from the proletariat for communist ideas (see Source M). Nothing could be further from the truth. It was achieved by a relatively small group of dedicated revolutionaries.

The majority of Russians, even in Petrograd and Moscow, were unaware of the Bolshevik takeover. So why were the Bolsheviks successful?

This was due to a variety of factors. In many respects, Lenin and the Bolsheviks were fortunate because of the mistakes of the Provisional Government. But Lenin ensured that the Bolsheviks took advantage of these mistakes. The appeal of Bolshevism and especially Lenin's slogan 'Peace, Bread, Land' brought support, while Lenin ensured that the timing of the revolution was just right. The main reasons for success were the careful Bolshevik preparations, under Trotsky, and the tactics used to seize the key points in Petrograd.

SOURCE M

A painting from 1937 showing the storming of the Winter Palace.

SOURCE N

The Bolshevik party was waging a determined struggle to win over the masses. The struggle was headed by Lenin, who frequently addressed mass rallies and meetings. Lenin's speeches, noted for their profound content and brilliant delivery, inspired the workers and soldiers. Bolshevik membership began to grow rapidly.

A Soviet historian, writing in 1981.

SOURCE O

The reality of the [November] Revolution was an armed rising by a revolutionary minority inspired by the political genius of Lenin against a government that had already lost control.

The view of a British historian in 1987.

QUESTIONS

1. Using Sources I and J and your own knowledge, explain why the Provisional Government lost support.
2. Is Source L a reliable view of Lenin's activities in 1917?
3. How useful is Source M as a view of the Bolshevik revolution?
4. How do Sources N and O differ in their interpretation of the Bolshevik revolution?

The establishment of communist rule, 1918–24

The success of the Bolshevik revolution surprised almost everyone. Few believed that Lenin would succeed in staying in power. Lenin faced several major problems. The Bolsheviks were a tiny minority in control of only a small part of Russia. How could they hold on to power? They faced a host of opponents, many of whom wanted to restore the Tsar. Russia was still at war with Germany. Should they make peace? The Russian economy was in turmoil. How could they restore stability and carry out Lenin's promises of 'Peace, Bread and Land'?

Peace with Germany – the Treaty of Brest-Litovsk

The first need was for peace. The Germans had invaded Russia and were threatening Petrograd. Lenin had long opposed the war and needed peace in order to carry out much needed economic and social reform, and to fight against the opponents of the Bolshevik regime. A cease-fire was arranged with the Germans. Trotsky, now Commissar of Nationalities, was sent off to negotiate peace terms. The Treaty of Brest-Litovsk was signed on 3 March 1918.

Terms of the treaty

The terms of the peace were very harsh. Russia was forced to give up large areas of the old Russian Empire. It lost 26 per cent of its population, 27 per cent of its farmland and 74 per cent of its iron ore and coal. Russia also lost the Ukraine, its main grain source. The Russians also had to pay 300 million roubles in reparations to the Germans and had to demobilise at once.

Opposition to the treaty

The peace with Germany was very unpopular. There was even opposition from some Bolsheviks such as Kamenev and Bukharin. But Lenin threatened to resign unless the harsh peace terms were accepted. He argued that the terms of the treaty were of minor importance in the fight for world revolution.

Russia's losses in the Treaty of Brest-Litovsk, March 1918.

Lenin's gamble proved justified. Germany's Western Front collapsed in August 1918 and this was followed by the almost total withdrawal of German troops from Russia. Most of the treaty was now meaningless. The struggle over Brest-Litovsk had strengthened Lenin's hold over the Bolshevik Party and provided the opportunity to consolidate Bolshevik power.

How did the Bolsheviks stay in power?

In the face of great opposition, Lenin and the Bolsheviks were able to consolidate their hold over Russia in the years after their successful revolution. Russia returned to autocratic rule, very similar to that of the Tsars.

The Constituent Assembly

This was the Assembly promised after the first revolution of 1917. It was to be elected by the people and was then to choose a form of constitution for Russia. The election results, however, proved disappointing to Lenin. The Bolsheviks won only one-quarter of the seats. Lenin realised that his party would not be able to rule alongside the Constituent Assembly. So, after the Assembly had met for only one day, the Red Guards dissolved it at gunpoint. Lenin would not tolerate any opposition to Bolshevik rule.

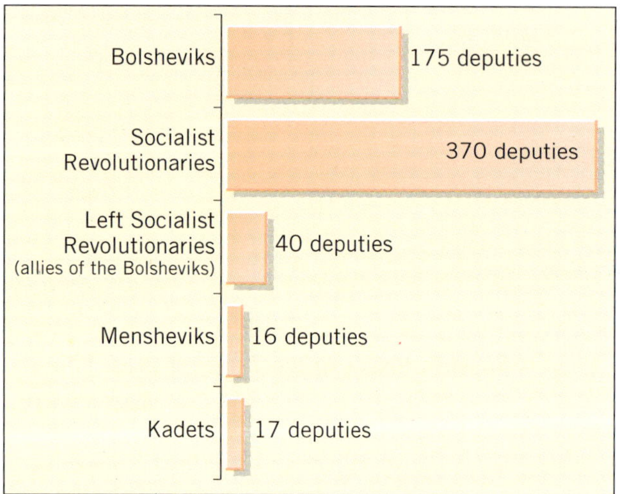

The results of the elections to the Constituent Assembly.

Communist dictatorship

Lenin now imposed a communist dictatorship, claiming that it was rule by the Bolshevik Party on behalf of the people. A new system of government was created. Instead of having government ministers as in Britain, commissars were appointed to take charge of foreign affairs, industry and so on. The equivalent to the British Cabinet was the Council of People's Commissars. In 1919, however, the Politburo was created. It was made up a few leading Bolsheviks, including Lenin, Trotsky and Stalin. It met every week and took important decisions.

Lenin also imposed one-party rule. Leaders of other political parties, such as the Mensheviks, the Social Revolutionaries and the Kadets, were arrested. By 1921 there was only one party, the Communist Party – the name adopted by the Bolsheviks in 1918. Only about 5 per cent of the population became party members. Candidates for elections had either to be Bolsheviks or belong to

SOURCE A

> When I made my speech in the assembly, every sentence of it was met with outcries, some spiteful, often supported by the brandishing of guns. Lenin showed his contempt for the Assembly by lounging in his chair and giving the impression of a man who was bored to death.
>
> *Written by Chernov, a Social Revolutionary.*

no party at all. All decisions at every level had to follow the party line. There was also a party youth movement called the Komsomol.

A secret police called the Cheka was set up to arrest real or imagined opponents of the party. It was founded in December 1917 and led by Felix Dzerzhinsky. In 1918 the Cheka began the 'Red Terror' in which enemies of the Bolsheviks were arrested, tortured and executed. By 1922 an estimated 200,000 people had been killed and 85,000 people sent to concentration camps.

Lenin also tried to gain early support by issuing a series of decrees:

- Businesses and trades were nationalised.
- Peasants were allowed to take over the land.
- Women were given equal rights to men.
- The government took the wealth of the Church.
- Different peoples in the Russian Empire were given the right to be independent.

These gave the Bolsheviks an important breathing space while they dealt with the threat posed by supporters of the Tsar.

QUESTIONS

1. Using the map on page 115 and your own knowledge, explain why many Russians were shocked by the Treaty of Brest-Litovsk.
2. How and why did Lenin set up a communist dictatorship in the years after the Bolshevik revolution?

The Russian Civil War, 1918–21

The main events of the Russian Civil War.

The threat to the Bolsheviks was increased by foreign intervention. The communist revolution and its threat of world revolution alarmed countries such as Britain, France, the USA and Japan. These countries were also annoyed by Lenin's decision to make peace with Germany and by his refusal to pay the Tsar's debts to foreign countries. They wanted Russia back in the war. These countries sent weapons. British troops landed at Murmansk in the north, and a combined British–Japanese force landed at Vladivostock in the far east. British and French troops landed in the south.

The Czech legion also joined the anti-communist crusade. This was a unit composed of Czechs who had been captured during the First World War and who had agreed to fight on the Russian side against their Austrian masters. They too wanted Russia back in the war. The Czech legion took control of the Trans-Siberian Railway.

The Bolsheviks faced a war of survival against supporters of the Tsar. This civil war lasted three years.

Causes of the civil war

The Bolsheviks had been able to seize power because their opponents were weak and poorly led. Once Lenin's enemies began to organise, the Bolsheviks faced a dangerous enemy. Opponents of the Bolsheviks were known as the 'Whites' and included many different groups: landowners who had lost land due to the Bolshevik revolution, religious groups who opposed the Bolshevik seizure of Church property, genuine royalists who wanted the restoration of Tsardom, and others. In the south of Russia, several army officers loyal to the old regime formed anti-communist armies. Admiral Kolchak and Generals Deniken and Wrangel became leaders of the White armies.

SOURCE B

Of all the tyrannies in history, the Bolshevik tyranny is the worst, the most destructive, the most degrading. The atrocities committed under Lenin and Trotsky are far more hideous and more numerous than anything for which the Kaiser was responsible.

Winston Churchill, British Secretary of State for War, giving his reasons for opposing Bolshevism in 1919.

The events of the civil war

In the north-west, the forces of General Yudenitch threatened Petrograd. The British assisted him. By 1920 he was within a few kilometres of Petrograd, and he was only driven back after Trotsky's appearance at the front inspired the Bolshevik forces.

In the south-west, the threat came from General Deniken and his successor, General Wrangel. In 1919, Deniken's advance on Moscow was stopped, and in March 1920 his forces were finally destroyed, apart from a small number later commanded by Wrangel. The latter's forces were finally defeated in the Crimea in November 1920.

Admiral Kolchak threatened from the east. He was extremely cruel, filling 'death trains' with Red Army prisoners. Kolchak's forces were defeated in 1919 and the leaders were arrested and later shot.

Amidst this civil war, another war was being fought against the Poles. Anxious to seize further territory from their traditional enemy, they had invaded Russia in spring 1920. Their invasion, led by General Pilsudski, went seriously wrong. They were driven back to the gates of Warsaw. The Poles and Russians finally signed the Treaty of Riga in March 1921.

Reasons for Bolshevik success

Despite foreign support, the Whites were eventually defeated due to a combination of their own weaknesses and Bolshevik strengths.

The Whites had several weaknesses. Their geographical location made co-operation between the different armies difficult. They also lacked a single leader. The White generals were jealous of each other and refused to co-ordinate their offensives. The Reds never had to face an attack by all their enemies at the same time. Some White leaders, such as Kolchak, were brutal and established a harsh rule over their territories. General Deniken slaughtered 100,000 Jews in the Ukraine. This 'White Terror' encouraged many Russians to support the Reds, especially when landlords were given back their lands.

The Whites did not have one aim and were unwilling to sacrifice their individual interests in order to form a united anti-Bolshevik front. Western aid did provide much-needed weapons, but made the Whites appear to be the puppets of foreign powers. The Red Army, through skilful propaganda, could claim that they were fighting for a Russia free from foreign control.

SOURCE C

Leon Trotsky, Commissar of War.

SOURCE D

A White Terror was begun, far worse than anything carried out by the Reds. Not just suspected Bolsheviks, but socialists of any kind, even Liberals and Democrats, were slaughtered in their thousands. In one village on the river Amur a number of Democrats had taken refuge. Kolchak's governor surrounded the place with White troops; a hole was made in the ice on the river and the entire population driven under the ice.

General W. S. Graves, US commander in Siberia, describes the White Terror.

The Bolsheviks had several advantages. They controlled the industrial centres and the extensive railway network, which enabled the Reds to rush supplies and troops to any part of their front under threat. They also had the key administrative centres of Moscow and Petrograd, and were concentrated in a much smaller area than their rivals.

SOURCE E

This Bolshevik propaganda poster shows France, the USA and Britain as evil capitalists who were trying to control Russia.

The Bolsheviks were also fighting for a cause – their communist revolution. They had superior morale, largely due to Trotsky's skills as an organiser and motivator. The Reds used extensive propaganda to portray the Whites as the tools of foreign powers. In contrast, the Reds were portrayed as defending Russia's national interests against foreign powers.

Trotsky's leadership of the Red Army proved decisive. He had formed this new army and turned it into a feared fighting force. When there were not enough officers, he conscripted Tsarist officers into the army. Discipline was harsh.

Victory also came due to Bolshevik ruthlessness. War Communism (see page 120) provided vital supplies. Cheka units in the countryside hanged, beat, shot and burned anyone who helped or fought for the Whites. The Tsar and his family were executed in case he was rescued from captivity and became a leader of the Whites.

Many Russians supported the Reds through fear. Others, however, genuinely preferred the Bolsheviks. The majority of peasants were annoyed when the Whites returned land to the landowners. Most of the proletariat did not want a return to the Tsarist regime.

SOURCE F

The Cheka became a fearsome instrument of Bolshevik power. In Kharkov, Chekists scalped the prisoners and took their skin, like gloves, off their hands. In Voronezh they placed a naked prisoner in a barrel punctured with nails and then set it in motion. In Poltava they impaled 18 monks and burnt at the stake peasants who rebelled. In Odessa they boiled officers and ripped them in half.

A British historian writing in 1981.

The consequences of the civil war

The civil war had disastrous effects on a population already devastated by over three years of war. Atrocities were commonplace on both sides. Prisoners were often tortured and killed. There had been 21 million deaths between 1914 and 1921. The fighting had seriously hindered both agriculture and industry. Land was only 50 per cent cultivated; steel production was down to 5 per cent of its pre-war output. Dirt and rats led to disease, and there was a serious shortage of doctors and hospitals.

There was a serious famine in 1921 and at times food shortages in the towns were so acute that the ration of bread fell to 30 grams a day. Industrial production dropped as workers left the cities for the countryside in the hope of finding more food. Those who stayed behind salvaged what they could by using the black market. It is estimated that about 5 million deaths were caused by the famine.

The Tsar and his family were murdered. They had been kept prisoner by the Reds in Siberia and then at Ekaterinburg in the Urals. In July 1918 Kolchak's White army was approaching the town, and the Reds were afraid that the Tsar might fall into White hands. The Red Guards forced the royal family into a cellar, shot them all, and burnt their bodies in a nearby mine.

Although the Reds won the civil war, they did not forget how close they had come to defeat by foreign armies. For years afterwards, the communist government remained suspicious of foreign, especially western, governments. Many communists believed they would only be safe if they helped bring about communist revolutions in other countries. In March 1919, during the civil war, the Communist International (Comintern) was set up. Its task was to help set up communist parties in other countries and to work for an international communist revolution. This made some countries even more suspicious of Russia.

SOURCE G

Sometimes a starving family eats the body of one of its junior members. Sometimes parents at night seize part of a body from the cemetery and feed it to their children.

Notes written by two doctors working in the Ufa region, one of Russia's worst famine areas.

QUESTIONS

1. Who were the main opponents of the Reds during the civil war?
2. How reliable is Source B as evidence of the effects of Bolshevik rule on Russia?
3. Was the Bolshevik success in the civil war due mainly to Trotsky's leadership?
4. Using Source G and your own knowledge, explain the main effects of the civil war on Russia.

Political, social and economic developments, 1918–24

War Communism

During the civil war, the Red Army had to be fed and equipped, and the government needed to boost the output of heavy industry, especially coal, iron ore and oil. In order to achieve this, in 1918 Lenin introduced the policy of War Communism, which brought the whole economy under government control. By the Decree of Nationalisation, all firms employing more than ten workers were nationalised (taken over by the government). But as a result, industrial production fell sharply, especially as factories were deprived of manpower due to conscription in the Red Army.

In agriculture, the main aim was to solve the problem of food shortages. Peasants were forced to provide more food. The richer peasants, known as kulaks, were accused of hoarding grain to keep prices high. In fact, they were simply trying to gain a reasonable price for their produce. Most peasants refused to co-operate and were forced to hand over their grain by the Cheka. This, in turn, led to widespread famine in 1921.

The Kronstadt rebellion

During 1920 and 1921 there were several rebellions against the harshness of communist rule in Russia. In March 1921 the most serious of these broke out in the naval base of Kronstadt, an island just outside Petrograd. The sailors at Kronstadt had been supporters of communism since the revolution, but now they were protesting against their harsh living conditions. They also demanded free elections, freedom of the press and an end to the seizure of grain to feed the army.

This rebellion seemed particularly serious and the Bolshevik leadership was determined to crush it. Trotsky sent the Red Army across the iced-up sea to attack the naval base. In a three-week struggle, many of the rebel sailors were killed and thousands were imprisoned or executed.

The rebellion was a great shock to Lenin and in March 1921 he announced the end of the very unpopular War Communism. This was to be replaced by the New Economic Policy (see page 122).

SOURCE H

Starving peasants buying and selling human flesh during the famine of 1921.

Lenin was also worried about the increasing number of arguments within the Communist Party. He issued a declaration on 'party unity'. In future, anyone who openly disagreed with the official policy should be 'purged' (sacked from the party). This was followed by even greater censorship. Newspapers, books and films were allowed only if they carried the correct Bolshevik message.

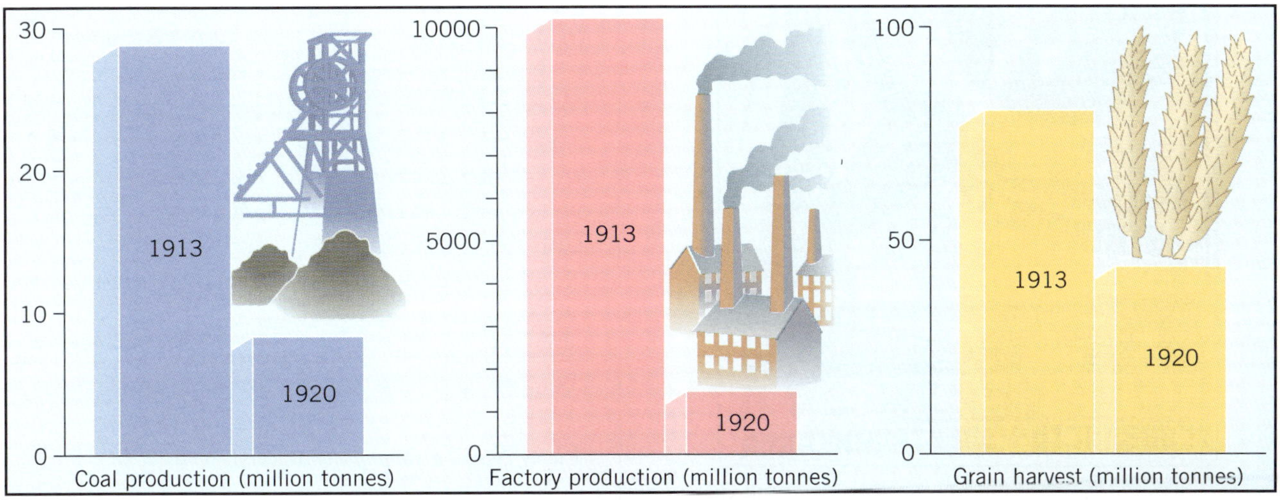

Production figures in 1913 and 1920, according to government sources.

The New Economic Policy

The problems created by War Communism led to the introduction of the New Economic Policy (NEP) in March 1921.

First, in agriculture, the government stopped the policy of forcibly taking food from the peasants. Peasants now had to supply a fixed amount of what they grew to the government. They were allowed to keep any extra or even sell it at a profit.

Second, in industry, small factories (employing fewer than twenty workers) were privatised. In other words, they were returned to private ownership. All the important industries, such as coal, steel, transport and foreign trade, remained nationalised for the benefit of everyone. Gosplan was established. This was a State Planning Commission, which aimed to formulate effective economic policies.

A new rouble was brought in to try to end inflation. A State Bank was introduced to advance loans and credit facilities. Finally, a programme of electrification was introduced and then extended to rural areas.

SOURCE I

A poster celebrating the electrification of Russia.

Reactions to the NEP

Lenin realised that to stay in power he would have to introduce the NEP. Communist ideals would have to be sacrificed in order to bring about economic recovery. Many communists, however, were horrified at what they thought was a step backwards to the old system with private ownership, private trade and profits.

In the towns, many complained about the appearance of 'Nepmen', who made a living by trading rather than making things. Communists argued that the NEP encouraged greed and selfishness, with people trying to make money for themselves rather than working for the good of everyone.

SOURCE J

Living conditions in Russia have enormously improved in the past two years. The essential fact is that everyone is much better off than during the 'black years' of 1920 and 1921. The industrial workers are relatively better off although hit by high prices and short time in many industries – at least they get paid regularly now.

From a report by Walter Duranty, an American journalist in Russia, 1921.

SOURCE K

In a few years' time the NEP restored to Russia an aspect of prosperity. But to many of us this prosperity was sometimes distasteful. We felt ourselves sinking into the swamp – paralysed, corrupted. There was gambling, drunkenness, and all the filth of former times. Classes were reborn under our very eyes. There was a growing gap between the prosperity of the few and the misery of the many.

Victor Serge, a former communist, writing in 1937.

Lenin admitted that he had moved away from communism, but he assured his critics that this was a short-term measure to preserve communism, not to destroy it. It was 'state capitalism' to strengthen Russia and make it easier for Russia to become socialist in the future. Lenin's ability to command loyalty prevented the party from splitting. Bukharin, a leading opponent of the NEP, changed his mind and became an enthusiastic supporter when he realised the new policy was increasing production.

SOURCE L

We are retreating, going back as it were, but we are doing this so as to retreat first and then run and leap forward more vigorously. We retreated on this one condition alone when we introduced our NEP, so as to begin a more determined offensive after the retreat.

Lenin speaking to party members in 1921.

How successful was the NEP?

The Soviet economy made a remarkable recovery under NEP. Between 1921 and 1927 the amount of cultivated land grew by 50 per cent. The grain harvest increased from 37.6 million tons in 1921 to 72.5 million tons four years later. By 1927 food production had returned to the level it had been before the First World War. In the towns, workers produced more and there was more to buy. The Soviet Union soon recovered from the terrible experiences of War Communism. The majority of people, in both the towns and the countryside, were more supportive of the communist government. However, not all the economic problems were solved. The output of industrial goods could not keep pace with demand, and prices rose.

The roles of Lenin and Trotsky

How important were Lenin and Trotsky to the success of the Bolshevik revolution of 1917 and the establishment of communism in Russia in the following six years?

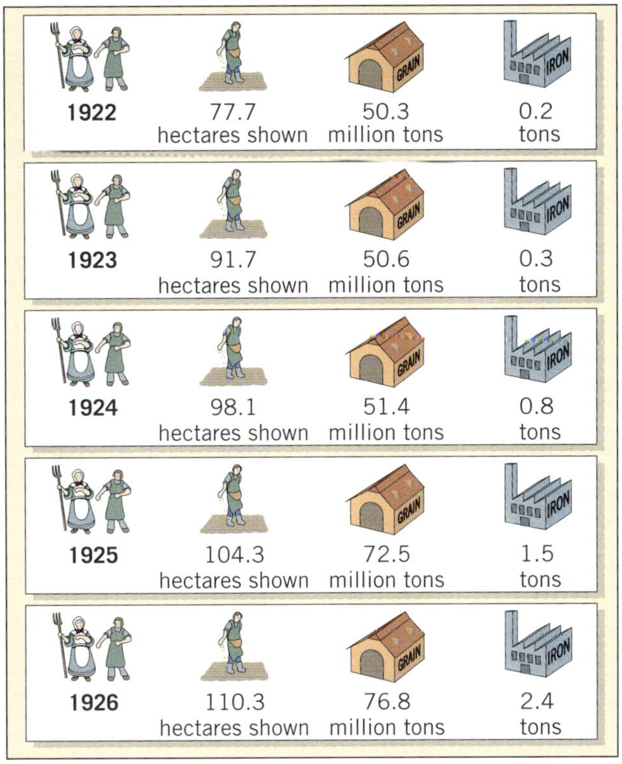

The effects of the New Economic Policy, 1922–6, according to government sources.

Lenin

In 1922, Lenin suffered a stroke and became severely disabled. He died in January 1924 at the age of 54. After his death, a 'Lenin Cult' developed in Russia. His image was everywhere – on statues, plaques and posters. Petrograd was renamed Leningrad in his honour. Some communists even christened their daughters 'Ninel', which is Lenin backwards. Lenin's body was not buried but embalmed and put on display in a mausoleum in Moscow's Red Square. It became a place of pilgrimage.

Did all this hero worship lead to an exaggerated view of Lenin's role in this period? There seems little doubt that without his leadership the Bolsheviks would not have been able to seize power in 1917. He had prepared the way by forging a determined, disciplined party, dedicated to revolution. When he returned to Russia in April 1917, it was Lenin who persuaded the Bolsheviks not to co-operate with the Provisional Government. His slogan 'Peace, Bread, Land' gained support and it was his sense of timing that took advantage of the confusion in Russia to push for a second revolution.

Lenin showed great determination in power, but was flexible too. He had the sense to realise that War Communism was not working and was not popular. He compromised his Marxist ideals with the NEP, but this ensured the survival of communism and improved the economy. It was only a short-term, emergency measure.

Trotsky

Trotsky also played a leading role in the period 1917–24. He was given the responsibility for organising the Bolshevik revolution. He trained and organised the Red Army. He drew up the plans to take key points in Petrograd in his role as Chairman of the Revolutionary Committee. Trotsky and the Red Guards successfully took control of the Winter Palace during the revolution.

He played an even greater role in ensuring Bolshevik success in the civil war. As Commissar of War, Trotsky organised a new Red Army of volunteers, and he enlisted officers from among the Tsarist commanders by arresting their families to guarantee their loyalty. In April 1918 he introduced conscription to increase the size of his army. He was a brilliant leader, well respected by his troops. During the civil war, he toured Russia in a special train to direct troop movements and keep up morale. He provided the strong leadership and unity that was lacking among the Whites.

SOURCE M

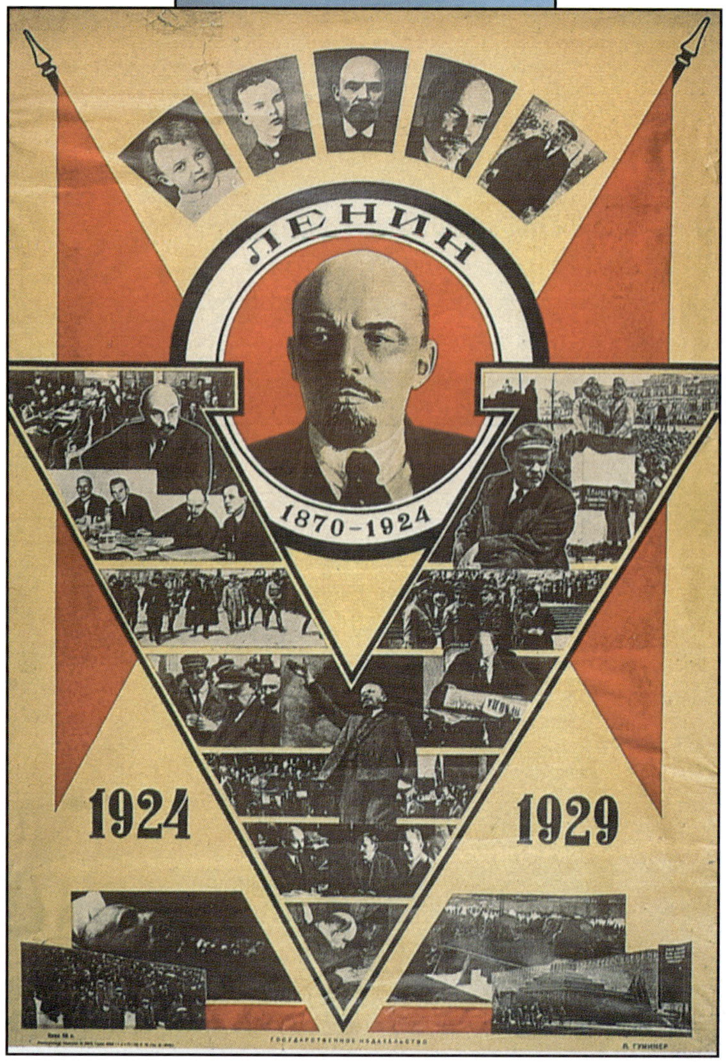

A Soviet poster produced in 1929, on the fifth anniversary of Lenin's death.

QUESTIONS

1. What effects did War Communism have on Russia in the period 1918–21?
2. How reliable are the charts on pages 121 and 123 as evidence of agricultural and industrial production in Russia?
3. Why do Sources J and K give different interpretations of the effects of the NEP?
4. Was there much change in economic policy in Russia during the period 1918–24?
5. 'Without Trotsky's leadership the Bolsheviks would have lost the civil war.' Do you agree or disagree?

Economic, social and political developments under Stalin, 1924–41

The struggle for power

After 1924 there was a power struggle to find Lenin's successor. Against the odds, Joseph Stalin emerged as leader. This was due to favourable circumstances, the weaknesses of his rivals and his own qualities.

SOURCE A

Joseph Stalin.

Early years

Josef Vissarionovich Djugashvili was born into a poor family in Georgia in 1879. He was educated in a religious college, but was expelled for revolutionary activities. He was soon an active member of the Bolshevik Party and organised bank raids to get money for party funds. By 1917 he had been arrested eight times and exiled on several occasions. In 1913 he changed his name to 'Stalin', meaning 'man of steel'.

Stalin was in Russia at the time of the March revolution in 1917 and was editor of the Bolshevik newspaper *Pravda*. But he was not a leading figure and did not play an important role in the Bolshevik revolution. After the revolution, Lenin promoted him. From 1917 to 1921 he was Commissar of Nationalities. During the civil war, he was the Bolshevik organiser for the Caucasus region.

General Secretary

Lenin made Stalin General Secretary of the Communist Party in 1922. This made Stalin very powerful because he could promote his own followers. Stalin presented himself as a moderate man, in the centre of politics. Meanwhile, however, he was strengthening his power base.

As Lenin's health declined, he grew worried that Stalin was becoming too powerful. In his 'Testament' or will, Lenin made it clear that he did not want Stalin to follow him as leader. Stalin knew that this document existed, but it was not shown to many leading Bolsheviks after Lenin's death. Stalin ensured that he made the arrangements for Lenin's funeral. Stalin made himself heir to the 'Lenin legacy'. He made it seem as though he would carry on Lenin's work.

SOURCE B

Stalin is too rude, and this fault ... becomes unacceptable in the office of General Secretary. Therefore, I propose to the comrades that a way be found to remove Stalin from that post and replace him with someone more patient, more loyal, more polite and more considerate to his comrades.

From Lenin's 'Testament'.

Stalin's tactics

In 1923, Russia was renamed the Union of Soviet Socialist Republics (the Soviet Union or USSR for short). There were many arguments about what path the country should take. Stalin's main rival, Trotsky, favoured 'world revolution'. He wanted the government to concentrate on spreading revolution to other countries. Stalin favoured 'socialism in one country'. He wanted the Soviet Union to concentrate on building up its own strength. In 1924 and 1925 many party members were sacked and replaced by Stalin's supporters.

In 1927, Stalin succeeded in having Trotsky, together with two other leading Bolsheviks, Gregory Zinoviev and Lev Kamenev, expelled from the party. Nobody now dared criticise Stalin.

Trotsky was expelled from the Soviet Union in 1929. He spent the 1930s in exile in foreign countries and eventually settled in Mexico. But Stalin had secret agents on his trail. In 1940 one found Trotsky and assassinated him by smashing his skull with an ice pick.

Reasons for Stalin's success

Stalin's opponents had failed to prevent his rise to power. They had all under-estimated him, thinking him not very clever. Trotsky lacked a genuine following because he was seen as too intellectual. Many viewed him as an outsider and were suspicious of his Jewish and Menshevik background. When Trotsky spoke out against Lenin's NEP and demanded world revolution, it seemed as though he was going against Lenin. This was made worse by his failure to attend Lenin's funeral.

However, Stalin's success was not just due to the weaknesses of his opponents. He had cleverly built up personal power in the Bolshevik Party in the years after 1917. In his position as General Secretary, he was able to remove rivals and replace them with supporters. He became the link between the party and the government and could monitor both policies and personnel. By 1924 he had firm control of the party machine and a sound power base.

He made skilful use of propaganda to convince people that he was Lenin's choice as successor. To the party members he appeared to be 'down to earth' and the heir to Lenin's achievements. Photographs of Lenin and Stalin together were published, and Stalin ensured that Lenin's 'Testament' was not published.

SOURCE C

This photograph has been put together from separate pictures of Lenin and Stalin. It makes it look as if they were photographed sitting next to each other.

The development of Stalin's dictatorship

Stalin was able to achieve total control of the Soviet Union through propaganda and a series of purges of the Bolshevik Party, armed forces, secret police and Soviet people in general.

Censorship

All books, newspapers, radio broadcasts and films were censored. Only the official Communist Party viewpoint was allowed. The party preached that it was service to the state, not freedom of the individual, that was important. Anyone suspected of acting 'individually' was thought to be committing treason.

Propaganda

Stalin made skilful use of propaganda to praise his own achievements, ensure support for his regime and exaggerate his own role in past Bolshevik achievements, notably the revolution of 1917.

Photographs were doctored to make it appear as though he was close to Lenin. Paintings were commissioned highlighting his role in the events of 1917–21. Stalin made frequent propaganda speeches to stress that he was the heir to Lenin's work. Propaganda was used to attack his rivals and promote his ideas of 'socialism in one country'. Trotsky was portrayed as a Jewish intellectual who was threatening to undo Lenin's achievements.

There were great parades to celebrate the glory of Stalin, the 'great' leader, and to impress Soviet people and the rest of the world. Expensive construction projects were undertaken to demonstrate the success of Stalin's regime. They included the construction of the Moscow Metro, the Dnieper Dam and the steel city of Magnitogorsk. Towns were named after Stalin: Stalingrad, Stalino and Stalinabad. Art and literature were allowed only if they glorified Stalin and his achievements. His name and picture were everywhere.

SOURCE D

An example of Stalin's propaganda against Trotsky.

The Purges

As Stalin became increasingly concerned about opposition to his rule, the word 'purge' took on a new and more sinister meaning. It came to mean not only dismissal from the party, but imprisonment and death. As early as 1928, fifteen mining engineers at Shakty were executed after being put on trial, accused of sabotaging the first Five-Year Plan (see page 133).

Why did Stalin carry out the purges?

There have been wide differences of opinion about this question. Some people think Stalin was simply mad or at best suffered from paranoia. He was certainly deeply suspicious of possible rivals and wanted to destroy any possible threat to his leadership. The purges also seemed to coincide with threats to Soviet security and were a means of rallying support to the regime from the armed forces and the people.

The purges were also a convenient way of excusing failures and setbacks. If the economic targets were not met, the failure was frequently blamed on sabotage. Stalin argued that 'enemies' of the Soviet Union had to be purged in order to save the party and the Soviet Union from their treachery.

There are many other theories. Some people think that the purges were intended to provide manpower for the forced labour camps. Fyodor Dan, a Menshevik, thought that Stalin was a sadist who genuinely enjoyed carrying out the purges. He often amused himself by cutting the throats of sheep at his own country home. Stalin's daughter thought that the purges had happened because Stalin was a weak character, too easily influenced by others – especially by Lavrenti Beria, who became the head of Stalin's secret police, the NKVD, in 1938 (see page 129).

SOURCE E

I cannot resist the conclusion that from his middle fifties Stalin was the subject of persecution mania to an extent which went a long way beyond reason.

C. P. Snow, British writer and politician, 1967.

The start of the purges

Stalin's terror really began in 1934. At the congress of leading party members that year, Sergei Kirov showed himself to be very popular. There were rumours that many would prefer him as leader. In December 1934, Kirov was assassinated in Leningrad. It was thought likely that the murder took place on Stalin's orders. At the time, the blame was put on fourteen men who had links with Kamenev and Zinoviev.

SOURCE F

Among the Trotskyites and Zinovievites fascism found faithful servants who were ready to work for the defeat of the Soviet Union in order to restore capitalism. Trotsky, Zinoviev and Kamenev had been in conspiracy against Lenin, the Party and the Soviet state ever since the October Revolution.

From Stalin's History of the Communist Party of the Soviet Union, *1939.*

Many people, well known and ordinary, were arrested. Famous communists were often persuaded or tortured into confessing to sabotage or spying. They confessed their crimes in public in a series of show trials, the biggest of which were held between 1936 and 1938. Zinoviev, Bukharin and Kamenev were all accused of plotting with Trotsky or with capitalist governments to overthrow the Soviet Union and Stalin. They were found guilty and executed.

Mass purges

Soviet Muslims, millions of whom lived in the central regions of the Soviet Union, were persecuted during the purges. Many mosques were closed and Muslim women were encouraged to remove their veils. Muslim practices, such as the pilgrimage to Mecca, were forbidden.

The rest of the Soviet population suffered during the 'Great Purges' of 1936–8. Stalin's agents arrested millions of people from all backgrounds, including doctors, writers, peasants and industrial workers. Neighbours or workmates informed the NKVD of 'enemies of the people'. As many as one in five of the population were known as Seksots or NKVD informers. Some used the purges to settle old scores. In 1935, one million people in Moscow and Leningrad alone were executed. Millions of others followed them.

SOURCE G

This French cartoon from the 1930s invites people to 'Visit the Pyramids of the USSR'.

The majority of those arrested were sent to labour camps, where conditions were very harsh. At Kolyma labour camp it was sometimes –60 °C. Torture was common, work was exhausting and living conditions were overcrowded. The same lice-infested clothes were worn for years. Food was terrible and many people suffered diseases such as scurvy.

Purges of the NKVD

The NKVD was purged in 1938 to prevent its leaders from becoming too powerful. Several leaders were arrested and shot, and finally the head of the NKVD, Nikolai Yezhov, was executed and replaced by Beria, a trusted henchman of Stalin.

Purges of the armed forces

Stalin's political control of the Soviet Union was not strong enough in itself to maintain his authority if the armed forces continued to be an independent force. It was essential that they were subservient to him. In May 1937, Marshal Tukhachevsky, hero of the Russian Civil War, and other high-ranking officers were arrested, tried in secret and shot for treason. Between 1937 and 1938, half of the Officer Corps and nine out of ten generals were purged.

The effects of the purges

The purges were a success for Stalin in that they enabled him to achieve absolute power. He gained control of the Communist Party and removed those from Lenin's time who might have proved to be a threat to his position.

In most other respects, however, they were a disaster. The cost in human lives was enormous. In 1988 the KGB, successor to the NKVD, allowed certain of its archives to be opened. From this evidence it has been calculated that 1 million people were executed in 1934. By 1937 there were between 17 and 18 million people in labour camps, 10 million of whom died. By 1939 another 5–7 million had been 'repressed'. In 1940 a further 2 million people were deported. Every family was affected.

Economically, the purges held back Soviet economic development. In industry, so many skilled workers and managers were purged that industrial production was seriously disrupted. There was no stability in the workforce. The workplace became a place of terror in which workmate informed on workmate.

SOURCE H

This picture was published in a US newspaper by followers of Trotsky in the 1930s. It shows the more prominent victims of Stalin's purges.

In agriculture, the effects were equally devastating. Stalin destroyed the efficiency of agriculture with his forced policy of collectivisation (see page 131). Many peasants, especially the kulaks, were executed, imprisoned, deported or sent to labour camps.

Perhaps the worst effects were on the armed forces. All three services were left understaffed by the loss of experienced officers during the purges. The 'missing' staff were usually replaced by inexperienced and/or incompetent staff. This crippled the Soviet military forces at a time when the country needed a strong defence. Indeed, much of Hitler's early success, in his invasion of the Soviet Union in 1941, was due to the weaknesses of the Red Army.

QUESTIONS

1. How reliable is Source B as evidence of Stalin's qualities?
2. Explain the methods used by Stalin to ensure success in the leadership struggle after Lenin's death.
3. Using Sources E and F, explain why Stalin carried out the purges.
4. How useful is Source G to a historian studying the purges?
5. What changes did the purges bring to Soviet society in the 1930s?

Collectivisation

Stalin was determined to modernise Soviet agriculture. His attempt to achieve this, through a policy of collectivisation, brought considerable opposition.

What was collectivisation?

In selected areas, peasants were to be persuaded to join their small farms together into collectives or kolkhozy. These farms were very large and run either directly by the government or, more often, by the peasants themselves. But they were managed by a Communist Party member. A Motor Tractor Station was set up in each area to provide mechanisation for harvesting and ploughing. The main duty of the collective was to provide a fixed amount of food to the government, which was then sold in the towns. The farm workers would share what food was left, after all the debts arising from their use of machinery were paid.

Some collectives had schools and hospitals for the workers. They were allowed small plots of private land on which they could grow a few crops or keep animals for their own use. However, the efficiency of the kolkhozy varied. From 1935, output could be raised only by allowing the peasants to have their own land and livestock.

Reasons for collectivisation

In the 1920s, Soviet agriculture was backward. Most peasants carried out subsistence farming and there was not enough grain to feed both the peasants and the town workers. Stalin wanted an efficient farming system to help serve the needs of industry as well as agriculture.

Stalin also supported collectivisation for political reasons. It would strengthen his control over farming and the peasantry. Most communists disliked the private land ownership encouraged by the NEP. They believed that, although many peasants were becoming better off under the NEP, they were only interested in themselves.

SOURCE I

What is the way out? The way out is to turn the small and scattered peasant farms into large, united farms based on the cultivation of land in common – not by pressure, but by example and persuasion.

Stalin speaking to the Communist Party conference in 1927.

Opposition to collectivisation

Most opposition came from the kulaks, or richer peasants. They burned their crops and killed their animals rather than hand them over. The government, afraid of food shortages in the towns, brought in bread rationing in 1928. Then it seized grain from the peasants, as it had during War Communism. Poorer peasants were encouraged to attack kulaks and take their property and belongings.

Food production fell. Stalin launched a propaganda campaign against the kulaks. He portrayed them as enemies of the people and said they had to be destroyed. Millions of kulaks were imprisoned, shot or sent to work in factories. About 4½–5 million were rounded up and by 1934 the kulaks had ceased to exist.

In 1930 there was so much opposition to collectivisation that Stalin called a temporary halt to the programme. But by the mid-1930s most of the Soviet Union's farmland had been collectivised.

The results of collectivisation

As far as Stalin was concerned, collectivisation was a great success. He had gained control of the countryside. The peasants never again openly rebelled against communist rule. Stalin had also ensured a steady supply of food for the towns. His main aim was to build up industry and this needed a guaranteed food supply for millions of townspeople.

SOURCE J

Workers on a collective farm, painted in 1934 by a Soviet artist.

SOURCE K

Millions of peasants, rather than give up their livestock to the collectives without compensation, preferred to kill and eat their cows, pigs, sheep and chickens. Many even slaughtered their horses out of sheer annoyance.

Hubert Knickerbocker, an American newspaper reporter in the Soviet Union, writing in 1930.

In other respects, collectivisation was a disaster. Over 14 million peasants were deported or killed for slaughtering livestock. The number of cattle fell from 60 million in 1928 to 33 million five years later. As a result of grain seizures and the deliberate slaughter of animals, there were over 7 million deaths from starvation between 1932 and 1933. By 1939, Soviet agricultural production had barely returned to the level of 1913. Soviet farmers still produced much less per head than farmers in the USA or western Europe.

SOURCE L

A Soviet anti-kulak poster.

SOURCE M

If you imagine that Stalin wanted to improve the harvest or the lot of the peasant, then you are just fooling yourself. Collectivisation was a bloody, terrible and monstrous means of the seizure of absolute power because the free peasant, the master of the land, was one barrier to the total power that Stalin wanted.

Lyudmila Saraskina, a Soviet writer, writing in 1994.

Industrialisation and the Five-Year Plans

The Soviet Union experienced massive industrial change after 1928.

Reasons for industrialisation

Like its agriculture, the Soviet Union's industry lagged far behind the rest of the world. Stalin feared invasion from the West and wanted a strong economy in order to deal effectively with this threat. A strong economy would make possible the build-up of the country's armed forces. Stalin also had political motives. To achieve full control of the Soviet Union, Stalin believed that he needed control of the economy. The survival of the Soviet Union and the revolution depended on the nation's ability to transform itself into a modern industrial society.

The nature of industrialisation

The first Five-Year Plan was started in 1928. Gosplan, the state planning authority, set targets for industry that had to be met in a limited time. These targets were very ambitious – many industries were to double their production within five years. The first plan concentrated on heavy industries, such as oil, coal, iron and steel.

In 1932, Stalin declared that the targets had been met ahead of schedule. Although Soviet statistics cannot be trusted, the results certainly seemed impressive. There was a threefold increase in heavy industry production and a fivefold increase in electricity.

The second Five-Year Plan started in January 1933 and ended in December 1937. Again it focused on heavy industry, but large quantities of tractors were produced for use in agriculture. Household goods, such as radios and bicycles, were also produced.

The third Five-Year Plan started in January 1938 but was abandoned in June 1941 when Germany invaded the Soviet Union. The increase in output continued, and new hydro-electric power stations, such as the Dnieper Dam, were generating seven times as much electricity as in 1927. More than 100 new towns had been created, such as Magnitogorsk and Sverdlovsk, and railways and canals had been expanded.

SOURCE N

We must create in our country an industry which would be capable of re-equipping and organising not only the whole of our industry, but also our transport and agriculture. We are 50 or 100 years behind the advanced countries. We must make good this lag in ten years. Either we do or we will go under.

From Stalin's Collected Works, 1931.

SOURCE O

A Soviet poster showing the benefits of a chemical factory, providing gas for warfare and fertiliser for farming.

Output	Coal	Oil	Pig iron	Steel
1927	35.9	11.9	3.4	4.1
1932	65.0	21.7	6.3	6.0
1937	130.1	29.01	14.7	18.0

Industrial improvements under the first and second Five-Year Plans (million tonnes).

Enormous efforts had to be made to meet the targets set by the Five-Year Plans. In 1935 a coal miner, Alexei Stakhanov, cut 102 tonnes of coal, fourteen times the usual amount, in a single shift. Using his unskilled comrades to carry away the coal and prop up the tunnel, he concentrated on the skilled job of cutting the coal. He became a national hero and everyone was encouraged to follow his lead. Nobody dared to point out that Stakhanov's success was due to the hard work of those around him.

Inflated output claims became normal practice. Factory owners altered their statistics to make Stalin think they had been successful. Stalin would alter the statistics again to exaggerate their success. This enabled him to claim that targets had been met earlier than planned.

The consequences of industrialisation

In the ten years or so after 1928, the Soviet Union was changed from a largely agricultural country to one whose power was based on industry. It did not suffer from the Great Depression of 1929 (see Chapter 7). There was no unemployment – rather, there was a shortage of workers. There were massive increases in heavy industry and machine building, and some growth in consumer goods.

There also seemed to be some improvement in the lives of workers and their families. Many were able to train for skilled, higher-paid jobs. All workers' children got a free primary education and increasing numbers of people had access to better medical facilities. Pensions and sickness benefits were guaranteed, and there were more doctors per 1000 people than in any of the major western nations. Illiteracy was cut from 50 per cent in 1924 to 19 per cent in 1939.

But all these improvements were at a cost. The concentration on heavy industry meant that light industries and consumer goods were often ignored. Quality was sacrificed for quantity. Training was often poor, while skilled workers were frequently removed due to the purges (see pages 127-30).

Workers had few rights and little or no freedom. In 1932 internal passports were introduced to stop people moving to find work without government permission. Living conditions in the towns were also very poor. There were high prices, food shortages and severe overcrowding. In 1935, 40 per cent of all families in Moscow were living in a single room.

SOURCE P

Industrialisation was cruel in its effects on millions of human beings, but still it laid the foundations for a richer economy, enabling Russia to withstand a foreign invasion and become a superpower.

The conclusion of a modern historian about industrialisation under Stalin.

QUESTIONS

1. Using Source I and your own knowledge, explain why Stalin carried out a policy of collectivisation.
2. How reliable is Source J as evidence of the effects of collectivisation?
3. Is Source O an accurate interpretation of the effects of industrialisation?
4. What changes did industrialisation bring to the Soviet Union in the period 1928–41?

The effects of Stalin's rule

In 1936 Stalin introduced a new constitution, which he called the 'most democratic in the world'. It guaranteed to people certain rights, including freedom of speech and religion. But this made little change to the lives of most Soviet people as the NKVD and the leaders of the government were not controlled by the constitution.

The lives of men and women

For most people, life was difficult and insecure in the Soviet Union of the 1930s. Almost everyone knew someone who suffered in the purges. But members of the Communist Party did quite well. The party had a list of 1 million approved members. When an important job became available, somebody from this list would be appointed.

There was little freedom. Trade unions were banned and there was strict censorship. All organised religions suffered under Stalin. Churches were closed and religious worship was condemned as distracting people from supporting the regime. Bishops were executed, imprisoned and deported.

Women were second-class citizens before the Bolshevik revolution. The Communist Party declared that they were equal to men. In parts of the Soviet Union, especially the Muslim areas, women received more personal freedom than ever before. In the 1930s, Stalin used propaganda to encourage women to work in the factories. He provided them with more nurseries, laundries and canteens to persuade them to help with rapid industrialisation. Families also received benefits to encourage them to have more children. But for most Russian women, life remained hard. Less than 20 per cent of the Communist Party were women, and very few women rose to high positions in the party or government.

Ethnic groups

Non-Russians in the Soviet Union had difficult lives. Stalin believed that non-Russians were not trustworthy. Few were given top jobs in government or the party. Non-Russian languages and traditions were discouraged.

For most people in the Soviet Union, life did not improve under Stalin. In many respects it got worse, as living and working conditions deteriorated and lack of freedom increased.

SOURCE Q

A Soviet propaganda picture from 1927 encouraging women to work.

SOURCE R

```
I can't find words to express my
gratitude to the Party and the
Government, to dear Comrade Stalin for
the care of us women. I have seven
children. My children are my joy. I've
never had an abortion, and I'm not
going to have any. I've borne children
and shall go on bearing them.
```

A letter from Tatanya Koval of the Lubchenko collective farm, Kieve district, to a magazine in May 1936.

Exam-style questions

These questions follow the pattern of questions set by AQA/SEG for Paper 3 of its current Modern World History syllabus.

Section A

1. The role of Lenin, 1917–24

Study sources A to E and then answer **all** parts of Question 1. To answer the questions, use the sources and your own knowledge. In your answers, you should refer to the sources by their letters.

Source B: Lenin returning to Petrograd in April, 1917

A painting made in the Soviet Union in the 1930s.

Source A: Lenin in 1917

> Hardly off the train, Lenin asked the Party comrades, 'Why didn't you seize power?' And at once he comes out with the April Theses. He is called mad and delirious … But suddenly it becomes apparent that he has the ear of the man in the street, and of the man in the factory and barracks! His whole genius consists in his ability to say what these people want to say, but do not know how to say.

From V. Serge's book, *From Lenin to Stalin*, 1937. Serge was a Bolshevik supporter in Petrograd in 1917.

Source C: Reactions to Lenin's speech on his return to Russia in April 1917

> Suddenly, before the eyes of all of us, completely swallowed up by the routine drudgery of the Revolution, there was presented a bright, blinding, exotic beacon … Lenin's voice, heard straight from the train, was a 'voice from outside'.

Written by a Soviet journalist in 1917.

Source D: An interpretation of Lenin

> We must realise that the violent zigzags in Soviet policy in the years after 1917 were caused by desperate, temporary necessities. We must not allow them to confuse our estimate of Lenin's purpose. In the Russia of 1918–20 when we recall that a large number of civil servants had deserted their posts, it appears almost a miracle that the government was able to carry on at all. We can appreciate more the sometimes crude methods which had to be used in War Communism.

A pro-communist historian, writing in 1947.

Source E: Another interpretation of Lenin

> Lenin has to take the total responsibility for the unnecessary suffering and wastage caused by War Communism. During the Civil War he strengthened the police state, established a one-party state and did away with the moderate form of socialist democracy.

An anti-communist historian, writing in 1987.

Question 1

(a) Using **Source A and your own knowledge**, explain why Lenin's leadership was so important in 1917 in the events leading to the Bolshevik revolution. *(5 marks)*

(b) Which is more useful to a historian studying Lenin's role in the events of 1917, **Source A or Source B**? Explain your answer using **Sources A and B** and your own knowledge. *(8 marks)*

(c) Is **Source C** a reliable view of Lenin's impact in 1917? Explain your answer using **Source C** and your own knowledge. *(6 marks)*

(d) Why do **Sources D and E** give different interpretations of Lenin's achievements, 1918–24? Explain your answer using **Sources D and E** and your own knowledge. *(7 marks)*

(e) 'Lenin was a success as Bolshevik leader between 1917 and 1924.' Do you agree or disagree with this interpretation? Explain your answer using **all the sources and your own knowledge**. *(10 marks)*

Section B

1. Why was there a revolution in Russia in March 1917? *(12 marks)*
2. Was there much change in Russian society under Lenin's government of 1918–24? *(12 marks)*
3. What effects did Stalin's economic policies have on the Soviet Union between 1928 and 1941? *(12 marks)*
4. How did Russian people react to Stalin's purges of the 1930s? *(12 marks)*

CHAPTER 5

Germany, 1918–39

Introduction

Germany entered the First World War in 1914 with great enthusiasm, but by the end of 1918 the German army was close to defeat, there was widespread discontent among the German people, the Kaiser had abdicated and a new republic had been set up.

The new republic, which met in 1919 in the southern German town of Weimar, soon became unpopular after signing the hated Treaty of Versailles in 1919. There was opposition from the left (the German communists, the Spartacists) and from the right (the Kapp and Munich *Putsches*). The Weimar governments faced serious economic problems and these resulted, in 1923, in the French occupation of the Ruhr and hyperinflation.

The Republic, under the direction of the Foreign Minister, Gustav Stresemann, recovered during the period 1924–9. The German currency was stabilised and industry began to develop, due mainly to US loans. German prestige increased abroad. There was less support for extremist parties.

All this changed after the Wall Street Crash in the USA. Germany was badly affected by depression, and unemployment had reached 6 million by 1932. Many Germans began to support either the communists or the Nazi Party led by Adolf Hitler. In the elections of 1932, the Nazis became the largest single party in the German parliament, the Reichstag, and on 30 January 1933 the German President, Hindenburg, invited Hitler to become Chancellor.

Hitler quickly established himself in power and by the end of 1934 he had set up a dictatorship of the Nazi Party. Under Nazi rule the German economy improved and there was full employment. The Nazis, however, established a police state with little freedom and strict censorship. Education, youth movements and propaganda were strictly controlled in order to convert the German people to Nazi ideals. The churches and minority groups, especially the Jews, were persecuted.

1918 Kaiser Wilhelm II abdicates
New republic set up

1919 Weimar constitution set up
Germany signs the Treaty of Versailles

1920 Kapp Putsch

1923 French occupation of the Ruhr
Munich Putsch

1924 Dawes Plan

1925 Germany signs the Locarno Pact

1929 Death of Gustav Stresemann
Wall Street Crash

1930 Brüning becomes Chancellor

1932 Nazis win 230 seats in Reichstag elections

1933 30 January: Hitler becomes Chancellor

1934 30 June: 'Night of the Long Knives'

1936 Olympics held in Berlin

1938 9 November: *Kristallnacht*

1939 1 September: Germany invades Poland

The nature and diversity of German society in 1918

Germany before the revolution

Before 1918 Germany was an empire that stretched across the centre of Europe. It was ruled by the Kaiser (Emperor), Wilhelm II, and was one of the most powerful countries in the world.

SOURCE A

Kaiser Wilhelm II.

German government

The Kaiser was the head of government. He appointed the ministers to run the country and was commander of the armed forces. He was also the King of Prussia, the largest of the 26 states of Germany.

Although the Kaiser held most of the power, German government had some democratic features. Men aged 25 and over had the right to vote for a parliament called the Reichstag. This voted on the laws that the Kaiser and his ministers drew up. But the Reichstag had no say in foreign or military affairs and could not appoint or dismiss ministers.

German industry

Germany had experienced rapid industrial growth in the second half of the nineteenth century and produced more iron and steel than any other country. As Germany's industries grew, so did the number of industrial workers. By 1914 over half of all Germans worked in industry. Many were unhappy with their situation because of their low wages and poor living conditions. More and more workers joined trade unions and supported socialist parties to try to improve their conditions.

German socialists

The socialists wanted power and wealth to be shared equally among the people. Some, the revolutionary socialists, wanted to get rid of the Kaiser and set up a government of the workers. Others, the parliamentary socialists, believed in winning power through parliament. They wanted to persuade Wilhelm II to give more power to the Reichstag.

The First World War

Germany went to war in 1914 as an ally of Austria-Hungary, fighting against France, Britain and Russia. At first there was great enthusiasm for the war and men rushed to join the army. But the war lasted far longer than expected and created widespread discontent in Germany.

The war created serious food shortages. The British navy blockaded German ports, stopping ships from bringing food and supplies from overseas. As a result, even basic foods were rationed. There were shortages of soap and washing powder, medicines, clothing and all kinds of lights. As living conditions worsened, more and more workers protested by going on strike.

The revolution of 1918

Causes

As winter approached in 1918, conditions grew much worse. Most adults were living at almost starvation levels. Fuel shortages led to power cuts and factory closures. The situation was worsened by a flu virus that killed thousands each week. In addition, the German armies on the Western Front were on the retreat and facing defeat.

The German commanders decided, in early October, to ask the Allies for peace. The Allies agreed on the condition that the German government was made more democratic. On 2 October, Wilhelm II allowed the main parties in the Reichstag to form a government.

Events

The revolution began on 3 November when the sailors at the port of Kiel refused to sail out and fight the British fleet. They believed it would be a suicide mission. After a thousand sailors were arrested, soldiers and sailors at Kiel held protest meetings. Supported by workers and socialists, they set up a workers' and soldiers' council, known as a soviet.

This mutiny soon spread and soviets were set up in many German cities and towns. On 9 November the Army High Command told Kaiser Wilhelm that the army could no longer support him. Kaiser Wilhelm had no choice but to abdicate. On the following day, Friedrich Ebert, leader of the largest socialist party, the Social Democratic Party, became president of a new republic. He arranged for elections to be held in January for a new national parliament. On 11 November 1918, the Germans agreed to an armistice (cease-fire) and the First World War came to an end.

The Spartacist Uprising

Causes

The Spartacus League, led by Rosa Luxemburg and Karl Liebknecht, was made up of German communists who opposed everything that Ebert did. They wanted Germany to be ruled by the soviets that had been created in the November revolution. On the last day of 1918 they renamed themselves the German Communist Party and made plans to seize power. Many Germans, especially the middle and upper class, feared a communist takeover in which they would lose their property, businesses and land.

Events

The Spartacists tried to seize power on 5 January 1918. They occupied public buildings, organised a general strike and formed a revolutionary committee.

SOURCE B

The Spartacus League is now fighting for total power. The government, which wants the people to decide their own future freely (by voting in the election), is to be overthrown by force. The people are not allowed to speak. You have seen the results. Where Spartacus rules, all personal freedom and security is abolished. The newspapers are suppressed. Traffic is at a standstill. Parts of Berlin are the scenes of bloody battles. Others are already without water and light. Food warehouses are being attacked. Food supplies are being stopped. The government is taking all measures necessary to destroy this rule of terror.

An extract from a document published by the Ebert government in January 1919.

Ebert did a deal with the army commanders that allowed the army to put down the Spartacists. In return, the Social Democrats agreed not to set up a new army that was sympathetic to the republic. The old army of the Kaiser's Germany remained in existence. Thousands of Spartacists were killed and Karl Liebknecht and Rosa Luxemburg were both shot.

Results

Ebert's government had been saved, but at a cost. The army, which never fully supported the republic, remained unchanged. The communists never forgot the Spartacist Uprising, and throughout the history of the republic, they saw the Social Democrats as their deadliest enemies. This was later to be of vital importance.

The problems of the Weimar Republic

German reactions to defeat and the Treaty of Versailles

Reactions to defeat

In later years, many Germans argued that Germany could have won the war in 1918. They said that the politicians of the new republic, who became known as 'the November criminals', had betrayed them when they agreed to an armistice. This 'stab in the back theory' won support among the army and German nationalists. In fact, the army commanders knew they were close to defeat and encouraged the government to sign the cease-fire. The new republic, however, was associated with defeat and this made it unpopular.

SOURCE C

This poster, produced by the Spartacists, was called 'What does Spartacus want?' *Neuer Militarismus* means 'new militarism', *Kapitalismus* means 'capitalism' and *Junkertum* means 'landowners'.

Reactions to the Treaty of Versailles

When the Germans signed the armistice, they believed that the treaty would be based on the Fourteen Points devised by President Wilson of the USA (see page 9) and would be fair and democratic. However, the Germans were not allowed to attend the Paris peace conference. They were not even told anything about the talks that took place there. But most German people still expected a reasonable peace treaty.

The hopes of the German people were dashed on 7 May 1919 when they were presented with a peace treaty much harsher than they had expected. Germany was held to be 'guilty' of causing the First World War and all the damage resulting from it. This was used to justify demands for reparations or compensation. Most Germans argued that Germany, alone, had not caused the war. However, the reparations were fixed at £6600 million in 1921.

Germans were equally angry about losing a large amount of territory in the peace settlement (see page 11). All Germany's colonies and over 70,000 square kilometres of its land were taken away and given to nearby countries. Germany was also severely cut back as a military power, with its army and navy greatly reduced in size and its air force scrapped. Further humiliation came when the area of western Germany known as the Rhineland had to be demilitarised by the Germans and was occupied by the Allies.

SOURCE D

This cartoon was published in a German magazine in 1919. It was called 'Clemenceau the Vampire' and shows the French Prime Minister sucking the blood from Germany.

A storm of protest greeted the treaty. Mass demonstrations took place against it. The German government insisted that it had no choice but to accept the treaty, as otherwise the Allied armies would occupy and possibly partition Germany. The popular press, however, called for revenge. On 28 June 1919 two ministers of the German government went to the Palace of Versailles, near Paris, and signed the Treaty of Versailles.

The new republic had got off to a bad start. Not only was it blamed for German defeat in 1918, but also many Germans did not forgive it for signing the Treaty of Versailles.

QUESTIONS

1. Why was there widespread discontent in Germany by October 1918?
2. How reliable is Source B as evidence of the aims of the Spartacists?
3. What does Source C tell us about the aims of the Spartacists?
4. Using Source D, explain why most Germans opposed the terms of the Treaty of Versailles.

The nature of the Weimar constitution

On 19 January 1919, 30 million Germans voted to elect a new parliament. This new parliament met on 6 February. Because of the fighting between Spartacists and the army in Berlin, it met in the southern German town of Weimar. Its first action was to elect Ebert as president. Its second was to devise a constitution for Germany.

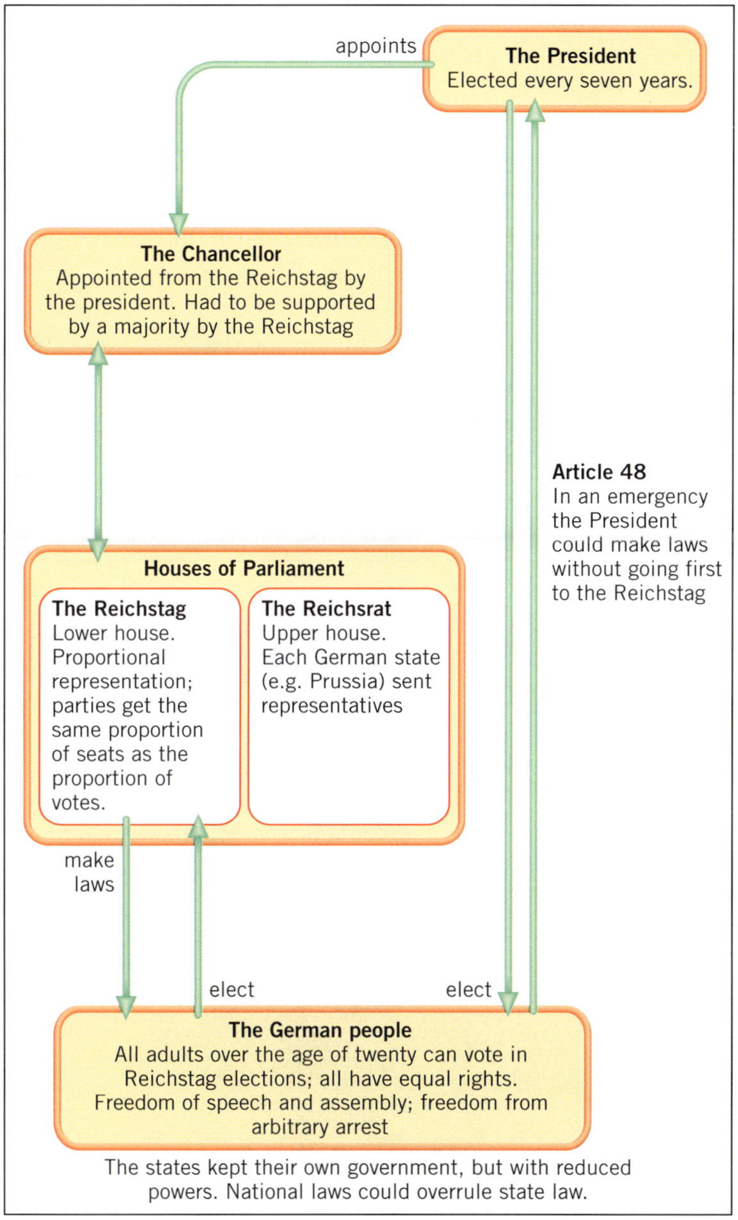

The Weimar constitution.

The constitution

When the constitution was published in August 1919, many people praised it. Germany was to be one of the most advanced democracies in Europe.

At a time when few other countries gave women the right to vote, the Weimar constitution gave all men and women over 20 years old the right to vote for members of the lower house of parliament, the Reichstag. The number of seats for each party in the Reichstag was to be based on the total number of votes won by that party. This is known as proportional representation. It gave small as well as large parties a share of seats. The head of government, or chancellor, had to have the support of a majority in the Reichstag.

Germany was to be a federation. This meant that each German state, such as Bavaria and Prussia, had its own state government. Each state sent a representative to the upper house of parliament, the Reichsrat.

The head of state, the president, was elected by the people. Finally, the constitution gave people many other human and civil rights. Germans now had the right to free speech, they could travel freely and hold political meetings, and they had freedom of religious belief.

Weaknesses of the constitution

The new constitution, however, had several fundamental weaknesses. The president had the power to appoint and dismiss the chancellor. If he considered that there was an emergency, he could use Article 48 to suspend democracy for a time and rule by issuing decrees or laws. This was to prove decisive in the breakdown of democracy in Germany after 1930. In addition, one of the German states, Prussia, had an overall majority of representatives in the Reichsrat. This meant that Prussia alone could veto (block) any changes in the constitution.

In addition, because of proportional representation, no party ever had an overall majority in the Reichstag. This meant that all governments were coalitions, which had to be put together from several parties. This, in turn, often led to weak governments that could not agree on policies. It proved disastrous in times of crisis, such as 1929–30. Proportional representation also encouraged the growth of extremist parties such as the Communists and National Socialists.

Opposition to the Republic

There were several important groups within Germany who never really supported the republic. They preferred the way that Germany was run before 1918, when the Kaiser was head of state. Army leaders, such as Hindenburg and Ludendorff, disliked democracy. The civil service slowed down some of the reforms attempted by the Weimar government. Finally, the judges and law courts were often more sympathetic to groups of the extreme right than to those of the left.

The causes, nature and consequences of disorder to 1924

Political instability

Most Germans quickly accepted the new form of government set up in 1919. However, extremists did not. The Treaty of Versailles had required the German government to cut back its armed forces, including the units of volunteer forces known as *Freikorps*. In March 1920, the Freikorps marched on Berlin and proclaimed Dr Wolfgang Kapp as Germany's new leader. The government fled from the city and Kapp set up a new right-wing government there. His aim was to recover the land taken from Germany by the Treaty of Versailles, and to rebuild Germany's military strength. In response, the German government called for a general strike of German workers in the essential services: gas, water, electricity and transport. Without these, Kapp could not hope to govern, and so gave up and fled abroad.

This '*putsch*' or uprising, however, showed that the Weimar Republic could not depend on the loyalty of the army, which refused to fight against Kapp and the Freikorps. No sooner had Kapp fled than workers in several parts of Germany tried to start a communist revolution. In the Ruhr industrial area, they formed a 'Red Army' and took control of many towns. This time the *Freikorps* and the army agreed to restore order and brutal fighting left a thousand workers dead.

Reparations and the occupation of the Ruhr

The Treaty of Versailles ordered Germany to pay reparations, which were fixed at £6600 million in 1921. The Germans paid the first instalment of this huge bill in 1921. In 1922, however, they announced that they could not afford any payments for the next three years. The French refused to believe this and invaded the Ruhr industrial region to take what they were owed by force.

The invasion began on 9 January 1923. About 60,000 French and Belgian soldiers took control of every mine, factory, steelworks and railway in the region. They set up machine-gun posts in the streets.

SOURCE E

A German poster from 1923. It says 'Hands off the Ruhr!'

The German government could not take military action because of the cuts in the size of its armed forces. They ordered the people of the Ruhr to carry out passive resistance against the foreign invaders. This meant the workers went on strike and refused to collaborate with the French. The French reaction was to expel 150,000 people from the region when they refused to take orders. In an eight month period, they shot dead 132 Germans, who refused to do as they were told including a seven-year-old boy. Industrial production in Germany ground to a halt.

Hyperinflation

Between 1921 and 1923 Germany experienced particularly severe inflation, known as hyperinflation. This meant that prices rose more and more quickly, and the value of the German currency fell drastically. The hyperinflation was triggered by the French occupation of the Ruhr. As the German government had told workers in the Ruhr not to work for the French, it had to pay them for the wages they had lost. It was soon paying out trillions of marks each week. The government also had to buy huge amounts of coal abroad, to replace coal from the Ruhr.

Date	Value
December 1918	0.54
December 1921	3.90
December 1922	163.50
January 1923	250.00
March 1923	463.00
June 1923	1465.00
July 1923	3465.00
August 1923	69,000.00
September 1923	1,512,000.00
October 1923	1,743,000,000.00
November 1923	201,000,000,000.00

The price of a loaf of bread in Berlin (marks).

The only way the government could raise enough money was to print huge numbers of banknotes. But the more money the government printed, the less value it had and the faster prices went up. By 1923, workers were being paid daily rather than weekly because the value of their wages was falling so quickly.

Hyperinflation forced up the price of essential goods, such as bread, eggs and butter, and caused terrible hardship for millions of people. The hardest hit were those on fixed incomes, such as pensioners. Middle-class Germans who had savings found that they had become poor overnight. Workers on strike had no income and faced starvation. Those with a wage found that they could not buy enough food. Some workers collected their wages in wheelbarrows.

SOURCE F

Two women were carrying a laundry basket filled to the brim with banknotes. Seeing a crowd standing round a shop window, they put down the basket for a moment to see if there was anything they could buy. When they turned round a few moments later, they found the money there untouched. But the basket was gone.

A German writer's memories of hyperinflation.

However, not everyone suffered from the hyperinflation. Many businessmen did well. High inflation led to big profits, especially as increases in wages did not keep pace with increases in prices. Also business debts were virtually wiped out by the collapse in the value of money. Price rises were also good for farmers – during serious inflation, food prices always rise highest. Foreigners in Germany suddenly had a huge advantage. People who had dollars or pounds could change them for millions of marks. They could afford things that ordinary Germans could not.

QUESTIONS

1. What were the main weaknesses of the Weimar constitution?
2. How accurate is Source E as an interpretation of the French occupation of the Ruhr?
3. What effects did hyperinflation have on Germany in 1923?

The recovery of the Republic, 1924–9

The crisis facing the Weimar Republic reached its peak in November 1923. For the next six years Germany went through a period of prosperity that is sometimes called the 'golden age of the Weimar Republic'.

The role of Stresemann

Gustav Stresemann was leader of the German People's Party (DVP). He became Chancellor briefly in 1923 and Foreign Minister from 1923 to 1929. As Chancellor, he introduced a new currency, the *Rentenmark*, to replace the old worthless mark. He ordered the striking workers in the Ruhr back to work and agreed that Germany should start paying reparations again. This made him unpopular and he was forced to give up the post of Chancellor in November 1923.

SOURCE G

Gustav Stresemann.

As Foreign Secretary, Stresemann did more than anyone else to make Germany acceptable again to the European powers. In 1929 he was awarded the Nobel Peace Prize. Stresemann was also important in countering extremism within Germany and did much to keep governments going during the 1920s. It was a tragedy that he died in October 1929 – at a time when Germany needed his special qualities.

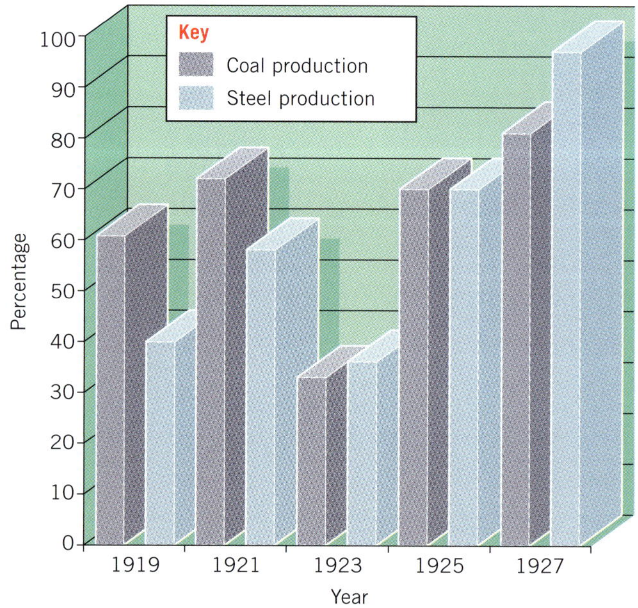

Steel and coal production in Germany, 1919–27 (100 stands for production in 1913, so a figure of 40 means that production had fallen to 40 per cent of what was produced in 1913).

Economic recovery

The introduction of the *Rentenmark* stabilised the German currency. To avoid another financial collapse in the future, other measures were also taken. In 1924 Germany agreed the Dawes Plan with the USA, Britain and France, in which the USA lent Germany 800 gold million marks. The Germans could use this to build new factories that would produce jobs and goods, and which would raise the standard of living of the German people. The Dawes Plan also spread the load of the reparation payments according to Germany's ability to pay. Over the next few years, Germany would make repayments starting at £50 million and rising to £125 million. Afterwards, payments would be linked to the prosperity of the German economy. The Dawes Plan did much to restore confidence in the German economy, and investment poured in from abroad. By 1925 all French and Belgian troops had been withdrawn from the Ruhr.

This seemed to be a period of economic prosperity as German industry produced more goods, exports rose, unemployment fell and most Germans were better off. The Young Plan of 1929 extended the deadline for payments of reparations for a further 59 years.

International relations

Other countries began to treat Germany as an equal. In 1925, Germany and France signed the Locarno Pact, in which they agreed never to try and change the border between them. In the following year, Germany was allowed to join the League of Nations. In 1928, Germany signed the Kellogg-Briand Pact with over 60 other countries. This said that these countries would never go to war against another.

Impact of recovery

The republic was now more stable than at any time since 1919. The result was a decline in support for extremist parties such as the Communists and National Socialists. The moderate Social Democrats, on the other hand, increased their support after 1924. It seemed that the Weimar Republic was safe.

People also had more money to spend. Berlin became the pleasure capital of Europe. Going to clubs and cafés became an important part of Berlin life. Artists flocked to Berlin. There was little censorship and people could do whatever they wanted.

The late 1920s saw a huge cultural revival in Germany. As the economy and politics became more stable, writers and artists had more chance to try out new ideas. The artist George Grosz used art to criticise society. Erich Remarque wrote the anti-war novel, *All Quiet on the Western Front*. Later it was made into a highly successful film.

A golden age?

Although Germany did experience economic recovery after 1923, there were still problems. The German economy now became very dependent on US loans. This was to have disastrous consequences in 1929 (see page 152). Much of the money borrowed from US banks was invested in projects that in the long term would pay off the loans and the interest. What was needed was time. Even as early as 1927, however, industrial growth had started to slow down and there was a depression in farming.

SOURCE H

A painting by the artist George Grosz.

Some critics saw the new Weimar Republic as 'decadent' and unpatriotic. Its new culture did not seem to represent the more traditional virtues of Germany. Many blamed the new wave of art for a decline of moral standards in the 1920s. Berlin had a huge number of nightclubs and there was more emphasis on sex in entertainment than in Paris.

QUESTIONS

1. Which is more useful to a historian studying the recovery of the Weimar Republic, 1924–9, the charts of industrial production on page 146 or Source H?
2. Was the recovery of the republic due to the leadership of Stresemann?

The growth of Nazi power, 1920–33

After 1929 Germany suffered from a severe economic depression that brought about the collapse of the Weimar Republic and Hitler's rise to power. Hitler spent the years 1920 to 1932 trying to build the Nazis into the largest party in the Reichstag.

The Nazi Party's beliefs and organisation

Hitler's background

SOURCE A

Adolf Hitler.

Adolf Hitler was born in Austria in 1889. As a student he lived rough in Vienna before joining the German army in 1914. He fought in the First World War and was awarded the Iron Cross, Germany's highest award for bravery. The end of the war saw Hitler in hospital in Munich recovering from gas poisoning. He was furious with the armistice and believed that the new republic had 'stabbed the army in the back'. Like many others, he thought that the soldiers' bravery and self-sacrifice had been in vain.

Hitler believed that if Germany was to be great again, the country would need decisive leadership. He thought he should be the man to provide that leadership.

The German Workers' Party (DAP)

The German Workers' Party was set up in January 1919 by Anton Drexler. It was one of many new parties that sprang up in Germany at this time. Hitler saw that he shared many of the party's ideas and joined in September 1919. He quickly showed a natural talent for public speaking and propaganda, and rose up the ranks of the party. Together with Drexler he wrote the 25-point programme that stated the party's beliefs. These can be grouped into three main themes:

- **Nationalism.** The German Workers' Party believed that Germany had been humiliated by the Treaty of Versailles and that the army had been stabbed in the back by the 'November Criminals'. They wanted all Germans to be united in a single country.

- **Socialism.** They hated socialists and communists and yet demanded that workers should be able to share in company profits. They thought that big companies should be taken over by the state, and land should be shared out for the benefit of everyone.

- **Anti-Semitism.** The DAP believed that Germans were racially superior to all other people. Non-German people were seen as inferior or 'lesser people' (*Untermenschen*) and should not be citizens of the Reich – the empire that the DAP wanted to build. Jews were regarded as the lowest of all the non-German races. This anti-Semitism was not new to Germany. It was common among many of the extreme parties. Hitler used Jews as a scapegoat and blamed them for most of Germany's problems.

Early organisation of the Nazi Party

In 1920, Hitler changed the name of the DAP to the National Socialist German Workers' Party or NSDAP, which was abbreviated to Nazi Party.

By 1921, Hitler had enough support to challenge Drexler and take over the leadership of the Nazi Party. He soon changed the party's image. It became the spearhead of a mass movement and became far more aggressive. Hitler was already regarded as the Führer or leader, and his followers owed him absolute allegiance.

SOURCE B

> Adolf Hitler has been the dominating force in the Nazi movement, and the personality of this man has undoubtedly been one of the most important factors contributing to its success. His ability to influence an assembly is uncanny. In private conversation he is a forceful and logical speaker. He has a fanatical earnestness which made a very deep impression on a neutral observer.
>
> *A US diplomat, writing in 1922.*

In 1921, Hitler set up a group known as *Sturm Abteilung* (Stormtroopers or SA). The SA attracted many ex-soldiers from the disbanded *Freikorps*. These men felt betrayed by the Weimar Republic. The SA offered them a new uniform in which to fight for Germany. Their job was to disrupt the meetings of opponents and often beat up opposition supporters. Their uniform was brown, so they became known as the 'Brownshirts'.

Hitler's new strategy seemed to work. Membership of the Nazi Party rose from 50 in January 1919 to 3000 in 1920, 6000 in 1921, and over 50,000 by 1923. The SA and the increased membership of the party gave Hitler the confidence to take his next step – an attempt to seize power.

The Munich Putsch, 1923

In 1923, Hitler attempted to seize power by force. The attempt failed, but it was to have significant consequences for the development of the Nazi Party.

On 8 November, Hitler surrounded a beer hall in Munich, the capital of the German state of Bavaria. In the hall, Gustav von Kahr, the new leader of the Bavarian state government, and General von Lossow, the commander of the Bavarian army, were addressing a meeting. Hitler, supported by General Ludendorff, burst in holding a revolver and announced that he was taking over the Bavarian government. He tried to persuade the two Bavarian leaders to support him. But they did not commit themselves and were allowed to go home.

Once out of the beer hall, von Lossow and von Kahr organised the army to stop Hitler. In the afternoon Hitler and 3000 supporters marched through the centre of Munich. In the Odeonplatz, armed police met them. In the struggle that followed, sixteen Nazis and four policemen were killed. Ludendorff was arrested, but Hitler fled the scene. He was arrested two days later.

Why did Hitler attempt the putsch?

Hitler had several reasons for carrying out the putsch or armed rising. He clearly wanted to destroy the Weimar Republic. He was greatly encouraged by Mussolini's success in Italy in 1922. Mussolini had organised a 'March on Rome' and taken over the Italian government. Hitler hoped to get the support of the Bavarian government and then march on Berlin.

He also hoped to take advantage of widespread discontent in Germany caused by the French occupation of the Ruhr and the effects of hyperinflation. Stresemann had given in to the French and agreed to resume paying reparations. Hitler was convinced that the German public wanted a new, strong government that would resist the demands of the wartime Allies.

Hitler also wanted to exploit the situation in Bavaria. Von Kahr came to power there during the Kapp Putsch of 1920, when a right-wing group seized power in Munich and set up a new Bavarian state government. Hitler was fairly confident that he would receive the support of von Kahr, a right-wing politician who did not support the Weimar Republic.

Consequences of the putsch

At first sight, the *putsch* seemed a disastrous failure. Hitler failed to win the support of the Bavarian leader, or the sympathy of the army and the police. He was also criticised for fleeing the scene of the gun battle. He was put on trial and sentenced to five years in prison. Von Kahr even appeared as one of the witnesses for the prosecution.

In other respects, however, the *putsch* had positive consequences for Hitler and the Nazi Party. It could be argued that the most successful part of the putsch was the trial. Ludendorff was declared to be innocent. Hitler used the trial to publicise the failures of the republic and to promote the ideals of Nazism. He admitted that he was guilty of trying to overthrow the Weimar system of parliamentary government. But he then set about showing how this was no crime, since he was trying to restore German greatness. Many Germans felt this was a convincing argument. The court seemed sympathetic to Hitler and sentenced him to only five years in prison despite being found guilty of treason. The judges also made it clear that he could expect an early release. When Hitler came to power, the Munich Putsch was portrayed as a heroic event.

SOURCE C

A painting of the Munich Putsch made later by one of the participants. The painting shows the police opening fire on the Nazis. Hitler is standing with his arm raised and Ludendorff is on his right.

In fact, Hitler served just nine months of his sentence. He was confined to Landsberg Prison, but received special treatment. He was allowed as many visitors as he wished and spent much of the time dictating the first part of his book, *Mein Kampf* (My Struggle). Imprisonment also gave Hitler the opportunity to reflect on the reasons for the failure of the *putsch*. In future, the Nazis would try to gain power by legal means. They would win votes rather than take power by force. The Nazi Party would now have to compete with the other parties for the support of the electorate. Hitler therefore changed his whole approach.

SOURCE D

> Instead of working to achieve power by armed coup, we shall have to hold our noses and enter the Reichstag against the opposition deputies. If outvoting them takes longer than outshooting them, at least the results will be guaranteed by their own constitution. Sooner or later we shall have a majority, and after that – Germany.
>
> *Hitler speaking in the mid-1920s.*

The lean years of the Nazi Party, 1924–8

Although the Nazi Party did not do well in elections during this period, Hitler did make progress in party reorganisation.

The Nazis performed badly in elections to the Reichstag. Although the Nazi Party won 32 seats in May 1924, four years later this number had fallen to 12. This can be explained by the fact that German people were more contented between 1924 and 1929 because of the economic prosperity of the Stresemann era. Most Germans voted for the moderate parties.

The Nazis did, however, make progress in other ways. On his release from prison in December 1924, Hitler immediately set about reorganising the Nazi Party. Branches were set up all over Germany and each regional organisation, known as a *Gau*, was placed under the control of a party official called a *Gauleiter* (regional leader).

SOURCE E

> Nazism appeared to be a dying cause. It had mushroomed on the country's misfortunes such as hyperinflation and the Ruhr invasion. Now that the nation's outlook was suddenly bright it was rapidly withering away. One scarcely heard of Hitler or the Nazis except as the butt of jokes.
>
> *Written in 1928 by William Schirer, a US journalist living in Germany.*

Hitler also defeated a possible threat to his leadership and tactics. Some Nazis, including Gregor Strasser, wanted to make the Nazi programme more socialist and concentrate on gaining more support from the working class. At a party conference at Bamberg, in Bavaria, in 1926, Hitler won the argument and strengthened his position.

Hitler also reorganised the SA and encouraged a larger number of young men to join. By 1925 the party's organisation and propaganda machine was far more effective than it had been in 1923.

The Nazis also began to win more support from farmers. Although the German economy recovered quickly from hyperinflation, agricultural prices slumped. Farmers were unhappy that they were suffering when other people were doing well.

QUESTIONS

1. Using Source B and your own knowledge, explain why Hitler was able to build up the Nazi Party between 1920 and 1923.
2. Is Source C reliable evidence of the events of the Munich *Putsch*? Explain your answer.
3. Was the Munich *Putsch* a total failure for Hitler and the Nazis?
4. How useful is Source E to an historian studying the fortunes of the Nazi Party between 1924 and 1928?

Growth in support for the Nazis, 1929–33

In 1929 the golden age of the Weimar Republic came to an end. This was caused by an economic crisis that created political problems. These problems in turn led to the total collapse of democracy in Germany. In 1928 the Nazis won only twelve seats in the Reichstag. By July 1932 they had become the largest single party there. This increased support was due to the effects of the depression on Germany and the appeal of Hitler and his party to the German electorate.

Economic causes

On 24 October 1929 the Wall Street Crash occurred in the USA. It triggered off the depression which quickly created serious problems for Germany. The German economic boom had been based on loans from the USA. Because of the crisis in the USA, American banks needed their money back, so they demanded that Germany repay its loans. As a result, German factories had less money to invest and industrial production slumped. Factories were producing less, so they were forced to sack some of their workers. This meant that people had less money to buy goods, so factories were able to sell even fewer goods. Even more workers were laid off. In 1928 there had been 1.8 million Germans out of work. By 1931 this figure had reached 4.8 million.

Unemployment reached a peak of 6 million by 1932. The result was social misery on a huge scale. Many people could no longer afford to rent their homes and had to give them up. They moved into makeshift dwellings in shantytowns. The streets became filled with people who had no work and no hope. The suffering seemed even worse because many German people had experienced some prosperity between 1924 and 1929. The memory of the earlier economic crisis of 1919–23 returned, leaving many people even more bitter.

German people began to lose faith in democracy when it would not provide them with a job. The moderate parties of the Weimar Republic seemed to have no solution. In desperation, more and more Germans began to support the extremist parties such as the Communists and Nazis, who seemed to offer them more hope.

Political causes

The economic crisis in turn produced a series of political crises that brought the collapse of democratic government.

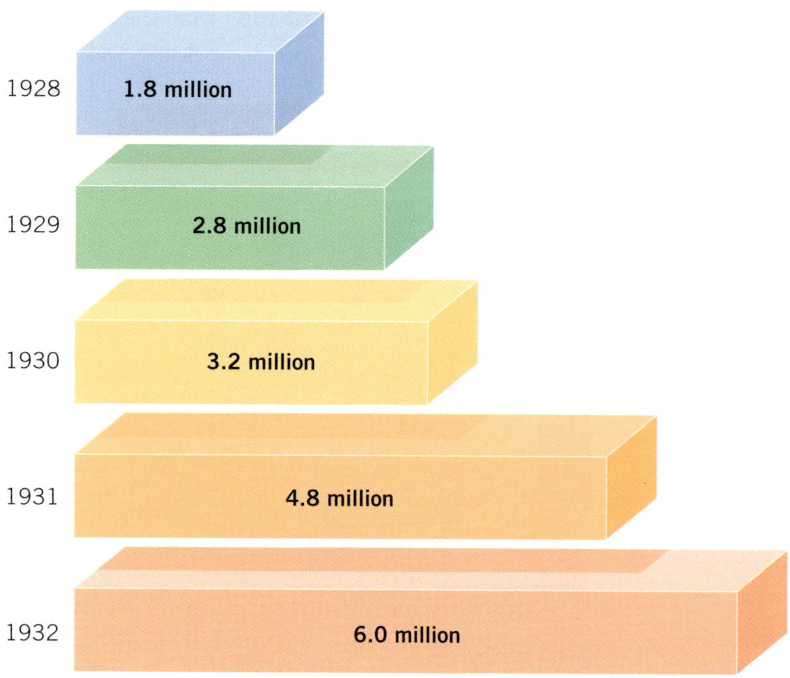

German unemployment, 1928–32.

With so many people out of work, the government had to pay out large sums of money in unemployment benefit. The government simply did not have enough money. It had three options: print more money and risk hyperinflation; cut unemployment benefit; or raise taxes.

Weimar coalition governments had worked well in good times, especially under the guidance of Stresemann. But he had died on 3 October 1929 and the two leading partners in the coalition, the Centre Party and the SPD, could not agree about what economic measures to take. Hermann Müller, leader of the SPD, refused to agree to cuts in unemployment benefit and resigned as chancellor. Heinrich Brüning, leader of the Centre Party, took his place, even though he no longer had the support of the majority of the Reichstag.

The only way Brüning could keep his government going was to ask the president to use Article 48 of the constitution. This stated that laws could be issued under emergency powers rather than having to be passed by the Reichstag. The president was Paul von Hindenburg, elected in 1925, who was sympathetic to the right wing and pessimistic about democracy. He was prepared to use Article 48 regularly between 1930 and 1932, and the Reichstag rarely met during this time. In effect, the Weimar democracy came to an end in 1930. This situation was to favour Hitler during the events of 1932–3.

Hitler's tactics

Support for the Nazi Party grew rapidly during the period 1929–32. Hitler's appeal was partly due to the Great Depression, but Hitler took full advantage of the situation to widen his party's appeal.

Throughout these years, Hitler campaigned vigorously. He showed his talents as a speaker to the full, touring Germany by air and speaking in halls and sports stadia. Loudspeakers relayed his speeches to people outside.

During the various election campaigns, Joseph Goebbels, who was in charge of propaganda, used posters, pamphlets and eight Nazi-owned newspapers to hammer home the Nazi message.

SOURCE F

Then came 1932. My mother and father went and heard Adolf Hitler make a great speech. The next morning they told us how he wanted to be on the side of the unemployed. My mother wept for joy. And my parents prayed dear God would give this man all the votes so that we could get out of need. There was no one else who promised that.

A German woman, interviewed in 1990.

SOURCE G

A Nazi poster from 1932, entitled 'We farmers are clearing out the muck'. The 'muck' is shown as socialists and Jews.

Hitler could not have afforded these campaigns without the help of wealthy supporters. Alfred Hugenberg, leader of the German National Party (DNVP) and a wealthy newspaper owner, worked closely with Hitler in opposing the Young Plan in 1929. Hugenberg gave Hitler access to the many cinemas he owned. Many powerful businessmen, such as the steel manufacturer Thyssen and the armaments manufacturer Krupp, were willing to lend their support to Hitler. With Germany in depression, these businessmen wanted to destroy the power of the trade unions and cut wages. They also feared that the crisis would lead to a communist takeover and the loss of their businesses. Hitler promised to destroy the trade unions and give businessmen a free hand. They, in turn, were willing to give money to Hitler.

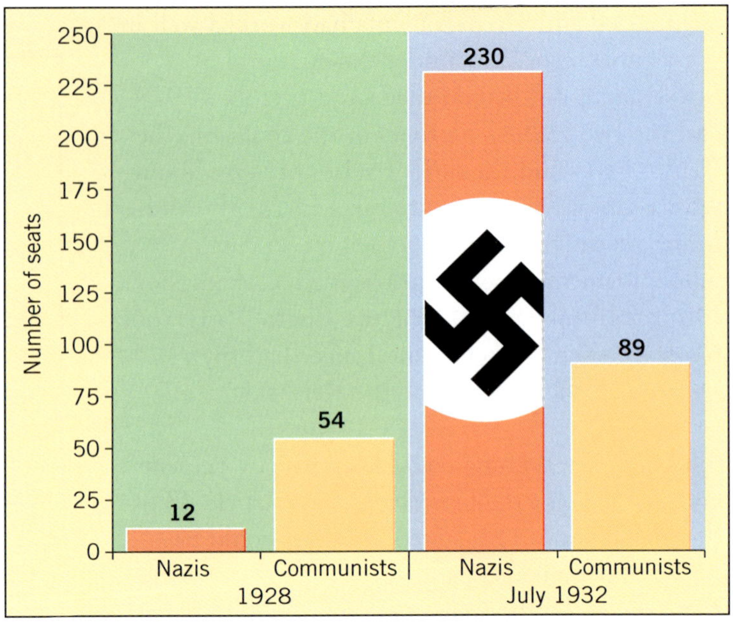

The election results of 1928 and July 1932 (number of seats).

Hitler made use of the SA, whose numbers had increased to 400,000 by 1932 with many recruits from the unemployed. They were used with increasing violence against Hitler's political opponents, especially the communists. Street battles between the two sides were commonplace. But many people were willing to overlook the brutality of the SA and give the Nazis a chance.

The appeal of Hitler and the Nazis

Hitler won widespread support because he appealed to the whole nation on issues that concerned everyone, while also appealing to sectors of the population on issues that affected them separately. First, he revived talk of the 'stab in the back' theory and the so-called betrayal of Germany in the Treaty of Versailles. He made many Germans once again feel resentful towards the treaty and the Weimar Republic that agreed to it.

He also exploited the Great Depression and the suffering it caused. He blamed the policies of the republic for bringing it about and promised an end to unemployment under the Nazis. He insisted that the Nazis were the one party that could unite the German people in times of crisis.

Finally, he continued to blame the Jews for Germany's problems. He accused them of being responsible for the Treaty of Versailles and the depression. He gave all social classes a scapegoat for Germany's problems.

In 1930 the Nazis won 107 seats, making them the second largest party. In the two elections of 1932 (held in July and November), the Nazis were clearly the largest party, winning 230 and then 196 seats.

Hitler's support

Most workers in the cities did not vote for the Nazis in large numbers. These workers were usually members of trade unions who continued to support the socialists and communists. However, outside the cities, most workers worked for small family firms. They did not belong to unions and were more willing to listen to Hitler's promises. These included reform of the economy to end exploitation by capitalists and measures to end unemployment.

In the countryside, there was increasing support from farmers badly affected by the slump in food prices and the depression of 1929. Middle-class people who did not work for the government also voted for the Nazis. They feared that the unemployed working class might lead a communist revolution that would destroy them. Hitler promised to eliminate the communist threat.

Many of the upper classes, such as former aristocrats, estate owners and wealthy businessmen, saw Hitler as a vulgar upstart and preferred the National Party. Hitler, however, successfully played upon their fears of communism as well as their opposition to the Treaty of Versailles.

The Nazis also appealed to women, who formed half the electorate. Some women disliked the changes under the Weimar Republic, including the move away from the traditional domestic role of women and the opening up of career opportunities. The Nazis made a special appeal based on the traditional family and re-emphasised the role of women as mothers and housewives.

Hitler becomes Chancellor

The Depression and Hitler's appeal had made the Nazis the largest single party in the Reichstag in 1932, but his rise to Chancellor came about because of political problems in Germany.

Political developments, 1932–3

In March 1932, Hitler challenged Hindenburg for the presidency. He lost by 19.4 million votes to 13.4 million. He now set his sights on the position of chancellor.

Faced with rising unemployment, Brüning resigned in May 1932 and was replaced by Franz von Papen, a leading member of the Centre Party. Von Papen called an election in July, hoping that the parties that supported the government would win a majority. Then they would be able to make laws democratically, rather than having to rely on presidential decree. But the party that opposed democracy, the Nazis, won 230 seats, far more than any other party. However, they did not have a majority of the Reichstag seats, so they could not govern on their own.

Von Papen continued as chancellor and held new elections in November to try to win more seats. For a second time the tactic failed, although the number of seats won by the Nazis fell to 196. President Hindenburg replaced von Papen with General Kurt von Schleicher, an opponent of democracy.

SOURCE H

Even at the height of its popularity, when the Nazis' position as a people's party was a mile wide, it was an inch deep. It remains one of history's most tragic situations that at precisely the moment when the Nazis were beginning to lose votes, Hitler was installed as Chancellor by politicians who had done so much to undermine the democracy in Germany.

The historian T. Childers explains the support for the Nazis.

Von Schleicher's government lasted less than two months. He resigned in January 1933 when Hindenburg refused to continue to govern by presidential decree. President Hindenburg asked Hitler to become chancellor on 30 January 1933.

SOURCE I

Hitler is with Papen, Strasser is with Schleicher (Papen's War Minister), Hugenberg (leader of the German Nationalists) is with Hitler, Papen is with Hugenberg, Hugenberg is with Hindenburg. Strasser will be Vice-Chancellor, Hitler wants the Defence Ministry. Schleicher wants this, Hindenburg that. Who can still find his way through such secretive politics that is being played without the German people?

A communist newspaper, 1932.

Hindenburg's role was crucial. Hitler would not have become chancellor if the president had allowed von Schleicher to govern by decree. But the leaders of the Centre Party, such as von Papen, wanted to rule Germany and hoped to use Nazi Party support to stay in power. They thought they could control Hitler.

Von Papen, who became vice-chancellor, encouraged Hindenburg to appoint Hitler and carried out the necessary negotiations. Hitler was appointed head of a coalition government in which there were only three other Nazis.

SOURCE J

THE TEMPORARY TRIANGLE.

VON HINDENBURG AND VON PAPEN (*together*)—
"FOR HE'S A JOLLY GOOD FELLOW,
FOR HE'S A JOLLY GOOD FELLOW,
FOR HE'S A JOLLY GOOD FE-EL-LOW,
(*Aside:* "Confound him!")
AND SO SAY BOTH OF US!"

A *Punch* cartoon showing Hitler with Hindenburg and von Papen.

Why did Hitler become chancellor?

Hitler did not become chancellor because of support from the majority of German voters. His party never gained much more than one-third of the votes cast in Reichstag elections. He eventually became chancellor because of the activities of Hindenburg and von Papen. However, other factors created the situation in which he would be invited to become chancellor.

As we have seen, the collapse of Weimar democracy, as a direct result of the effects of the depression, created a situation in which many Germans began to look to the extreme parties to solve their problems.

Hitler played an important role himself. Without Hitler there would have been no Nazi government in 1933. He gave the ideas of the Nazi Party their peculiar slant. Above all, he was responsible for their strongest single element, anti-Semitism. Hitler inspired the party in its early years through his speeches and propaganda techniques. His speeches and charismatic appeal did much to gain support in the years after 1932.

Varied reactions among German people to the rise of Hitler

Although popular in January 1933, Hitler did not have the support of the majority of German people and there were varied reactions to his rise to power.

SOURCE K

The Nazis promised higher wages to the workers, higher profits to industry, and well-paid jobs to the unemployed. They promised to outlaw strikes and at the same time supported every strike to win the support of the workers. They criticised capitalism and yet bargained with the industrialists and capitalists behind the scenes.

A communist, Jan Valtin, writing in 1941.

Working-class reactions

Some workers were pleased about Nazi success because they hoped that the Nazis would end the depression and provide schemes to reduce unemployment greatly. They had lost faith in a democracy that had brought massive inflation in 1923 and huge unemployment after 1929.

However, most were not enthusiastic. Many were socialist or communist supporters who wanted a left-wing solution to Germany's problems. Working-class communists had already suffered at the hands of the SA and feared for their future freedom under a Nazi regime.

Wealthy businessmen and industrialists

Most people in this group felt relief at Hitler's rise to power. They feared a communist take-over, which in turn would threaten their business empires. Some had already ploughed money into the coffers of the Nazi Party and hoped the economy and their businesses would flourish under Hitler's regime. They had lost confidence in a democracy that did not seem to be able to solve major economic crises, such as those of 1923 and 1929.

German nationalists

Most German Nationalists were pleased because of Hitler's promises to destroy the Treaty of Versailles and revive German greatness. They saw the Weimar Republic as guilty of signing the treaty and blamed the politicians for 'stabbing the army in the back' in November 1918. The majority of the traditional army officer corps, however, were suspicious of Hitler and his private army, the SA. Like Hindenburg, they probably believed that Hitler could be used and controlled by more moderate politicians.

Racial minorities

The Jews, in particular, had experienced little or no discrimination under the Weimar governments. Hitler's rise to power alarmed most of this group. He had made them the scapegoat for Germany's problems since 1919 and his anti-Semitic views made it obvious that they would lose many of their rights.

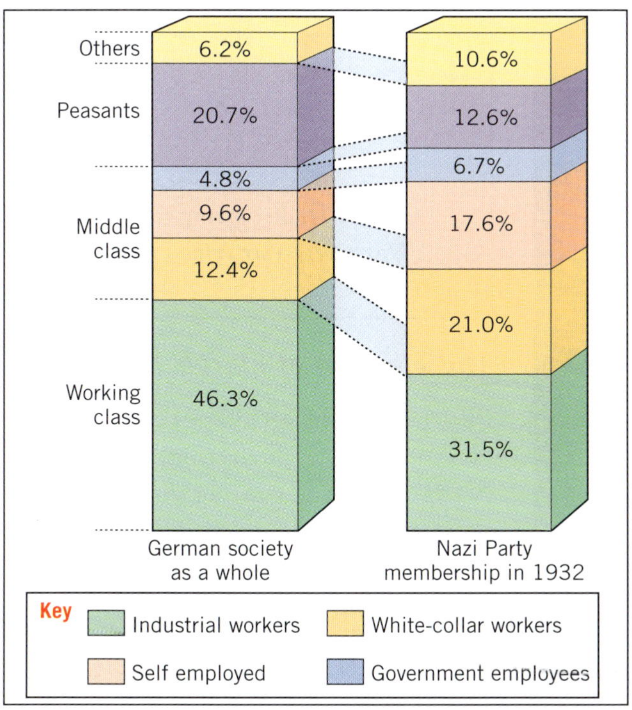

Comparison of Nazi Party membership and German society, 1932.

Women

Women had mixed reactions to the Nazi take-over. Hitler's promise to promote the family and the role of women in the household appealed to some. On the other hand, women's rights had improved during the Weimar Republic as more and more women had been encouraged to go out to work. Career-minded women were therefore cautious because of Nazi opposition to female employment.

The young

Many strong Nazi supporters were young people who were disappointed with democracy and the failures of the Weimar governments. Some were attracted by the vision of the Nazis and the prospect of being important and useful at a time of mass unemployment. Others were impressed by the organisation and activities of the Hitler Youth (see page 164).

QUESTIONS

1. Using the chart on page 152 and your own knowledge, explain the effects of the depression on Germany between 1929 and 1932.
2. Is Source F more useful than Source G as evidence of Nazi methods of gaining support in this period? Explain your answer.
3. Does Source I provide a reliable view of the political events in Germany between 1932 and the end of January 1933?
4. 'Hitler came to power because of popular support.' Do you agree with this interpretation? Answer the question using Sources I, J and K, the chart on this page, and your own knowledge.

The Third Reich, 1933–9

The Nazi consolidation of power, 1933–4

Although Hitler became chancellor in January 1933, he was leader of a coalition government in which there were only four Nazis. Between 1933 and 1934, Hitler used his powers under the constitution to consolidate his position and convert Germany into a Nazi dictatorship.

The Reichstag fire

On 27 February 1933, the Reichstag building burnt down. The authorities arrested a young communist, Marinus van der Lubbe, at the Reichstag. He was carrying matches and firelighters, and admitted that he was guilty. Hitler and other Nazi leaders did not believe that van der Lubbe had acted alone. They declared that the fire was part of a communist plot. As a result, leading communists were put in prison. Hitler persuaded Hindenburg to declare a state of emergency under Article 48 of the constitution. This was used to prevent other parties, especially the Social Democrats and the Communists, from putting their ideas across to German voters during the March election campaign.

Some historians believe the Nazis set fire to the Reichstag themselves to have an excuse for declaring an emergency. Others believe it was van der Lubbe alone. He denied any connection with the Communist Party, but the Nazis did not miss the opportunity to accuse the communists of trying to start a revolution.

SOURCE A

The Reichstag building on fire.

SOURCE B

On the occasion of a lunch on the Führer's birthday in 1943, the people around the Führer turned the conversation to the Reichstag building. I heard with my own ears how Göring broke into conversation and shouted: 'The only one who really knows about the Reichstag is I, for I set fire to it.'

General Hadler giving evidence to the Nuremberg war crimes trial, 1946.

The election of March 1933

Hitler hoped to get 50 per cent of the votes in the March election, so that the Nazis could rule without coalition partners. He had advantages over his rivals. He had used the Reichstag fire to arrest leading communists and have a state of emergency declared. Herman Göring, a leading Nazi, was Prussian Minister of the Interior. This meant he controlled the police in about two-thirds of Germany. The police were instructed to leave the SA alone. This meant they could attack their opponents without being arrested.

SOURCE C

> The Nazis had nothing to do with the burning of the Reichstag. The young Dutchman, van der Lubbe, did it all alone, exactly as he claimed.
>
> *The British historian, A. J. P. Taylor, writing in 1961.*

Results of the March 1933 election.

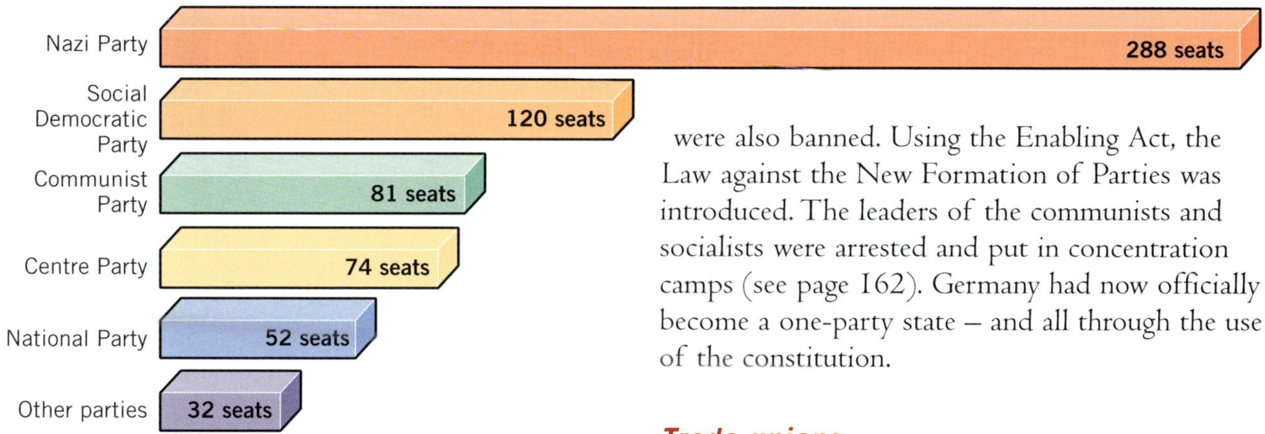

The Nazis gained seats in the March election, but they still had less than half the seats in the Reichstag. To change the German constitution legally, Hitler needed a two-thirds majority. He already had the backing of the Nationalists and also won the support of the Centre Party by promising to defend the interests of the Catholic Church. This, together with the outlawing of the Communist Party, gave him the necessary two-thirds majority.

The Enabling Act

Hitler could now legally make his first change to the constitution. In March 1933 he introduced the Enabling Act. The Act gave Hitler the power to make any law he wanted without needing a vote in the Reichstag. The presence of the SA and the SS, who lined up at the exit and along the walls of the Kroll Opera House, the temporary home of the Reichstag, persuaded a large majority to vote for the Act. It was supported by 444 members of the Reichstag, with only 94 against. This meant that Hitler no longer depended on either the president's emergency decree or a majority in the Reichstag to pass new laws. To put it another way, the Enabling Act gave Hitler the power of a dictator.

Political parties

Hitler now set about removing all political opposition to the Nazi Party. The Communist Party had already been banned after the Reichstag fire, and it was followed in May by the socialist party, the SPD. In July the other parties, some of whom had helped Hitler to become chancellor, were also banned. Using the Enabling Act, the Law against the New Formation of Parties was introduced. The leaders of the communists and socialists were arrested and put in concentration camps (see page 162). Germany had now officially become a one-party state – and all through the use of the constitution.

Trade unions

Back in 1920 the trade unions had great power, but by early 1933 they were weak. During the depression they had lost both members and the will to resist. On 2 May 1933, trade union offices across Germany were occupied by the Nazis. Their leaders were beaten up or arrested. The unions were merged into the Nazis' own labour organisation, the Labour Front.

The Night of the Long Knives

In 1925, Hitler had formed his own personal bodyguard, known as the Schutzstaffel (SS). On the night of 30 June to 1 July 1934, Hitler used the SS to arrest and shoot leading members of the SA, including its leader Ernst Röhm. Over the next few days, Gregor Strasser and leading members of the SA were also shot. Up to 200 people were killed, including politicians such as von Schleicher. These events have become known as the 'Night of the Long Knives'.

SOURCE D

A cartoon from the *Daily Herald*, 3 July 1934.

Why did Hitler purge (clear out) the SA? There were several reasons. Ernst Röhm and some other SA leaders felt that Hitler was introducing change too slowly. They began to press him to take over the Reichswehr, the German army, and merge it with the SA. Hitler feared that any attempt to do this would encourage the army to take immediate action to remove him. He believed it was better for him to win the support of the army by removing Röhm and the SA. The army would then support Hitler as the next president.

Furthermore, the SA had outlived its usefulness. It had been used to intimidate opponents of the Nazis, such as the communists, and to hold large meetings and demonstrations. By 1934 it probably had 2 million members, many of them from the unemployed. Their continued violence was giving a bad reputation to the Nazi regime.

Finally, Hitler had a ready-made replacement for the SA – the SS, his personal bodyguard. Heinrich Himmler, leader of the SS, wanted it to become a separate organisation and saw Röhm as an obstacle to achieving this ambition. Late in the evening of 28 June, Himmler told Hitler that Röhm and the SA were planning to seize power immediately and replace Hitler.

On 2 August 1934, President Hindenburg died. Hitler now combined the offices of chancellor and president. From this time onwards he was known as the Führer or leader. His search for total power was complete.

As a result of the Night of the Long Knives, Hitler had removed potential opponents such as Röhm, Strasser and von Schleicher. On 20 June 1934, the SS was established as a separate organisation from the SA. Himmler now took orders from Hitler. A month later, the *Reichswehr*, which was grateful to Hitler, swore an oath of personal loyalty to him. In 1935 the *Reichswehr* was reorganised into the Wehrmacht, a new army directly under Hitler's control.

Methods of control and repression

Hitler wanted the German people to obey him. He aimed to achieve this obedience through propaganda and terror. Germany became a police state. If people would not accept Nazi ideas through choice, then had to be forced to accept them. The police were given the power to do as they wanted.

The SS

The SS was more carefully disciplined than the SA and its members wore black uniforms. In 1934 the SS was used to destroy the SA and replaced it as the most important military group within the state. The SS was eventually divided into three sections. The Sicherheitsdienst (SD) was responsible for state security. It had to search out and deal with enemies of the Nazis. The Waffen SS comprised units who fought alongside the army. The Death's Head Units took control of the concentration camps.

The Gestapo

The Geheime Staatspolizei (Gestapo) was the secret police. It was first set up by Göring in 1933 when he was Prussian Minister of the Interior. In 1936 the Gestapo was given power in the whole of Germany, and Hitler's deputy, Reinhard Heydrich, became its head. Like the SD, the Gestapo's job was to search out opponents of the Nazis. It could arrest anyone and send them to concentration camps without a trial. It used informers to uncover any attempts to organise opposition and used torture to extract information and confessions. By 1939, 162,000 Germans had been imprisoned without trial.

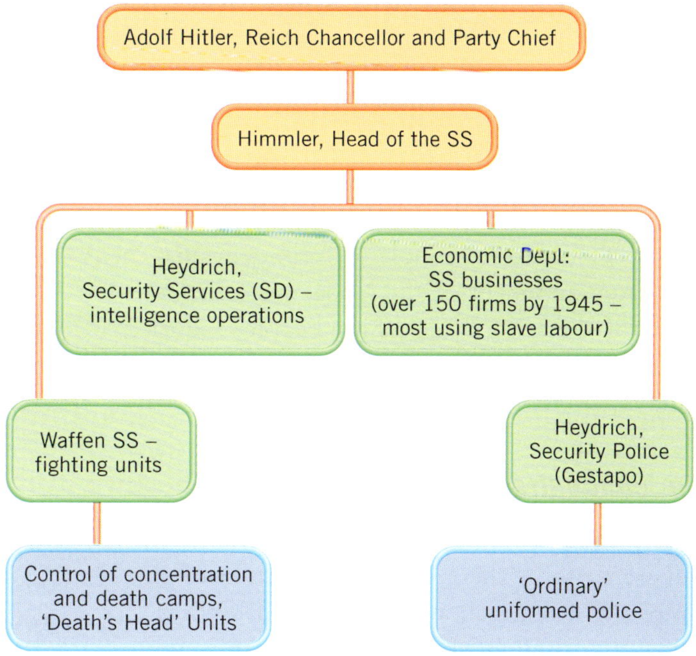

The structure of the Nazi police state.

SOURCE E

Political prisoners are led by SS men to the concentration camp in Oranienburg in about 1933.

The courts

The Nazis abolished the right of trial before imprisonment. The SD and the Gestapo could put people in concentration camps without a trial. The courts were 'Nazified' – justice became part of the Nazi state. The judges were replaced by Nazi supporters. Hitler had no time for the idea of justice being neutral. In 1934 he set up the People's Court to try people for 'crimes against the state'. Any opponent of the Nazis was called an enemy of the state. By 1939 the People's Court had sentenced over 500 people to death and sent many others to concentration camps.

The concentration camps

These were prisons set up for Hitler's enemies, and they were run by the SA and SS. The first of the camps was at Dachau, opened in 1933. Others followed, including Mauthausen, Sachsenhausen, Buchenwald and Auschwitz. They were supposed to 'correct' opponents so that they stopped opposing the Nazis. The camps were places of torture and brutality, and many prisoners died in them. They were filled with 'undesirables', such as intellectuals, communists, homosexuals and Jews. During the Second World War, many of these concentration camps were turned into extermination camps.

QUESTIONS

1. Why do Sources B and C give different interpretations of who caused the Reichstag fire of February 1933?
2. What changes took place in Germany as a result of the Enabling Act of March 1933?
3. How useful is Source D to an historian studying the Night of the Long Knives?
4. Using the diagram on page 161 and your own knowledge, explain the effectiveness of Hitler's police state.

Propaganda

Hitler was determined that Germans would be 'converted' to Nazi ideals through the use of propaganda and censorship. The state would put across its own ideas and squeeze out those of their rivals or opponents.

Goebbels

Joseph Goebbels had been responsible for the highly successful Nazi propaganda campaign of 1929–33. Together with Hitler he realised that the way to success was to present the public with a few simple ideas, sum these up in short slogans and repeat these slogans endlessly. Hatred of the Jews, destruction of the Treaty of Versailles, making Germany great – these ideas were put across in posters, newspapers, film and radio, and by word-of-mouth.

In 1933 Goebbels was put in control of a new Ministry for People's Enlightenment and Propaganda. He controlled the press, radio, publishing, films and the arts. The ministry was responsible for the entire organisation of propaganda. No book could be published without Goebbels' permission. He also ordered the public burning of those books that disagreed with Nazi views. Some newspapers were closed down. The remaining newspapers had to get their news and their opinions from the Nazi news agency. The Nazi publishing company, *Eher Verlag*, also bought up newspapers so that by 1939 it owned two-thirds of Germany's newspapers.

Methods of propaganda

Goebbels made very effective use of the radio. It enabled Hitler to get access to most German homes. In his first year as chancellor, Hitler made 50 radio broadcasts. German industry produced cheap radios and by 1939, 70 per cent of German families possessed a radio. More Germans owned radios in proportion to their population than even the prosperous Americans. However, these radios had a short range to prevent Germans picking up foreign stations and hearing different views.

Goebbels was also aware of the importance of the cinema in putting across Nazi ideas. Nazi films would often portray the SA or members of the Hitler Youth as heroes, and communists and Jews as villains. However, Goebbels realised that people would soon become bored if all films simply showed Nazi propaganda. So he also ordered Hollywood-style musicals and epic films that would simply entertain people.

Image was also important in Nazi propaganda. People would have to believe that Hitler was making Germany great if they could see it. Huge marches and rallies were organised to advertise the power and achievements of the Third Reich. Every year a party rally was held at Nuremberg. Its sheer size gave the image of greatness.

SOURCE F

A Nazi poster from the 1930s. It says 'All of Germany listens to the Führer on national radio.'

Why was Nazi propaganda so effective?

This was partly due to Goebbels' ability to put out propaganda on a national scale through control of the media, especially the radio and press. Censorship proved very effective. It was very difficult for Germans to hear alternative ideas and views.

Children and young people were particular targets of Nazi propaganda. As well as in posters, Nazi ideas could be put into toys and things they read, especially books.

Education and control of the young

Hitler wanted to ensure that the young were converted to Nazi ideals.

Education

Young people were constantly exposed to Hitler's ideas through the school system.

Children had to attend school until the age of 14. Boys and girls were taught in separate schools.The whole purpose of schooling was changed. Instead of being to open the minds of the students and encourage free thinking, it was to create closed minds indoctrinated with Nazi beliefs.

The curriculum was changed so that subjects taught Nazi beliefs. In history, students were taught the Nazi version of the past, such as the view that the German army had been 'stabbed in the back' by the Weimar politicians at the end of the First World War. Biology lessons taught that Germans, as members of the Aryan race, were superior to all other races. Boys were taught military skills, while girls were taught domestic skills concerned with turning them into perfect mothers and housewives.

SOURCE G

8.00	German (every day)
8.50	Geography, history or singing
9.40	Race study or ideology (three days each)
10.25	Break
11.00	Domestic science with maths
12.10	Eugenics or health biology
Afternoon	Sport

A girls' school timetable. German children went to school for six days a week, including Saturday. Eugenics is the study of how to 'improve' the race through breeding.

The Hitler Youth

Hitler also wanted to control the young during the hours when they were not in school. He did this through youth organisations, which children had to belong to after 1936. The Hitler Youth consisted of a variety of levels. Boys aged from 6 to 10 joined the *Pimpf* (Little Fellows) and were involved in activities such as hiking and camping. At 10 years old, boys took a test to enable them to move into the *Deutsche Jungvolk* (German Young People). Here they learnt more about Nazi ideology and military matters. Between the ages of 14 and 18 they were enrolled in the Hitler *Jugend* (Hitler Youth), which concentrated on military discipline.

The *Bund Deutsche Mädel* (League of German Girls, or BDM) was the girls' version of the Hitler Youth. It also organised camping and hiking, but aimed to make girls fit enough to be strong mothers. For some girls, who had lived a sheltered existence, the BDM allowed them to take part in activities that

SOURCE H

Girls from the League of German Girls salute Hitler in 1931.

had previously been for boys. It opened up the eyes of some girls to new horizons. About 1.5 million girls were members of the BDM.

Opposition to the Hitler Youth

Reactions to the Hitler Youth varied considerably. We know that the numbers in the movement gradually increased, but the recollections of former members contain very mixed feelings. Some were upset by the emphasis on absolute obedience. Others enjoyed the comradeship.

The Nazis banned all alternative youth organisations. However, during the late 1930s and the Second World War, unofficial youth organisations emerged. Their members were rebellious and posed a threat to the Nazis. Some groups deliberately developed an unacceptable appearance. They grew their hair long and imitated characteristics from abroad, especially England. They became involved in jazz music from the USA.

Other groups became gangs, such as the Navajos Gang, the Kittelbach Pirates and, most famously, the Edelweiss Pirates. They went looking for the Hitler Youth and beat them up. During the Second World War, the Edelweiss Pirates, who wore a metal badge of the edelweiss flower, collected propaganda dropped from Allied aircraft and pushed it through letterboxes. They also helped Allied airmen, shot down over German territory, to escape.

Nazi economic policies

Hitler had three main aims in his economic policies. The first was to get Germany out of the depression and greatly reduce the level of unemployment. In the long term, however, he wanted to create an economy that could bring about major re-armament and turn Germany into a major military power. Finally, he wanted to ensure that Germany was self-sufficient in essential raw materials to avoid being starved out of a future war. This was known as autarky.

Unemployment

Hitler had promised, in his election campaign of 1929–32, to remove unemployment. Creating jobs for the many people out of work would increase his popularity and ensure solid support for the Third Reich. Unemployment peaked at 6 million in 1932. By 1939 it had fallen to less than 0.5 million. This was due to a variety of policies.

After 1932 Germany made no more reparation payments. This meant that money that had been going to France and Belgium could now be invested in the German economy and used to create more jobs. Hitler sought to create jobs through government spending on construction. Germany built a network of autobahns (motorways) across the country. These not only created jobs, but also helped make German industry more efficient by increasing the speed at which goods could cross the country. Huge public buildings were constructed, such as the Olympic Stadium in Berlin. Such buildings created jobs and seemed to show that Hitler was making Germany great again.

The Reich Labour Service was set up. This provided men to build autobahns, drain marshes so that they could be used for farmland, and build sea walls to protect coastal areas from flooding. The government also invested money in the car industry. This produced the Volkswagen or people's car. An expanded car industry created jobs by cutting imports of foreign cars.

The drive for re-armament also created jobs, but was only really significant after 1936. It was not simply that money was being spent on building weapons. Heavy industry grew and needed additional workers, and far more men were recruited into the armed forces. In 1933 the German army was limited to 100,000. This number had swollen to nearly 1 million by 1939.

The economy under Schacht

In 1934 Hjalmar Schacht was made Economics Minister. He was not a Nazi and had been head of the Reichsbank. He aimed to improve Germany's level of raw materials by making trade deals with less developed countries. These countries would be paid in German manufactured goods. He also gave priority to those raw materials that were vital to re-armament. Imports of cotton and wool were cut, while imports of iron ore increased.

Schacht's policies enabled Germany to pay for re-armament and encouraged the growth of German industry. They did, however, make Germany more dependent on imported raw materials. Hitler soon grew impatient with Schacht, who insisted that faster re-armament would only interfere with the growth of the German economy.

Göring and the Four-Year Plan, 1936–40

Schacht resigned as Economics Minister in 1937. The year before, Göring had drawn up a Four-Year Plan for the economy. This set much higher targets for re-armament. It also tried to move Germany closer to autarky. Experiments were begun to try to produce artificial replacements for vital raw materials that could only be obtained from abroad. The chemical company IG Farben was paid to try to develop a method of extracting oil from coal. Attempts were also made to develop artificial rubber.

The Four-Year Plan brought a considerable increase in spending on armaments and in the size of the German army. The experiments with artificial raw materials were not a success. They did not reduce the amount of goods that Germany imported. Göring had said that in the decisive hour it would not be a question of how much butter Germany had, but how many guns. Many felt that he was sacrificing the standard of living of the German people for the build-up of heavy industry.

SOURCE I

This picture, entitled 'Hurrah, the butter is finished!', was produced by a communist. It makes fun of Göring's claim that Germans had to choose between guns and butter.

QUESTIONS

1. Was it control of the radio that made Nazi propaganda so effective?
2. Using Source G and your own knowledge, explain the effects on schoolchildren of Nazi control of education.
3. Is Source I reliable as evidence of the effects of Göring's Four-Year Plan?
4. How far did the German economy change under Nazi control, 1933–9?

Racial policy

Hitler's racial theory had been explained in *Mein Kampf*. Anti-Semitism was an important Nazi belief, used by Hitler to gain support in the years before 1933. Once he was in power, racial policies were given absolute priority.

Racial theory

Although Hitler believed that the German people were of Aryan descent and therefore the master race, he felt that they needed to be purified by a programme of selective breeding. The German people would also have to be indoctrinated into accepting these racial views.

The programme of purifying the German people was entrusted to the SS. It recruited its members only from men with the correct Aryan physical appearance – tall with fair hair and blue or grey eyes. These men were only allowed to marry women whose racial background had been checked. The SS set up a series of race farms using Aryan women, who were to breed children fathered by SS officers.

Racial theory was taught in schools and universities. Scientists were ordered to promote racial studies not only in Biology but also in Physics and Chemistry. New paintings and sculptures were produced to show the German people their racial background and future.

Persecuting the Jews

The Jews were seen as the most inferior race and were persecuted as soon as Hitler came to power. They were easy targets, as in 1933 Jews made up just 1 per cent of the German population. However, they made up 16 per cent of all lawyers and 10 per cent of doctors. Many Germans were jealous of their success. There had, in any case, been a long history of anti-Semitism in Germany. There were three quite distinct stages in Hitler's policies against the Jews.

The first phase, from 1933 to 1938, was to deny Jews their rights as German citizens. As early as April 1933, Hitler ordered the SA to turn customers away from Jewish shops. They also smashed up some windows in Jewish shops. People were ordered to stop using Jewish lawyers, and Jewish doctors and nurses were ordered to look after only Jewish patients. In April 1933 Jewish civil servants were dismissed and in September of the same year they were prohibited from inheriting land.

SOURCE J

Nazis campaigning to stop Germans buying from Jewish shops.

The Nuremberg Laws

In 1935 the Nuremberg Laws were passed. These made it illegal for Jews to marry non-Jews. Jews were deprived of German citizenship and so lost the right to vote. Jews were stopped from using swimming pools, restaurants and other public facilities. A Jew was defined as anyone who had at least one Jewish grandparent. In school, children were taught to hate Jews, and Jewish children were humiliated in front of the class. Between 1933 and 1938 nearly one-third of all Jews emigrated from Germany.

The anti-Jewish campaign was relaxed in 1936. Germany was host to the Olympic Games and did not want to attract criticism of its racial policies from the outside world.

Kristallnacht

From 1938 the position of the Jews deteriorated rapidly. This was partly because the German regime had much greater control over Germany by this time. Also Nazi indoctrination appeared to have converted many Germans to anti-Semitism. The turning point came when a German diplomat in Paris was shot dead by a Jew.

The German response to the murder was to launch an attack on Jews and Jewish property on the night of 9 November 1938. This became known as *Kristallnacht* – a reference to all the broken glass resulting from the destruction. Some 7500 Jewish businesses were destroyed and over 30,000 Jews were sent to concentration camps.

After 1938 the Jews lost their last remaining liberties. They were no longer allowed to trade and they were even deprived of the right to choose their children's names. In 1941 they were forced to wear a large, yellow six-pointed star sewn on their coats, and they were segregated into ghettos. These were areas where Jews only lived.

Before 1941 there was no scheme for the mass destruction of the Jewish people. This was introduced later in the Second World War and is known as the Holocaust.

SOURCE K

Mob law ruled in Berlin throughout the afternoon and evening, and hordes of hooligans indulged in an orgy of destruction. I have seen several anti-Jewish outbreaks during the last five years, but never anything as sickening as this.

Racial hatred and hysteria seem to have taken complete hold of otherwise decent people. I saw fashionably dressed women clapping their hands and screaming with glee, while respectable mothers held up their babies to see the 'fun'. The fashionable shopping centre of the capital has been reduced to a shambles, with the streets littered with the wreckage of Jewish shops and offices. No attempt was made by the police to stop the rioters.

An account of Kristallnacht from the Daily Telegraph, *12 November 1938.*

SOURCE L

Berlin, 10 November 1938: The announcement of the death of the diplomat and party member vom Rath by the cowardly hand of the Jewish murderer has aroused spontaneous anti-Jewish demonstrations throughout the Reich. In Berlin, as in other parts of the Reich, drastic anti-Jewish demonstrations have taken place. In many places Jewish shop windows have been smashed and the showcases of Jewish shopkeepers wrecked. The synagogues from which teachings hostile to the state and people are spread have been set on fire and the furnishings destroyed.

An account of Kristallnacht from a German newspaper.

The Nazis and religion

In 1933 the majority of Germans were Christians, belonging to either the Catholic or Protestant churches. Hitler was against these churches because Nazi ideals were almost totally contrary to those of Christianity. Christianity preached help for the weak; Nazism supported only the strong. Christianity spread the gospel of peace; the Nazis believed in violence and war. Hitler also disliked the Catholic Church because its head was not Hitler, but the Pope.

SOURCE M

Neither Catholic nor Protestant has any future left. At least not for the Germans. Nothing will stop me stamping out Christianity in Germany. One is either a Christian or a German. You can't be both. Do you really believe the masses will ever be Christian again? Nonsense. Never again.

Hitler speaking to a colleague in 1933.

The Catholic Church

The Catholic Church was very strong in southern Germany, especially in the Nazis' home state of Bavaria. At first, the Catholic Church supported the Nazis. It hated the communists, who wanted to destroy Christianity. Hitler seemed the only hope in the struggle against communism. Many Catholics believed that Germany had become an immoral country under the Weimar Republic. They thought that the Nazis would restore the family and traditional moral standards. In 1933 Hitler signed the Concordat with the Pope. By this agreement the Nazis left the Catholic Church alone. In return, the Church stayed out of politics and did not criticise Nazi policies.

The Catholic Church soon discovered that it could not trust the Nazis. It was not left alone. Many parents sent their children to the Catholic Youth, in direct competition to the Hitler Youth. In 1937 the Catholic Youth was made illegal. Many children attended Catholic schools where they would not be subjected to Nazi propaganda. The schools were taken out of Church control. In 1937 the Pope protested to Hitler.

Many Catholic priests opposed Nazi policies. At least 400 were put in a special block at Dachau concentration camp. The Catholic Church itself did not openly oppose the Nazis as this would have led to severe punishment. Catholic churches, however, were packed every Sunday.

SOURCE N

'The Reichsbishop inspects Christianity.' A poster produced by a communist critic of the Nazis.

The Protestant churches

Some Protestants, such as Bishop Meiser, supported the Nazis because of their fear of communism. Others, such as the Confessing Church, led by Pastor Martin Niemöller, opposed the Nazis. He was arrested and spent seven years in concentration camps. Another leading

Protestant, Dietrich Bonhöffer, tried to organise resistance to the Nazis during the Second World War. He was imprisoned in 1943 and murdered two years later by the Gestapo.

Nazi Church

The Nazis set up their own Reich Church so that they could gain control of Christianity. It was not well supported. The Faith Movement was a further attempt to reduce the influence of the Christian churches. The Nazis also set up a pagan, non-Christian religion which fitted in well with many Nazi ideas, especially their theory of race.

Culture in the Third Reich

Culture was used by the Nazis to indoctrinate the German people into Nazi ideals, especially their theory of race. This applied especially to painting, sculpture and architecture.

Nazi art

Many German people disliked modern art because they did not understand it. Hitler called it 'degenerate art' and blamed it on the Jews. Art was now used as propaganda to show Nazi views. According to the Nazis, Weimar paintings undermined racial purity, so the work of 'degenerate' artists was attacked. Many German artists decided to leave Germany.

Painters and sculptors of the Third Reich produced works designed to show Germans what the Nazis wanted them to believe. Hard work was shown as heroic. Illness and poverty were not shown. Nazi pictures highlighted the perfect Aryan. Young German men and women were shown as having perfect bodies. They were better than any other races. Men were shown as armed, alert and ready to fight; women as submissive and totally dependent on the protection of men.

The best-known Nazi artists were Ivo Saliger, Arthur Kampf and Adolf Ziegler. Exhibitions of art were held every year. In 1937 an exhibition of 'degenerate' paintings was held to make fun of modern art.

Nazi architecture

Hitler used architecture to show the power and success of the Third Reich. He wanted to put up buildings that would last a thousand years. His greatest plan was to rebuild Berlin totally and rename

SOURCE O

'The Family', a painting by the Nazi artist Walter Willrich.

it 'Germania'. Huge buildings, monuments and two great highways would replace the old buildings.

Cultural life in the Third Reich was rigidly controlled. The best of Nazi culture was very mediocre and there was little freedom of expression.

QUESTIONS

1. How useful is Source J as evidence of Nazi policies against the Jews during the period 1933–9? Explain your answer.
2. Why do Sources K and L give different views of the events of *Kristallnacht*?
3. Using Source M and your own knowledge, explain why Hitler persecuted the German churches.
4. What changes did the Nazis make to German culture?

The effects of Nazi rule

The lives of women

During the Weimar Republic, women had made considerable progress towards equal rights. They had been given the right to vote and had been encouraged to work and have careers. This was to change under the Nazis.

The Nazis believed that the place for women was in the home, as child-bearers and supporters of their husbands. Girls were taught this in school. As a result of Nazi policies, women were squeezed out of a large number of jobs shortly after Hitler came to power. The first to go were women doctors and civil servants. The number of women teachers also declined, and no more were admitted to lectureships at universities. From 1936 no woman could be a judge or prosecutor, and women were even removed from jury service.

Women were encouraged to have as many children as possible. The production of children was vital for the Nazis. They would be the first generation to grow up in a Nazi world. The Nazis introduced a series of laws to encourage women to have more children. Loans of 600 marks were made to women who gave up work in order to get married. These loans did not have to be paid back if the woman had at least four children. As a result of these policies, the birth rate did rise. There were 970,000 babies born in Germany in 1933. This had risen to 1,413,000 by 1939.

Women reacted in different ways to these policies. Some had always believed that their role was in the home. Others might well have been converted by Nazi propaganda. Many perhaps were resentful, but accepted their role because they had no choice. A few women joined opposition groups such as the communists. They criticised Nazi policy because it deprived them of vital experiences, especially if they had talents for certain types of employment.

In fact, more women were employed in the Third Reich in 1939 than in 1933. This was because the economy was set up for war. Large numbers of workers were needed in industry. The Nazis needed women to work in factories to replace men who were conscripted into the armed forces.

SOURCE P

Within months of Hitler coming to power, many women doctors and civil servants were sacked from their jobs. Then women lawyers and teachers were dismissed. By 1939 there were few women left in professional jobs.

Josh Brooman, an historian, writing in 1985.

SOURCE Q

In 1933 almost 5 million women were in paid employment outside the home, whereas the figure had risen to 7.14 million by 1939. Labour shortages and rising wages thus drew many females into industrial employment, despite the ideals of the Nazi Party.

Dick Greary, an historian, writing in 1993.

The lives of men

These varied considerably depending on men's class or group. Most industrialists and businessmen did well under the Nazis. Trade unions were abolished, giving employers more control over working conditions and pay. Some big firms got massive re-armament contracts and made huge profits. Chemicals, steel and weapon industries did especially well. Some, however, disliked the high production targets set by the Four-Year Plan and disliked government control of profits, imports and foreign currency.

Industrial workers also seemed to benefit from the Nazi regime. Hitler restored full employment. The German Labour Front, set up to replace trade unions, ran 'Beauty of Labour' schemes to help employers improve working conditions. It also organised 'Strength Through Joy' leisure activities such as cruise holidays.

SOURCE R

The gypsy question can be considered solved only when the majority of the asocial and unproductive are placed in large labour camps and the further reproduction of this half-caste population is terminated.

Dr Robert Ritter, head of the Nazi Institute of Criminal Biology.

QUESTIONS

1. What effects did Nazi rule have on the lives of women, 1933–9?
2. Why do Sources P and Q give different interpretations of Nazi policies towards women?
3. Are you surprised by what is said in Source R? Explain your answer.

These benefits, however, were outweighed by several disadvantages. Wages rose more slowly than production in Nazi Germany, so workers were putting more into the economy than they were getting out. The length of the working day increased by an average of 10 per cent between 1928 and 1939. Most people worked 49 hours per week. Many unemployed people had to do hard, poorly paid work in the Reich Labour Service. Only a small proportion of workers had access to the 'Beauty of Labour' schemes. Without trade unions, workers had no rights in respect of working conditions and pay.

Social and ethnic groups

The Jews were not the only minority group to suffer discrimination. The gypsies were unpopular with many Germans before Hitler came to power. They did not settle in an area and have regular jobs. In 1935 they were classified as 'aliens' and subjected to the Nuremberg Laws (see page 168).

Mental patients were also considered a threat to Aryan purity. The first step was to sterilise them, so that they could no longer have children, while later measures included euthanasia or 'mercy killing' by means of injection or carbon monoxide gas.

There were few black people in Germany, but they were also seen as inferior and subjected to the Nuremberg Laws. Germans were not allowed to marry them. The Nazis treated black people in much the same way as gypsies.

Tramps and beggars were also targeted. They were called 'community aliens' and were forcibly integrated or removed. Most were rounded up and put to forced labour. Many were sterilised in case they 'polluted' German women.

Exam-style questions

These questions follow the pattern of questions set by AQA/SEG for Paper 3 of its current Modern World History syllabus.

Section A

1. The Hitler Youth

Study Sources A to E and then answer **all** parts of Question 1. To answer the questions, use the sources and your own knowledge. In your answers, you should refer to the sources by their letters.

Source A: A member of the Hitler Youth

How did we live in Camp S---, which is supposed to be an example to all other camps? We practically didn't have a minute of the day to ourselves. This isn't camp life, no sir! It's military barrack drill. Drill starts after a meagre breakfast with marmalade. We would like to have athletics, but there isn't any. Instead we have military exercises, down in the mud, till the tongue hangs out of your mouth. The few hours when there isn't any military service are filled by lectures called 'political and cultural teachings'. They tell you about 'the genius of the Führer' and the 'soldier spirit of National Socialism'.

A private letter written in 1936.

Source B: Hitler Youth poster

A poster published in 1933.

Source C: Hitler's views on the Youth Movement

There were times when the ideal young man was the chap who could hold his beer and was good for a drink. But now his day is past and we like to see not the man who can hold his drink, but the young man who can stand all weathers – the hardened man. Because what matters is not how many glasses of beer he can drink, but how many punches he can stand.

Hitler speaking at the Nuremberg party rally, September 1934.

Source D: An interpretation of the Hitler Youth

The discipline of the Hitler Youth is very much shaken. Many no longer want to be commanded, but wish to do as they like. Usually only a third of the whole group appears for roll-call. The level of the evening meetings is very low. They sing soldiers' songs and make a lot of noise, without doing any constructive work.

Germany Today magazine, published in Britain in May 1938.

Source E: Another interpretation of the Hitler Youth

> What I liked about the Hitler Youth was the comradeship. I was full of enthusiasm when I joined the Jungvolk at the age of 10. I can still remember how deeply moved I was when I heard the club mottoes: 'Jungvolk boys are hard, they can keep a secret, they are loyal; Jungvolk boys are comrades; the highest value for a Jungvolk boy is honour.' Is there anything better than enjoying the splendours of the homeland in the company of your comrades?

Memories of a Hitler Youth leader recorded after the Second World War.

Question 1

(a) Explain why Hitler set up a Nazi youth movement. Answer the question using **Source A** and your own knowledge. *(6 marks)*

(b) Is **Source A** reliable as a view of the Hitler Youth? Explain your answer using **Source A** and your own knowledge. *(6 marks)*

(c) How useful are **Sources B and C** to an historian studying the Hitler Youth movement? Explain your answer using **Sources B and C** and your own knowledge. *(7 marks)*

(d) Why do **Sources D and E** give different interpretations of the Hitler Youth movement? Explain your answer using **Sources D and E** and your own knowledge. *(7 marks)*

(e) 'The Hitler Youth Movement was popular with all Germans between 1933 and 1939.' Do you agree or disagree with this interpretation? Explain your answer using **the sources and your own knowledge.** *(10 marks)*

Section B

1. Was there much economic and political change in Germany, 1919–24? *(12 marks)*
2. Why did Hitler become chancellor of Germany in January 1933? *(12 marks)*
3. What effects did Nazi rule have on the churches and culture, 1933–9? *(12 marks)*
4. How did German men react to Nazi rule, 1933–9? *(12 marks)*

Introduction to coursework

Students entering Modern World GCSE History with the Southern Examining Group must take two written papers. One is covered in Chapters 1–3, the other in Chapters 4 and 5. But there is also a Coursework Study Unit from which two assignments have to be produced. There is a choice of study units, but most students choose the First World War, the USA 1918–41, or the Second World War.

Students must cover the whole study unit of their choice, and Chapters 6–8 provide the basic information for studying one of these three units. However, the nature of the coursework assignments involves studying particular topics in greater depth, using research skills. Hence students will need to supplement the information provided here by using other sources. On the Objective 2 (essay) assignment, detailed information will be needed to secure the highest marks. On the Objective 3 (sources) assignment, in addition to source analysis skills, the student's own knowledge is needed to provide extra reasoning.

The First World War, 1914–18

In 1914, Britain, France and Russia went to war against Germany and Austria-Hungary. The failure of the Schlieffen Plan (the German attempt to defeat the French quickly) led to trench warfare and stalemate for the next three and a half years on the Western Front. Both sides launched major offensives during this period, all of which failed, despite the development of new weapons such as gas and tanks. The stalemate was finally broken in 1918 with the failure of a series of German offensives in the spring, followed by successful Allied counterattacks, which were assisted by the arrival of US troops.

At home, the British government greatly extended its powers over rationing, censorship, propaganda, industry, agriculture and trade. Lloyd George, who became Prime Minister at the end of 1916, inspired a policy of total war.

The USA, 1918–41

At the end of the First World War, the USA was the world's richest country. Its strong position was highlighted by the key role of President Wilson at the Paris Peace Conference. In the 1920s, the USA experienced a boom. Ordinary people could buy consumer goods such as cars and radios, and had more money and leisure. This was 'the Roaring Twenties' – the age of jazz, Prohibition and gangsters. But farming and some traditional industries remained depressed. Blacks and immigrants suffered racial prejudice and violence from the Ku Klux Klan. The USA became isolationist, raised tariffs on foreign goods and cut back on immigration.

The Wall Street Crash took the 'roar' out of the 1920s. The Depression set in, businesses collapsed and unemployment soared. The Republican government offered no speedy solution, so the voters elected a Democrat, Franklin D. Roosevelt. His 'New Deal' had some success in overcoming the Depression. But only the stimulus of the Second World War solved the USA's long-term economic difficulties.

The Second World War, 1939–45

The Second World War was more global than the first, yet for the first two years activity was centred on Europe. Hitler's invasion of Poland in September 1939 forced Britain and France into action. Germany's actions then brought in other European countries and the Soviet Union. The entry of the USA into the war, following Japan's attack on Pearl Harbor, was vital in determining the outcome of the war in 1945.

The casualties from fighting were not as huge as in the First World War, but there were many more civilian casualties. Fire bombs were intended to maximise civilian casualties, and the V rockets launched by Germany on Britain were terrifying in their indiscriminate aim. The development of new weapons culminated in the USA dropping atomic bombs on Hiroshima and Nagasaki in Japan.

Chapter 6

The First World War, 1914–18

The Western Front, 1914–17

When war broke out in 1914, most people expected it to be over by Christmas. But the failure of the Schlieffen Plan, the impact of new weapons and the use of trenches led to a position of stalemate, and the war did not end until 1918.

The Schlieffen Plan

The German Head of General Staff, Count Alfred von Schlieffen, drew up the Schlieffen Plan in 1905. In the event of war, the plan aimed to solve the problem of Germany having to fight on two fronts at the same time – against Russia in the east and France in the west. The plan was that Germany would attack France through Belgium and Holland, avoiding the heavy French defences on the border with Germany. France would then be defeated within six weeks. Once the French had been defeated, the Germans would turn east and defeat Russia.

Assumptions

The plan made several assumptions:

- The Belgians would not resist the German invasion.
- If the British became involved, their small army, the British Expeditionary Force (BEF), would arrive too late to play any part in the German attack on Belgium and France.
- Few German forces would be needed in the east. The size of Russia and its poor transport system meant that it would take the Russians at least six weeks to be ready for war. In addition, Austria planned to send large forces across the Russian border at the outbreak of war, so Russia would be contained.
- The German army in the west would remain strong.
- There would be no difficulty in moving Germany's large armies the necessary distances.

The failure of the Schlieffen Plan

On 4 August 1914 the Germans launched the Schlieffen Plan. At first, their attack was successful. But the Belgians resisted and their forts, especially at Liège and Namur, held up the German advance. The last Belgian fort fell on 16 August. Belgium's resistance, however, slowed down the German advance and gave the British time to send the BEF, commanded by Sir John French, across the Channel. This small force of 100,000 troops arrived in France on 21 August 1914.

Two days later, on 23 August, the BEF met the German army at Mons. The battle that followed held up the German advance by a day. At first, the BEF was forced to retreat because of lack of support, but on 26 August they fought the Germans at Le Câteau and delayed them again.

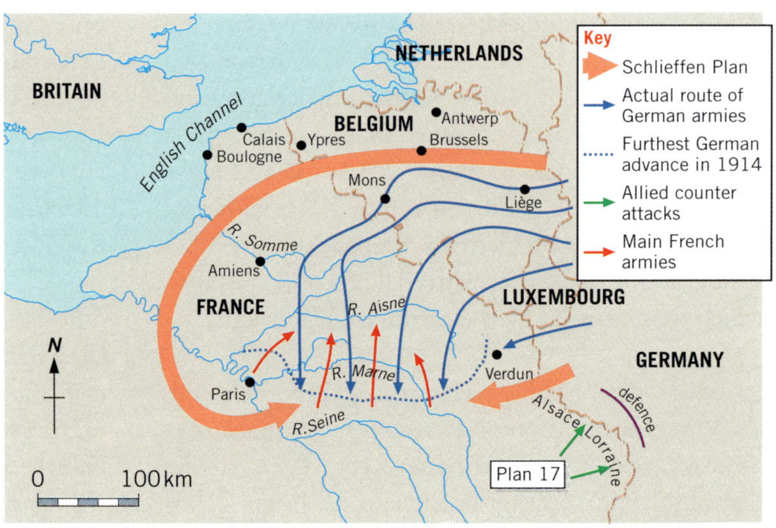

The Schlieffen Plan.

The actions of the BEF had provided a further breathing space for the French armies. The French abandoned their own plan to attack through Lorraine, which was being defended by the German army, and decided to concentrate on the defence of Paris.

On 25 August, the German commander, General von Moltke, made a crucial mistake. He withdrew 100,000 troops from Belgium to defend Germany's eastern border against Russia's expected attack. In doing this, he weakened the right flank of Germany's attack. At the same time, the Germans were having difficulty in keeping their armies supplied because they were advancing too quickly.

The system of trenches at the end of 1914.

Battle of the Marne

The German armies were eventually stopped at the Battle of the Marne, 5–11 September 1914, and this prevented the fall of Paris. The commander of the German armies on the right flank ordered his troops to cross the River Marne and instead of passing to the west of Paris, as originally planned, to move to the east. The French commander, Field Marshal Joffre, attacked from Paris and forced a gap between the two German armies on the right flank. The BEF poured into this gap. In order to close the gap, the German armies retreated northwards to the line of the River Aisne. Paris had been saved. The Schlieffen Plan had failed.

The establishment of the Western Front in 1914

There was one more battle before the war settled into stalemate. The first battle of Ypres took place between 12 October and 11 November 1914. Control of Ypres was vital in any advance on the Channel ports. The BEF resisted the German attack at a cost of 50,000 men, but prevented the German army occupying the Channel ports. This ensured that British troops and supplies could be easily transported to France.

The 'war of movement' was over – as were all hopes of a quick war. Both sides decided to dig themselves in for the winter of 1914–15 and prepared to resume fighting in the spring of 1915. The Germans dug the first line of trenches in order to hold on to what they had gained in 1914. It stretched for 650 kilometres from the Channel coast in the north, to the border of Switzerland in the south. They intended to hold on to the parts of France and Belgium that they had already occupied. The Allied forces (British and French) dug their trenches too. The war now developed into a long slog. The stalemate had begun. There was little movement either way for the next four years.

The nature of warfare on the Western Front, 1915–17

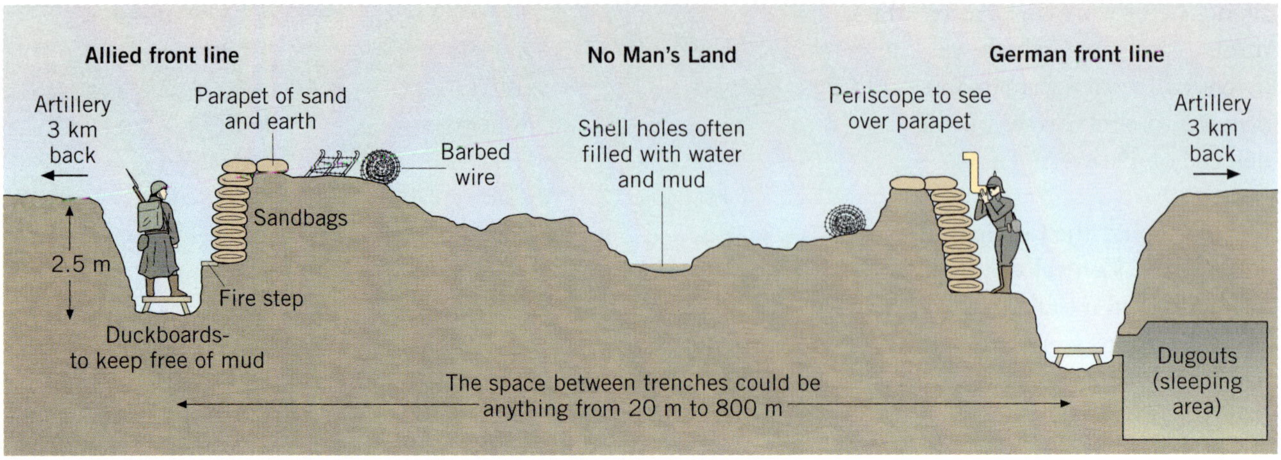

A cross section of the trench system.

The trench system

Trenches were built to house the troops and as a base from which to launch attacks on the enemy. The trench system became more complex as the war progressed, as each side tried to strengthen its defences. In time, more lines of trenches were dug behind the original front line. For every 1.5 kilometres of front, there were eventually 48 kilometres of trenches. Attacks were launched from the front-line trenches, with men 'going over the top' and trying to break through enemy lines. Behind the front-line trenches were a series of support trenches, which provided more equipment and manpower. A third line of trenches held all the reserves of food and equipment. Running between all these trenches were communication trenches, vital for moving goods and men.

In between the trenches was No Man's Land – an area that was being fought over. All trees and buildings had been destroyed in this area, which soon became a mass of shell holes. The holes often filled with rainwater, and many troops drowned in them during offensives. The enemy could be as much as 800 metres away; in a few places, he was just 20 metres away.

Inside the trenches, wooden duckboards were built to keep the soldiers out of the mud that gathered on the ground. Sandbags helped support the sides of the trenches and a fire step was built so that soldiers could step up to fire over the top, without exposing themselves to enemy guns. A parapet of earth and sand was built at the top of the trench to provide extra protection. It was difficult to watch the enemy without being shot at by snipers, so periscopes were used.

Conditions in the trenches

The soldiers slept in dugouts at the back of the trench. These places were usually damp, dark and cold. The soldiers had very little variety in their diet. All the food had to travel down the supply lines, which could take weeks, so there were no fresh vegetables or fruit. The soldiers' staple diet consisted of bully beef (meat similar to corned beef), bread, biscuits, bacon, tea, jam, cheese, potatoes and a small quantity of salt, pepper, mustard and sugar. Cooking facilities were basic. All food was generally cooked in the same few pots, so it all tasted the same.

SOURCE A

Lice, rats, barbed wire entanglements, fleas, grenades, bombs, caves, corpses, blood, drink, mice, cats, gases, cannons, filth, bullets, machine guns, fire, steel. That's what war is! Nothing but the devil's work.

Otto Dix, a German, describes the trenches.

For most soldiers, life in the trenches was a horrifying experience. Apart from the danger of being killed or wounded, soldiers endured awful living conditions. The water supply was very limited, so washing facilities were poor. Many soldiers wore the same clothes for weeks, so they were riddled with lice.

One of the most common diseases suffered by soldiers in the trenches was known as trench-foot. It was caused by standing for long periods in mud and water. The feet would swell and go completely numb for a few days. Then they would become extremely painful and begin to rot. Sometimes the feet had to be amputated. Other illnesses, such as bronchitis, were also common.

Some men could not cope with conditions in the trenches. Over 50,000 British troops suffered from shell shock – a nervous breakdown caused by being in the front line. A few soldiers tried to run away: their punishment was execution by a firing squad. Others gave themselves a 'blighty wound' in order to get sent back to blighty (home).

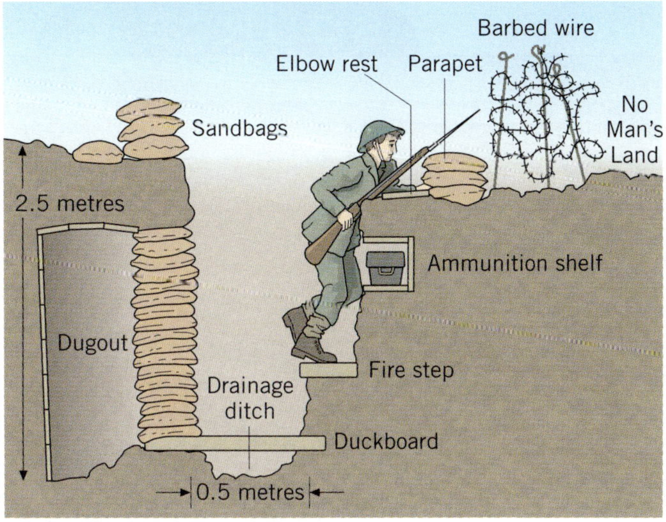

A cross section of a trench.

Methods of offence and defence

Until the First World War, most military leaders believed that battles and wars were won mainly by cavalry charges, with the infantry (foot soldiers) following behind the cavalry. But the cavalry was of no use in trench warfare. Horses were easy targets for the rapid fire of machine guns, especially when they tried to gallop across the mud of No Man's Land.

Many generals believed that the way to win the war on the Western Front was to take over the enemy's trenches and drive their forces back until they surrendered. For four years the army generals followed the same tactics in their attempts to create a breakthrough. For days beforehand, the artillery (heavy field guns) would bombard the enemy night and day. The idea was that the shells would destroy enemy wire and trenches, making attack easier. In wet weather, however, they turned No Man's Land into a sea of mud, making it harder for men to get across.

QUESTIONS

1. Explain three reasons for the failure of the Schlieffen Plan in 1914.
2. At the end of 1914, both sides dug trenches. What were the following:
   a dugouts
   b No Man's Land
   c duckboards?
3. What was shell shock?
4. Why did some soldiers give themselves a 'blighty wound'?

SOURCE B

Kitchener is firmly convinced that we waste ammunition here. I told him quite plainly that neither he nor his advisers had any idea of what modern war was really like. The enemy's trenches must be broken down, his wire torn up, and the machine-gun resistance reduced by artillery fire and an unlimited supply of ammunition.

From the diary of Sir John French, commander of the BEF until December 1915.

SOURCE C

A British field gun used in the First World War.

Even in dry weather, an attack would cause huge casualties. The initial bombardment warned the enemy that an attack was coming. When it stopped, the attack began. An officer blew a whistle and the men went 'over the top' of the trench and ran towards the enemy. On their backs the men carried their personal kit, including clothing and weapons, which weighed at least 28 kilograms. All too often, the enemy's machine guns just mowed them down. The generals were trying to fight an offensive war, but the defences were too strong.

The war developed into a stalemate with neither side able to break through these strong defences. The trenches proved easy to defend. Machine guns, which could fire 600 or more rounds a minute, were ideal defensive weapons. The trenches were further protected by barbed wire, and when artillery shells hit it, they often bounced back to where they had come from. By 1917 the Germans had developed a new trench system, the Hindenburg Line, which was nicknamed 'the Siegfried Line' by the British. This was made of four lines of trenches and concrete bunkers 10 metres below ground level, which were extremely strong and difficult to capture.

Developments in strategy, tactics and weapons

Both sides developed new tactics and weapons, but none of these was able to break the stalemate between 1915 and 1917.

The creeping barrage

The British developed the 'creeping barrage' in September 1916, during the Somme offensives. The purpose of the creeping barrage was to avoid the gap between the end of the artillery bombardment and the infantry going over the top. The artillery fired in front of the soldiers as they crossed No Man's Land. This meant that the enemy front-line soldiers had to man their trenches during the bombardment rather than remaining in the relative safety of their dugouts till the bombardment ceased. The tactic needed extreme accuracy and many men were killed by their own artillery. It was, however, used successfully when capturing two villages during the Battle of the Somme.

Poison gas

The Germans used a horrifying new weapon at the second battle of Ypres in April 1915 – poison (chlorine) gas. The gas attack took the Allies by surprise and caused panic in the trenches. The Germans began to advance, but the wind changed direction and blew the gas towards the German lines, causing more casualties among the Germans than among the Allies. Soon both sides were using gas.

SOURCE D

A painting showing men blinded by gas, queuing for treatment.

Chlorine gas irritated the lungs, and many of those affected died of suffocation. The Germans later used phosgene, which was more powerful, and in 1917 began using mustard gas, which had no smell. The gas temporarily blinded its victims, burned their skin and poisoned their lungs.

Gas, however, was not a war-winning weapon. It became largely ineffective when gas masks were introduced to protect soldiers against it. Attacking troops often feared the gas being blown back into their own trenches. Furthermore, as the British navy had formed a blockade, the Germans were seriously short of the chemicals needed to produce poison gas during the last year of the war.

Tanks

In 1916, at the Battle of the Somme, the British introduced their new weapon, the tank. As early as 1914, Ernest Swinton of the Royal Engineers had seen that tanks might break through enemy lines in a way that men could not. They were not affected by machine-gun fire, they could cut through enemy wire and they could drive straight over trenches. This new weapon was secret, but it was too large to hide. So it was given the code name 'tank' because it looked like a large water tank.

SOURCE E

British tanks and infantry advancing at Cambrai in 1917.

General Haig used 50 of these 'Mark I' tanks at the Somme in 1916, but they proved mechanically unreliable and most got stuck in the mud. However, Haig could see their potential for getting across No Man's Land and the lines of trenches, so he ordered 1000 of them quickly. In November 1917 nearly 400 British tanks broke through the German lines at Cambrai and pushed them back 8 kilometres. But there were few infantry to follow up this breakthrough due to British losses in offensives earlier in the year.

The Germans were slow to realise how useful the tank could be. It was spring 1918 before they had tanks in battle and they did not perform well. The biggest Allied tank attack came late in the war, in August 1918, when enemy lines were broken. By then, the war was nearly over. It had taken too long to develop the tactics necessary for a successful mass tank attack. But tanks were to become an important weapon in warfare in the future.

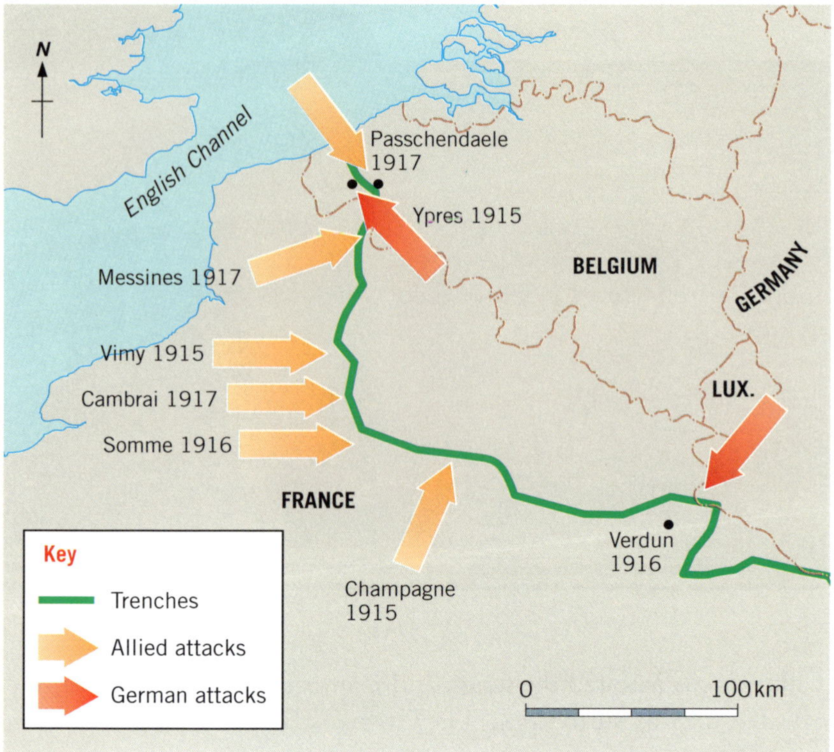

The major offensives on the Western Front, 1915–17.

QUESTIONS

1. Why was the machine gun an ideal defensive weapon?
2. What was the Hindenburg Line?
3. Why was gas not a war-winning weapon?
4. When and where were tanks first used on the Western Front?

The major battles and their importance

Between 1915 and 1917 there were several attempts by both sides to break the stalemate. The Allies launched most of them, as the Germans were occupying parts of France and Belgium.

As early as March 1915, a British attack at Neuve Chapelle broke through the German front line, but poor communications and lack of ammunition led to a delay. This gave the Germans time to recover and build a second line of defence using sharp-shooters mounted on bicycles. The same mistakes were repeated in the British offensive at Loos in September 1915.

Verdun

In February 1916 the Germans attacked the French fortress of Verdun. Falkenhayn, the successor to von Moltke, believed he could defeat the whole French army at Verdun because they would defend it to the last man. The Germans succeeded in taking some of the outer forts, but the main fortress held firm under the leadership of General Pétain, who famously claimed 'Ils ne passeront pas' ('They shall not pass'). Nevertheless, the French suffered greatly at Verdun and urged the British to launch their offensive on the Somme as early as possible, to relieve the pressure on Verdun.

The Somme

Sir Douglas Haig, the British commander, planned a major attack on the Germans. This was partly intended to relieve the pressure on the French at Verdun, but it was also part of Haig's strategy of attrition. He believed that victory on the Western Front would only be achieved by constantly attacking and wearing down the Germans until they gave in.

The place chosen was the River Somme, where the British and French armies joined. Haig had planned for a joint offensive, but action at Verdun meant there was little help from the French. In any case, the Somme was not an ideal battleground for the British. The land sloped upwards towards the German lines, so the German trenches were on higher ground. In addition, the land was chalky, so the Germans had dug very deep front-line trenches, some with dugouts 10 metres below ground level.

The Germans knew the attack was coming. For seven days, British artillery pounded the German front line. But the shells mostly fell on empty trenches. The bulk of the Germans were safe in their dugouts.

The attack began at 7.30 a.m. on 1 July 1916. It was a sunny summer morning. The plan was that over 500,000 men would cross No Man's Land and capture the enemy line. When they had broken through, the cavalry would ride straight through the gap opened up by the infantry attack. The British troops were ordered to walk in a straight line across No Man's Land. They were told by their commanders that they would not meet any resistance as the German defenders had been killed by the bombardment.

However, as soon as the bombardment ended, the German troops clambered back to their front-line position and manned their machine guns. There was no British breakthrough. Instead, the British suffered approximately 60,000 casualties, including about 20,000 deaths, on the first day of the attack alone. Haig realised that a major breakthrough was unlikely and settled for a long war of attrition in the Somme.

By November 1916, both sides were exhausted and the Allied attacks had ground to a halt in the dreadful clinging mud. In some areas they had advanced 15 kilometres, but in others they had gained no land at all, and at a terrible cost in men killed.

How disastrous was the Somme campaign?

Haig has been heavily criticised for the Somme campaign, which cost so many lives and saw few gains. However, many historians feel that this is unfair. German accounts from the time show how the German army was seriously weakened by the Allied attack. The Germans called off their Verdun offensive in September 1916 and remained on the defensive throughout 1917.

The Somme also saw the introduction of new tactics that were to prove decisive in 1918. The creeping barrage was used for the first time by British troops in September 1916 and succeeded in capturing the two villages of Beaucourt and Beaumont Hamel. Tanks were introduced in the same month and, although they were not successful, Haig insisted on their development for subsequent campaigns.

Britain	420,000
France	200,000
Germany	650,000

Total casualties for the Somme campaign.

SOURCE F

The officers were in front. When we started firing we just had to load and reload. They went down in their hundreds. You didn't have to aim; just fire into them.

A German machine-gunner describes how easy it was to shoot down British soldiers in the Somme.

The offensives of 1917

The Allies launched all the offensives of 1917. The French appointed a new commander, General Nivelle, who decided to launch a major offensive against the German lines. He used the same kind of mass attacks that had failed in the Somme campaign, aiming at the newly constructed Hindenburg Line. Once again there was no breakthrough and heavy French casualties resulted. In early May 1917, several divisions of French troops mutinied and refused to advance. The British supported the French offensive with an attack on Arras. The attack included a brilliant victory by the Canadians at Vimy Ridge.

SOURCE G

Cleaning the mud off a horse in 1917.

Third battle of Ypres/Passchendaele

Although the Germans were unaware of the French mutinies, General Pétain restored discipline in the French army by promising that there would be no more offensives in 1917. Britain now had to shoulder the responsibility on the Western Front. Yet another attack was planned for 31 July at Ypres. For ten days beforehand, the British shelled the Germans: in all, over 4 million shells were fired. The main effects were to warn the Germans that an attack was imminent and to destroy the drainage system.

To make matters worse, it was a wet summer. In August alone, there was twice as much rain as usual. Tanks sank in the mud. Men slipped off muddy duckboards and drowned in shell holes full of clinging mud. But Haig would not give up. In October 1917, he launched a new phase of the attack – to capture the little village of Passchendaele. By the time Canadian troops reached the village on 6 November, it was mostly rubble. Four days later, the offensive ended.

The Allies had advanced just 8 kilometres and gained Passchendaele. Five months later, the Germans recaptured it. The British lost 250,000 men in the Ypres offensive of July–November 1917, and their morale was seriously weakened. On the other hand, the offensive took the pressure off the French, who were given a much needed breathing space to recover from the mutinies of May. It also badly affected German morale, with German losses at 200,000.

QUESTIONS

1. Why were most of the offensives between 1915 and 1917 launched by the Allies?
2. Was the Battle of the Somme a total failure? Explain your answer.
3. Why did the British launch an offensive at Ypres at the end of July 1917?
4. What caused the attack to slow down?

Changing circumstances, 1917–18

The entry of the USA

Until 1917 the USA did not take part in the war. People originally from Britain and Germany had formed the two largest groups of settlers in the USA, and the US government did not want a European war to stir up trouble between them. It had little or no interest in European conflicts, although it did supply weapons and money to the Allies. In April 1917, however, the USA declared war on Germany. This was due mainly to the activities of German U-boats (submarines).

The Lusitania

In May 1915 an incident took place that stirred up great anti-German feeling in the USA. A passenger liner, the *Lusitania*, was struck by a torpedo from a German U-boat off the Irish coast and 1198 passengers were drowned, 128 of them US citizens. The Germans claimed that the *Lusitania* was carrying munitions to Britain, which made it a fair target, but the US public felt it was a vicious attack on a defenceless passenger liner.

After the outcry against the sinking of the *Lusitania*, the Germans cut down on their U-boat activity and eventually called off unrestricted warfare, which involved sinking any ships sailing in or out of the British Isles. By January 1917, however, the Germans felt the best chance of winning the war was by cutting off British supplies, so they resumed unrestricted U-boat warfare. The USA was furious.

SOURCE A

An artist's impression of the sinking of the *Lusitania*.

SOURCE B

> If America joins the war, we make the proposal of alliance to Mexico. Mexico is to reconquer lost territory in Texas, New Mexico and Arizona.
>
> *From the Zimmermann telegram.*

The Zimmermann telegram

Matters came to a head when a telegram sent by the German Foreign Secretary, Arthur Zimmermann, to the German ambassador in the USA, was intercepted. The telegram said that if the USA joined the war, Germany would seek an alliance with Mexico and support its claims to land it had lost to the USA in the nineteenth century.

The knowledge that Germany was seeking an alliance with Mexico, and the increasing U-boat activity, caused the US government to send an ultimatum to Germany demanding that it abandon submarine warfare against passenger and freight-carrying vessels. But the Germans refused to abandon their campaign, so war was declared between the two countries.

Consequences of US entry

The entry of the USA into the war had significant consequences on the Western Front. However, it took some time for the USA to recruit, train, equip and transport the necessary troops. It was over a year before US troops arrived in numbers.

In the short term, the entry of the USA forced the Germans to gamble in the spring of 1918. They launched a series of offensives designed to force a breakthrough and victory on the Western Front before the Americans arrived in great numbers.

In the long term, the USA's entry greatly strengthened the Allied war effort. It provided a great morale booster at a time when many were growing tired of the stalemate. It also gave access to the rich economic and financial resources of the USA. US industries had expanded greatly during the war and its economy had flourished. In 1917 the USA was the richest country in the world – its gold reserves had increased by £300 million since the start of the war. With the manpower and resources of USA at their disposal, victory for the Allies was inevitable.

The withdrawal of Russia

While the USA entered the war on the Western Front, Russia was being defeated in the east. The war had been going badly for the Russians for some time. As early as 1914 the Germans had defeated them at the Masurian Lakes and Tannenberg. On 15 March 1917, Tsar Nicholas II abdicated and was replaced by a Provisional Government (see page 110). The new government continued the war effort, but a major Russian offensive in June 1917 was defeated.

SOURCE C

The inexplicable stupidity of the Germans in provoking a quarrel with America and bringing that mighty people in the War against them just as they had succeeded in eliminating another powerful foe – Russia.

From the War Memoirs of David Lloyd George.

In November 1917, Lenin and the Bolsheviks (communists) overthrew the Provisional Government. Lenin was determined to withdraw from the war and agreed to all the German demands. In March 1918, Russia and Germany signed the Treaty of Brest-Litovsk, by which the Germans took control of huge areas of Russian territory (see page 115).

The withdrawal of Russia left the Germans to concentrate on the war on the Western Front. They were able to transfer a million troops from east to west.

The German spring offensives of 1918

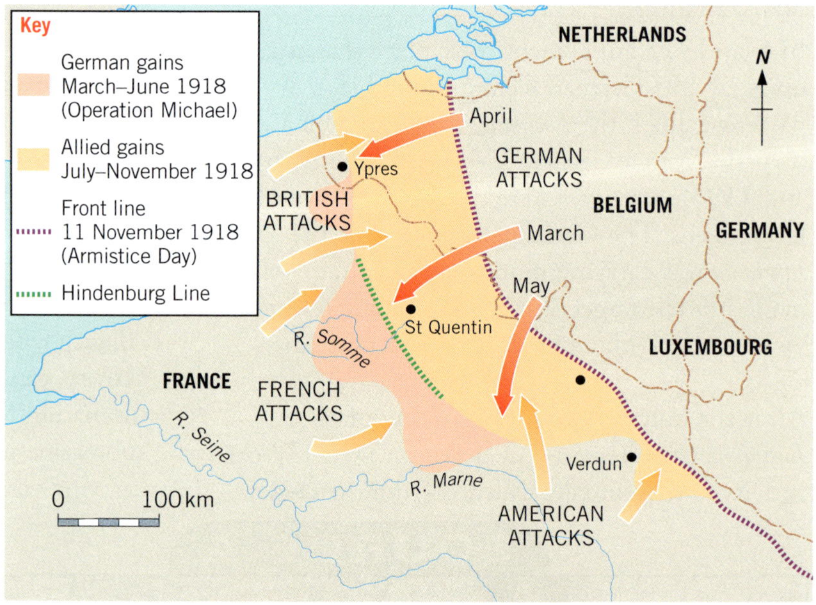

German offensives and Allied counter-offensives, 1918.

In 1918, the German general Ludendorff decided on a major offensive designed to achieve a decisive breakthrough on the Western Front. He realised that Germany must win the war before the US forces entered Europe, and he now had one million extra troops available from the Eastern Front. The British naval blockade of Germany was slowly starving Germany out of the war. By early 1918 the Germans were seriously short of vital iron and steel supplies, chemicals and, most importantly, food supplies.

Operation Michael

Ludendorff believed that a breakthrough against the strongest of the Allied armies, the British, would lead to the collapse of the weakest, the French. He launched the first part of his offensive (code-named 'Operation Michael') in March 1918 at St Quentin, near the Somme. This took the British by surprise, as they were expecting the Germans to attack further north in Flanders. Early German attacks were aided by fog, but the offensive ran out of steam and there was no breakthrough. The British hastily formed a new defence line and rushed troops there from Italy and the Middle East. This stemmed the German advance.

In April, Ludendorff turned north and attacked the British at Flanders. Again there were early German successes with the possibility of a breakthrough to the Channel ports. The British commander, Field Marshal Haig, issued his famous 'backs to the wall' orders (Source D).

SOURCE D

> There is no other course open to us but to fight it out. With our backs to the wall and believing in the justice of our cause, each one of us must fight to the end.
>
> *Haig's 'backs to the wall' orders, 1918.*

The German advance was halted with the aid of French and newly-arrived US troops. Finally, in May 1918, Ludendorff attacked the French in the Champagne area and drove them back to within 65 kilometres of Paris. Again, however, the advance was stopped without any decisive breakthrough. The British were able hastily to set up a new defence line.

Consequences of the offensive

Ludendorff's gamble had failed and left the Germans much weaker. They had suffered twice as many casualties as the Allies and were exhausted after three months of continuous fighting. The Germans had made huge gains in territory, but this only gave them a much greater area to defend. Morale among the German troops began to fall. Not only were they exhausted, but also when they captured Allied trenches they found much better supplies than they were given.

The Allied response

The Allies put their armies under the leadership of one man, the French commander General Foch. He counter-attacked using tanks, and by late July 1918 the German forces were retreating. The British, under Haig, attacked near Amiens with tanks, aircraft and the creeping barrage. On 8 August, the German army was pushed back 11 kilometres.

In September, Belgian troops attacked the Germans and drove them back to the Belgian port of Ghent, while US troops enjoyed similar success around Verdun. On 26 September, Allied troops broke through the Hindenburg Line – the last line of German defences. Just a week later, the German Chancellor asked the USA to arrange a ceasefire. They carried on talking while Germany's allies collapsed: Bulgaria had made peace in September, Turkey gave up in October and Austria-Hungary surrendered on 3 November.

SOURCE E

> 8 August was a black day for the German army in the history of the war. This was the worst experience that I had to go through. I was told of deeds of glorious valour, but also of behaviour which I should not have thought possible in the German army. Whole groups of men surrendered to single troopers.
>
> *From the memoirs of General von Ludendorff, 1938.*

The war ends

Events in Germany itself brought an end to the conflict. At home, German people were dying in an influenza epidemic. Many Germans were also starving. Food shortages were so serious that butchers were selling crows. A typical day's food for an adult provided just 1000 calories.

At the end of October, the navy mutinied and some soldiers on the Western Front also laid down their arms. Riots broke out in Munich on 9 November, and two days later people were protesting in the streets of Berlin. The Kaiser abdicated on the same day, and he later fled to Holland. The war ended on 11 November 1918. At about 5 a.m., an armistice was signed. Fighting would end at 11 a.m., Paris time.

SOURCE F

In the end we could hardly buy a pea without a ration card. No fat, no milk, no eggs. Fritz and I needed them so urgently. Our growing bones were bare of flesh and only covered with greyish skin. Day after day we had to queue up for the barest necessities of life. Shivering with cold and weariness, I looked more like a scarecrow than a little girl.

A German woman, Lio Linke, remembering the German food shortage at the end of the war.

QUESTIONS

1. What was the significance of the Zimmermann telegram?
2. Why did Ludendorff decide to launch a series of offensives in the spring of 1918?
3. What were the 'backs to the wall' orders of April 1918?
4. How did the German revolution of October–November 1918 begin?

Reasons for the military defeat of Germany

1. The failure of the Schlieffen Plan in 1914 meant that Germany was committed to a war on two fronts.
2. The development of the trench system with its strong defences drew Germany into a long conflict that helped to drain Germany of essential supplies.
3. The British blockade of Germany's navy and coastline was very effective during the last year and a half of the conflict. Although Sweden and Denmark did not get involved in the fighting, Sweden agreed to limit exports of iron and steel to Germany, while the Danes reduced their food supplies.
4. The blockade, in turn, drove Germany to resume unrestricted U-boat warfare in early 1917 in a desperate attempt to break the blockade. In addition, Ludendorff's 1918 spring offensive was a last-ditch effort to win the war before Germany was starved out of the conflict and the USA entered.
5. The entry of the USA eventually proved decisive. It gave the Allies access to the vast industrial production of the USA and a supply of fresh troops. It also greatly increased the morale of the Allied troops. At the same time, the failure of Ludendorff's offensive left the Germans with a much greater area to defend.
6. US reinforcements and the effective use of tanks and the creeping barrage brought success to the Allies in the counter-offensives of July to September 1918.

The Home Front in Britain, 1914–18

When the war began, no one expected there would be much change at home. But the need for more men, arms and munitions, together with the shortages experienced at home because of the German U-boat campaign, led the government to take more control over the lives of British people.

British society at the outbreak of war

Before the First World War, most politicians believed that governments should interfere as little as possible in people's lives and in the running of the economy. This was one reason why conscription was delayed until 1916. Britain had been ruled by a Liberal government since 1905, which had introduced a series of social welfare measures, including pensions and National Insurance against sickness and unemployment.

However, the Prime Minister, Herbert Asquith, had faced serious threats to order and democracy in the years before 1914. The Suffragettes, the militant organisation fighting for votes for women, had stepped up their campaign with arson and bomb attacks. Many were arrested, went on hunger strike and were force-fed. Meanwhile, trade unions representing unskilled workers had grown in number in the early years of the twentieth century. Between 1910 and 1912 there were strikes by the three biggest unions – the miners, railway workers and transport workers. They, in turn, set up the Triple Industrial Alliance, in 1914, with the threat of sympathetic strikes.

Economically, Britain still led the world, especially in coal mining and shipbuilding. There was increasing competition from the USA and Germany, however, with the latter leading the way in the production of chemicals and electrical goods.

The changing attitudes of civilians and soldiers to the war

The outbreak of war produced a huge wave of patriotic support for the government in 1914. Men rushed to join up, and one million had volunteered by the end of 1914. By 1916 over 2 million men had been recruited to the armed forces.

SOURCE A

Whitehall was full of people highly excited ... cries of 'Down with Germany' and 'Berlin by Christmas' were heard. Hundreds were buying Union Jacks. There was a deafening roar when the King appeared at the balcony of Buckingham Palace.

An eyewitness describes the scene in London on 4 August 1914.

SOURCE B

An army recruitment office in London, 1914.

As the war continued, volunteers became fewer: in December 1915 only 55,000 volunteered compared to 436,000 in September 1915. This was due to a number of reasons. People at home became weary of the war, sickened by the news of casualties at the front, suffering shortages at home and worried by attacks on Britain by air and sea. Civilians learned about the war through letters sent home. For the first time, people in Britain could see what the war was like from newsreel film of the trenches, although most of this was taken in training trenches away from the front line. Newspapers were full of the names of the dead, especially after big offensives, such as the first day of the Somme in 1916.

The troops had set off in August 1914, believing that the war would be over by Christmas. By Christmas 1916, however, the fighting was still going on. Few people even then thought an end was in sight.

On the Western Front, the armies battled it out over the same stretch of land, turning it into a wilderness. The Battle of the Somme had a great effect on the troops. Many now doubted the ability of their leaders. They felt betrayed. As a result, they lost some of their enthusiasm for the war.

SOURCE C

Don't swallow all that the papers say about the 'great push'. When you read of German battalions being destroyed, don't forget that English battalions get wiped out too.

From a letter home, written in September 1916 by Lieutenant Edward Chapman. He went to France during the Battle of the Somme.

Government policies

The First World War saw a massive increase in the role of the government. The government believed that it needed greater control over people's lives in order to try to ensure victory against Germany and its allies.

DORA

In August 1914 the government passed the Defence of the Realm Act (DORA). It gave the government greater powers over people's lives than ever before.

People could be told where to work. Railways and coal mines were taken over by the government because they were essential to the war effort. British Summer Time was introduced: clocks went forward an hour to provide more daylight working hours. In 1916, bank holidays were cancelled. So was Bonfire Night.

DORA affected people's lives in many other ways, too. Pub opening hours were cut and the beer was watered down so workers would not take time off work as a result of drunkenness. It was forbidden to buy someone else a drink – or to feed bread to an animal. DORA even restricted the kind of kite you could fly. These measures were effective. For instance, by 1918 convictions for drunkenness had dropped to 10 per cent of their 1914 number.

Censorship and propaganda

Throughout the war, it was important for governments to keep the support of the public. Without support for the war at home, the war effort would crumble. Governments sought to achieve this support through the use of censorship and propaganda.

DORA gave the government control over the newspapers. All news had to be approved by the government's press office, and newspapers were not allowed to tell the truth about the conditions on the Western Front. Instead they told stories of heroic deeds and victories. A newspaper could be taken to court if it used unauthorised material. However, censorship was relaxed to enable the newsreel film of the Somme to be shown (page 191).

In 1914, the British government wanted men to fight Germany. At the same time, it wanted neutral countries to stay friendly with Britain. To achieve its objectives, it used propaganda. Propaganda means the spreading of ideas and beliefs. Its aim is to get everyone to accept these ideas, whether they are true or not. The British did this through spreading rumours and lies.

The Germans were nicknamed 'Huns' – the name of a barbarian tribe in the fifth century AD. The British government wanted people to believe that the Germans were cruel and evil. Many British newspapers reported that they crucified enemy soldiers; they raped nuns; they bayoneted babies.

SOURCE D

An anti-German poster issued by the British government stresses how Zeppelin raids killed innocent people (see page 195).

Propaganda was used to encourage men to join the army. There were posters everywhere urging men to sign up. But the propaganda campaign was not just aimed at men. Campaigns called for women to volunteer for nursing jobs, to work in factories, or simply to 'Eat less bread'.

As casualties mounted and men did not return, the government was forced to adopt a more subtle approach. So in 1916 it released the official film of the Battle of the Somme to prepare people for the realities of war. Some people fainted in cinemas. But the film did not come close to showing the real horrors of war.

Recruitment

In 1914, Britain had a problem. Both Germany and France had introduced conscription, forcing their young men to join the forces. As a result, the German army had over 2 million men. By comparison, the British army was tiny and needed to be enlarged. The British government did not want to force men to join, so Lord Kitchener, the War Minister, had to ask for volunteers. His original aim was 100,000 men, but by the end of September 175,000 men had volunteered, and from then on an average of 125,000 men per month were recruited.

SOURCE E

A British army recruitment poster of 1914. Kitchener points the finger.

In August 1914, few people thought the war would last much longer than a few months. Most men probably volunteered because they thought it was their patriotic duty: Britain had to defend Belgium and teach the Germans a lesson. War also seemed to promise adventure – it was a chance to escape from poverty and unemployment.

Many went to fight in what were called 'Pals Battalions'. These were made up of men who already knew each other. They usually trained together and went off to France together. Old school-friends marched side by side into the attack. Whole 'Pals Battalions' such as the Leeds Pals were wiped out on the first day of the Somme campaign.

Men came under considerable pressure to volunteer. In London, women handed out white feathers, a sign of cowardice, to any man not in uniform. Recruitment took place in village halls and town squares. Public speakers whipped up emotion in the crowd, patriotic songs were sung, and men were encouraged to sign up there and then, amidst the cheering crowds. Music-hall stars also encouraged their audiences to enlist. By March 1916, over two and a half million men had volunteered.

SOURCE F

A British government poster issued in 1914.

SOURCE G

Oh we don't want to lose you,
But we think you ought to go,
For your King and your country
Both need you so.
We shall want you and miss you,
But with all our might and main,
We shall cheer you, thank you,
kiss you,
When you come back again.

A recruitment song from 1914.

Conscription

Although the recruitment campaigns were very successful, by 1915 thousands of men had died on the Western Front and the army badly needed more men. The country needed 5000 volunteers a week to fill the gap. In addition, the number of volunteers began to fall as more and more people realised the horrors of life in the trenches.

In January 1916 the government passed the first Military Service Act. This said that all single men between the ages of 18 and 41 could be called up into the army. In May, another Act of Parliament enlisted all married men in the same age group.

However, some men were allowed to stay in Britain. They included those who were not fit enough, as well as people like miners and engine drivers, whose work was essential to keep the country going.

Conscientious objectors

Special tribunals (courts) were set up to listen to the cases of men who refused to join up because they thought it was wrong to fight and kill. These men were called conscientious objectors or COs. The tribunals were not very sympathetic to them; the newspapers called them 'slackers' or 'shirkers'.

Altogether there were about 16,000 COs. Many of them took on jobs such as driving ambulances and helped in the war effort. But about 1500 refused to have anything at all to do with war. They were sent to prison, where they were not allowed to speak. 71 COs died in prison or as a result of their treatment during the war; another 31 became mentally unstable. In 1918, COs were banned from voting for five years.

QUESTIONS

1. What did DORA stand for?
2. Why did many men rush to volunteer for the army in August 1914?
3. What were 'Pals Battalions'?
4. Why did the government introduce conscription in 1916?

Rationing

During the war, British farmers were not able to produce enough food for the whole population. A great deal of food was imported by ships, mainly from the British Empire. All sugar, chocolate and cocoa, and most cheese, wheat, fruit and butter came from overseas.

The German U-boat campaign (see page 195) reduced the amount of food being imported into Britain, so food prices went up. But food only became scarce later in the war. White bread was banned in 1916 because grain was in short supply. In 1917 people were asked to eat only 1.1 kilograms of meat a week. But for many people, this was actually more than they could afford to eat anyway.

The government was not keen to introduce rationing and preferred people to reduce voluntarily the amount of food they consumed. For example, in 1917 the royal family announced that it would be cutting its food consumption by a quarter. But in the end, the government had to act. On 1 January 1918, sugar was rationed. By the spring, butter, tea, jam, margarine, meat and bacon had all been added to the ration list.

In the same month, the government passed the Public Meals Order of January 1918. This stated that for two days a week people should not eat meat; meat should not be served for breakfast; people over ten years old should only drink milk in hot drinks; guests should bring their own sugar with them; and no more than 42 grams of bread, cake, scone or biscuit should be served for afternoon tea.

The role of women

The war had a major impact on the position of women in British society, and on their attitude towards themselves. In 1914 women did not have the vote and were considered by many men to be second-class citizens, whose role it was to look after the home and bring up the children.

War work

During the war, 5 million men joined the army. With a large percentage of the male population abroad fighting, many women stepped into jobs traditionally done by men. Soon women were working in factories and steel mills, driving buses, building ships or working in agriculture in the Women's Land Army.

SOURCE H

A British government poster from 1917 encourages women to join the Women's Land Army.

Most importantly, large numbers of women worked in the munitions factories, making the bullets and shells for ammunition. The number of women working in this industry increased from 200,000 in 1914 to 900,000 by 1918. This was highly dangerous work. Some factories blew up. Many women were nicknamed 'canaries' because the chemicals that they worked with turned their skin yellow. But the work was well paid by pre-war standards. A female industrial worker could expect to earn £3 to £5 a week, which was a huge sum compared to the £2 per month paid to a domestic servant before the war.

SOURCE I

Women working in a munitions factory in May 1917. They are doing skilled precision machine work, turning brass nose cones for shells.

Social attitudes

For large numbers of women, employment during the war was the first time they had received their own wage packet and the first time they had been financially independent of their husbands. Many women gained a greater sense of their place in society. Being part of the workforce meant that women could change their social behaviour. They wore more practical clothes, including trousers. Many women went to pubs on their own, drank alcohol and smoked.

SOURCE J

> I was doing some crochet work in my teatime when I heard the alarm. We had to push through a crowd of men who shouted to us not to go near. The exploding cartridges were making a fearful noise. Most of us were struck by bullets but were only bruised; there was not much power in the hits.
>
> *From a woman munitions worker's diary.*

In the services

From the spring of 1917, women were able to do many jobs in the armed services. About 100,000 women served in the various sections of the armed forces: the Women's Army Auxiliary Corps (WAAC), the Women's Royal Naval Service (WRNS, or Wrens) and the Women's Royal Air Force (WRAF). Here they took over the clerical and administrative jobs normally done by men. This released men to fight at the front.

About 23,000 women served as nurses close to the fighting and a further 15,000 volunteered to serve as assistants in the Volunteer Aid Detachment. This provided cooks, kitchen maids, laundry workers and motor drivers to assist the war effort. The work was hard and often unpleasant.

SOURCE K

> Women became more independent. Women munitions workers paid for their round of drinks at the pub. Fashion changed for practical reasons: never again did skirts sweep the ground. The petticoat disappeared, though not for good. Women's hats became neater. A few women cut their hair.
>
> *A British historian writing in 1965.*

During the war, women proved that they played a vital part in the nation's welfare. The war forced men to change the way they regarded women. More people realised that women could make greater contributions in the workplace as well as the home.

At the end of the war

The government recognised the role that women had played in the war. Before 1914 the Suffragettes had been campaigning for the vote. During the war, they called off their campaign as women gave their full support to the war effort. But at the end of the war, in 1918, the Representation of the People Act gave the vote to women aged 30 or over. (Men could vote at the age of 21.) In 1919 women were allowed to do jury service, become lawyers and join the Civil Service. Two years later they were able to claim unemployment benefit and were entitled to pensions.

On the other hand, when the war ended, women were forced to give up the jobs they had been doing. When the men returned, they took back what few jobs there were in the post-war economic slump. In 1921, 31 per cent of the female population had a job – 1 per cent less than in 1911. Women under 30 were disappointed with the Representation of the People Act. They had expected the same voting rights as men.

QUESTIONS

1. What was the first product to be rationed in January 1918?
2. Many female munitions workers were nicknamed 'canaries'. Why?
3. What were the WAAC, WRAF and WRNS?
4. What did women gain from the Representation of the People Act, 1918?

The impact of enemy action on the civilian population

This was the first war in which enemy action had a direct effect on British civilians. People on the east coast of Britain received a shock in December 1914 when German ships shelled Hartlepool, Scarborough and Whitby. There were over 500 civilian casualties in these raids, which created the fear of a German invasion. But the raids also helped to unite the British people and build up a hatred towards the Germans. The government made full use of this in its recruiting campaign.

The civilian population was also affected by the German U-boat campaign. The Germans used their submarines to try to starve Britain out of the war. In 1915 and again between 1917 and 1918, the Germans carried out unrestricted U-boat warfare. They sank any ships sailing in and out of the British Isles. By April 1917, Britain was down to its last six weeks' supply of grain. This led to food rationing.

Air-raids

The danger of invasion also came from the air. The Germans had developed Zeppelin airships. The first air attack on Britain was in January 1915 when two Zeppelins bombed Great Yarmouth and King's Lynn, killing two people and damaging houses.

Further Zeppelin attacks in 1915 and 1916 concentrated on London. Zeppelin raids were replaced by German bomber attacks in 1917. Bombs dropped by German Gotha planes killed over 1000 people in these raids and damaged many shops and houses.

Because of improved British defences such as anti-aircraft fire against fighter planes (see page 196), the Germans switched to night attacks, especially on London, which they reached by following the moonlit River Thames. Towards the end of the war, the raids increased. From September 1917 to May 1918 there were 19 major attacks on London, during which over 300,000 people sought refuge in Underground railway stations.

The effect of these raids on the war effort was not great. More important was the effect on people's morale. Britain was an island and had always been safe from invasion. For the first time, British civilians realised that they were vulnerable, and that not only those fighting at the front were affected by war.

British counter-measures

The government had to take measures to defend its citizens from further attacks. The British fleet guarded the east coast against further attacks by sea. It also blockaded the German coast and forced the German fleet to remain in port. In May 1917 the British government introduced the convoy system – merchant ships sailed in groups with the protection of the navy. This made them less vulnerable to attack and ensured that British people did not starve.

The British also developed defences against air attack. They used barrage balloons to defend themselves against Zeppelins and sent fighter planes to intercept them. They also illuminated the sky with searchlights, so that the Zeppelins could be easily spotted and fired at. If a Zeppelin was hit, it burst into flames because it was filled with hydrogen. Further defences were introduced against bomber attacks, including anti-aircraft guns and the blackout, where street and house lights were turned off and windows blacked out to make it more difficult for the German bombers to see their targets. Improvements were also made to British aircraft, so that they could launch attacks on German towns.

SOURCE L

The whole street seemed to explode. There was smoke and flames all over, but the worst of all were the screams of the wounded and dying and mothers looking frantically for their kids.

Description of an air-raid on Folkestone in May 1917.

SOURCE M

A German postcard of 1916 shows the effect they hoped Zeppelin raids would have.

The role of Lloyd George

When war began in 1914, a Liberal government led by Asquith governed Britain. By May 1915, however, serious criticisms had emerged about the way the government was managing the war. Some people were concerned about the extreme shortage of shells and others felt that many of the military campaigns, especially on the Western Front, had been badly managed. In response to these criticisms, Asquith set up a coalition government that contained people from all the main parties.

Minister of Munitions

David Lloyd George was made Minister of Munitions. He completely changed the munitions industry by bringing in successful businessmen to run the industry. Women were encouraged to work in the factories. The results were startling. Machine-gun production rose from 6000 in 1915 to 33,000 in 1916. The monthly output of shells increased from 20,000 in May 1915 to one million by July 1916.

Despite Lloyd George's achievements, however, there was growing criticism of Asquith's leadership. Many people felt that Asquith was too old to organise the war effort; others believed that he did not put enough energy into the war and that he was out of touch with the army and its leaders. Matters came to a head in December 1916 when, as a result of this opposition, Asquith resigned and Lloyd George became Prime Minister of a new coalition government.

SOURCE N

David Lloyd George.

'Total war'

Lloyd George showed much greater energy than Asquith and organised the country for 'total war'. He introduced a much smaller war cabinet, which was able to make decisions much more quickly. Lloyd George also further increased the role of the government over industry and agriculture. In 1917 he set up the Ministries of Food, Pensions, Labour and Blockade. The Corn Production Act of 1917 gave wide powers of control over farming. Compulsory rationing was introduced in January 1918.

Lloyd George also influenced the war effort. The leading admirals of the navy were reluctant to bring in the convoy system to combat the threat posed by the German U-boats. The Prime Minister forced the issue in May 1917. Lloyd George also opposed the slaughter on the Western Front. He did not want a repeat of the Somme, in 1916, and tried to prevent Haig from launching his major offensive at Ypres in July 1917.

However, Lloyd George was not totally successful and made several mistakes in military matters. In 1917 he supported the new French General, Nivelle, as overall commander on the Western Front. Nivelle's offensive, in April 1917, was a total failure which led to mutinies in the French army (see page 184). Because Lloyd George was unable to remove Haig as commander of the British forces on the Western Front, he retaliated by deliberately reducing the number of new recruits sent to the front. This left the British defences weak during Ludendorff's offensives in the spring of 1918.

The effects of the war on British society

The war brought many changes in British society. Before the war, it was rare for an upper-class or middle-class woman to go out alone. A chaperone accompanied her everywhere. During the war, the women were out helping in the war effort. The war brought in quaint national customs such as British Summer Time and afternoon closing of public houses.

SOURCE O

The wartime business girl is to be seen any night dining out alone or with a friend in the restaurants in London. Formerly, she would never have had her evening meal in town unless in the company of a man friend. After a modest dinner, cigarettes follow, and then there is talk of typing, 'governors', theatres and dress.

Daily Mail, *17 April 1916.*

Cigarette smoking became much more popular, but the average beer remained permanently weaker and more expensive. In 1918 alcohol sales were only half those of 1900.

The most devastating effect of the war was the large number of deaths, mainly of young men. Of over 6 million serving soldiers, sailors and airmen, over 700,000 were killed – nearly 12 per cent. This led to an increase in the proportion of women, and of widows, in the population.

Social progress

Nevertheless there was great social progress during the war. Life expectancy at birth rose, between 1911 and 1921, from 49 to 56 years for men and from 53 to 60 years for women. The war saw a fall in infant death rates, partly due to improved maternity care. There was more work and better pay for most of the population. State benefits of all kinds were extended, including the provision of school meals for children and health insurance for members of the armed forces, whose wives also received maternity benefits.

Wage rates improved and the average working week was reduced from 55 to 48 hours. The trade union movement also gained from the war. Membership more than doubled between 1914 and 1920, and the unions' reputation improved as they were consulted by the wartime governments and co-operated with the war effort by banning strikes.

The effects of the war on the economy

In 1914 London was the financial capital of the world. Britain's main industries – coal, cotton, shipbuilding and iron – were booming. Britain had 42 per cent of the world's exports. Government spending and taxation were quite low.

All this changed as a result of the war. The war was very expensive, costing £7 million a day by 1918. Income tax, which was 6p in the pound in 1914, had to be raised to 30p by 1918. The national debt (the amount that the British government owed abroad) rose from £706 million in 1914 to £7481 million in 1918. Much of this money was borrowed from the USA. Britain's share of the world's exports fell during the war, partly due to the sinking of millions of tons of shipping.

The main industries, which were essential for the war effort, were overproducing once the war ended because less was needed. Coal, cotton and shipbuilding began a long period of decline. Unemployment, which had been very low before 1914, reached one million in 1921 and did not fall below that level in the 1920s and 1930s.

QUESTIONS

1. Which towns on the English east coast were raided by German warships in the early months of the war?
2. What were Zeppelins and Gothas?
3. Why did Britain introduce the convoy system in 1917?
4. What effects did the war have on Britain's heavy industries?

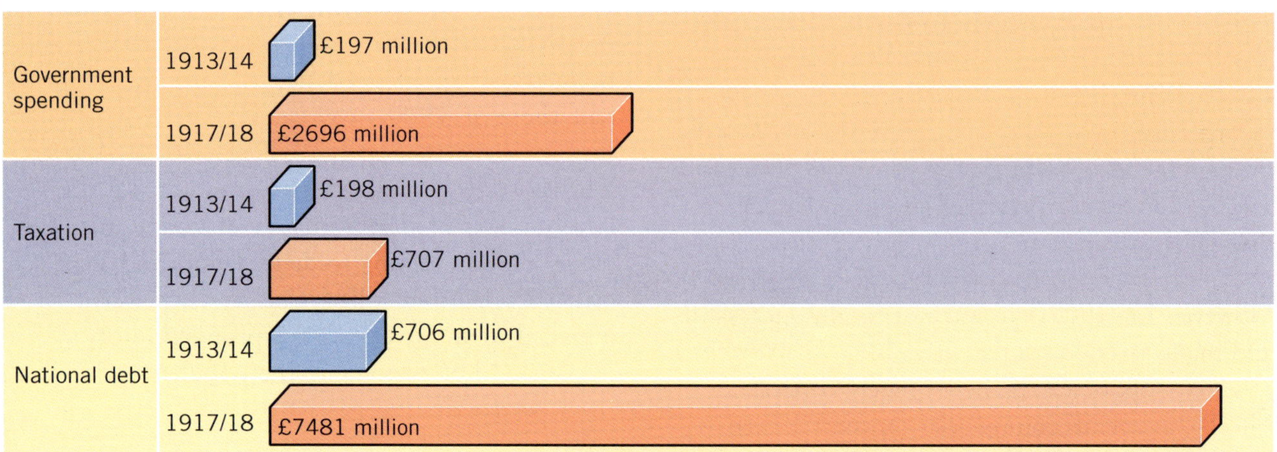

Government spending, taxation and the national debt, 1914–18.

Coursework/Paper 1–style questions

The First World War 1914–18

Assessment Objective 2

Aspect 1 Causes and/or consequences

1. Explain why the Battle of the Somme **or** Verdun **or** Third Ypres came to be fought.
2. What were the consequences of the Battle of the Somme **or** Verdun **or** Third Ypres?
3. During 1917 first Russia surrendered then the USA joined the war on the side of the Allies. What were the consequences of these events for the war on the Western Front?
4. Many believed the First World War would be over by the end of 1914. Why did this not happen?
   Explain your answer.
5. The First World War had a greater impact on civilian life than any war before that time.
   Explain why.

Aspect 2 Change and continuity

1. The Western Front during the First World War is generally seen to be a time of stalemate and lack of military innovation. How far **did** fighting methods change from 1915 to 1918?
   Explain your answer.
2. How great were the changes to women's lives in Britain during the First World War?
   Explain your answer.

Aspect 3 People's ideas and attitudes

1. During the First World War people in Britain had different opinions about how the war was being conducted.
   Explain why this was the case.
2. At the end of 1917 British soldiers were still entrenched on the Western Front.
   Explain the reactions of British soldiers fighting on the Western Front to the progress of the war at that time.

Aspect 4 The role of the individual

1. How important was Field Marshal Sir Douglas Haig in achieving victory for the Allied forces in the First World War?
   Explain your answer.
2. Was Lloyd George more important than Field Marshal Haig in helping Britain play its part in achieving victory in 1918?
   Explain your answer.

Assessment Objective 3

Assessing the Battle of the Somme, 1916

Source A

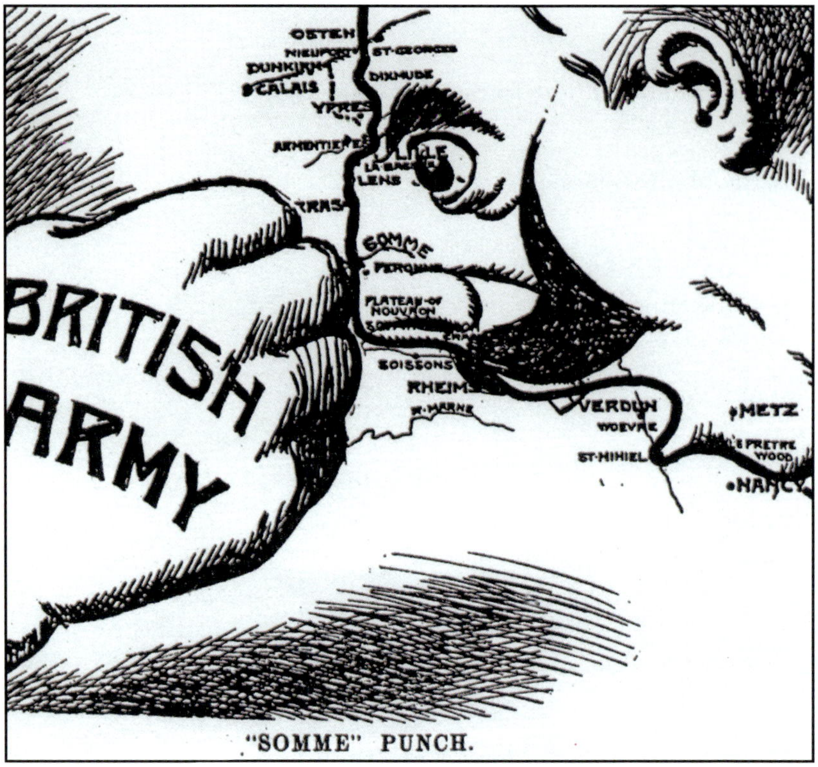

A contemporary cartoon, commenting on the Battle of the Somme.

Source B

6 July, 1916

My Dear Murray,

I suppose you will have heard of the very severe losses sustained by the 17th HLI on the 1st of July.

Up till now, I have made it a rule to write to the next of kin of any of our men who have fallen out here, but in the present circumstances it is beyond me to continue this practice. I have, therefore, no course open to me but to ask you to send this letter to the Glasgow papers for publication.

I should like to express to all the relatives of those who have died, my sincere sympathy with them in their present great sorrow, and to assure them that all the remaining Officers, NCOs and men share their grief with them.

It may be some consolation to them to know that the battalion walked into action as steadily as if it had been on the Parade Ground, and I cannot adequately express my feeling of admiration for the spirit, gallantry, and daring with which all faced this terrible task. …

(Signed) David S. Morton, Lt.-Col.,
Commanding 17th HLI
(Glasgow Chamber of Commerce Battalion)

A letter sent to James W. Murray, President of the Glasgow Chamber of Commerce. Many of the 17th Battalion of the Highland Light Infantry had been men who in peacetime worked in Glasgow businesses.

Source C

A photograph of soldiers advancing on the first day of the Battle of the Somme.

Source D

> The fate of the infantry battalions on the 1 July had very little to do with the attack formation they used. On the southern area of the line units took all their objectives, whether they advanced in an extended line or not. On the northern part of the attack they failed disastrously no matter whether they went over the top shoulder to shoulder or used fire and movement tactics. The key to success was artillery.

An historian, Dr John Bourne, writing in 1997.

Source E

> David said he talked to Haig as a father to a child, and as he had never been talked to before. At lunch he gave Haig his frank opinion. He said that there was a feeling of uneasiness in the country about our military operations. We have been talking of 'great victories' for the last few months, but in the end it only means that we have advanced five or six miles. We have been using up all our splendid men and our ammunition, and it has resulted in gaining only six miles at the most. The people feel they would like to see a little more imagination, inventiveness and originality and they are getting a little impatient. David said Haig listened very carefully to what he said to him.

From the diary of Frances Stevenson, secretary and mistress of Prime Minister David Lloyd George. This was written on 23 November 1916.

Source F

> The three main objectives with which the great offensive had begun in July had now been achieved. And this success had been obtained in spite of the fact that the heavy autumn rains had prevented full advantages being taken of the helpful situation created by our advance. These rains came at a time when we had good hopes of achieving yet more important successes.
>
> Verdun had been relieved; the main German forces had been held on the western front; and the enemy's strength had been very considerably worn down.
>
> Any of these three results was in itself, in the view of Field Marshal Haig, sufficient to justify the Somme battle. Success in all three of them afforded ample compensation for the splendid efforts of our troops and for the sacrifices made. They had brought us a long step towards the final victory.

From *The History of the Great European War*, written in Britain in 1917.

1. **Sources A and B** were both produced at the time of the battle, but give different viewpoints about what happened.
   Explain why they differ **using Sources A and B and your own knowledge.**
2. How reliable is **Source C** for an historian studying the tactics used during the first day of the battle?
   Explain your answer **using Source C and your own knowledge.**
3. **Source D** is a recent interpretation of the battle. How useful is this interpretation to an historian studying the tactics used during the first day of the battle?
   Explain your answer **using Source D and your own knowledge.**
4. Study **Source E.** Frances Stevenson was very close to Lloyd George. Does this mean that her account of the meeting with Field Marshal Haig cannot be trusted?
   Explain your answer **using Source E and your own knowledge.**
5. **Source F** is an interpretation which was written in 1917 whilst the war was continuing. How far does this affect its value as an interpretation of the Battle of the Somme?
   Explain your answer **using Source F and your own knowledge.**
6. 'There was nothing to show for the thousands of lives that had been lost. If this was victory, it was indeed a strange one.' Is this interpretation of the Battle of the Somme a fair one?
   Explain your answer **using all the sources and your own knowledge.**

Assessment Objective 3

Home Front propaganda in Britain

Source A

THE BATH CHRONICLE, SATURDAY MARCH 6 1915

FOR KING AND COUNTRY.

BRAVE BATH LADS WHO HAVE ANSWERED THE CALL.

DRIVER JAMES GORE

Serving with the A.S.C. Driver Gore is a son-in-law of Mrs. Derrick, of 38, Locksbrook Road, whose five sons are also serving. Their photographs are here given.

DRIVER JAMES DERRICK

Serving with the A.S.C.

DRIVER THOMAS DERRICK

Serving with the A.S.C.

TROOPER CHARLES DERRICK

Serving with the 15th Hussars.

TROOPER WILLIAM DERRICK

Who is serving with the 15th Hussars, has been wounded, but has since returned to active service.

DRIVER JOHN DERRICK

Serving with the Royal Engineers.

From a British local newspaper, 6 March 1915
It shows five brothers and their brother-in-law.

Source B

I went to the cinema ... we were all mopping our faces in the heat, fanning ourselves with newspapers and wondering about Mons. Then the lights went off and, instead of the film we expected, a girl appeared on stage, unannounced. The orchestra gave a few chords and she set off with a rush into a patriotic song about the French marching off to war. ... Someone started singing 'The Boys of the Bulldog Breed', and a soldier called for a big cheer for the King. Then we had three cheers for the French and three for the Russians and three for the Belgians, and three for all the others we thought were on our side, but were not so sure about. Then three for the Army, and three for the Navy, and three for the flying men. Then the girl on stage capped the lot by calling for three for Kitchener's volunteers. Finally we started to sing the National Anthem and we all stood to attention. My back seemed straighter than I remembered it. I felt six inches taller. Carried away by the emotion in that hall, the emotion of a great many young men all patriotically and suddenly determined to do their damnedest – die if necessary – I'd decided there couldn't be anyone more fitted than I for soldiering.

Extracts from a novel, *Covenant with Death*, by John Harris (1961).

Source C

Surrender! British Cavalry Beat and Cow the Hun

In April 1917 our cavalry had not had the full opportunity for which it was reported 'they burn and are ready', nevertheless they had many occasions to tighten their girths for a gallop and try conclusions with enemy patrols and rearguards. They rode into the burning ruins of villages and found scattered Germans, left behind to snipe or to complete the work of devastation, and at these they charged full tilt, so hot with wrath that they hoped the wretched creatures would not be too terrified to put up some sort of resistance, and would not answer to the shout of 'Surrender!' with a whimpered 'Kamerad!'

From *War Illustrated*, a British wartime magazine (1917).

Source D

A British propaganda poster from the early years of the war.

Source E

I'm thinking, Mrs Atkins, now that Tommy's gone away,
You'll be sending a letter from Home.
Don't tell him all your troubles, though for instance yesterday
The children's boots you bought took half your separation pay.
The eldest boy wants trousers and the rent is overdue,
You're planning and you're scheming for of debts you've got a few!
But don't you write and tell him, for here's my advice to you:

When you send him a letter from Home,
Send him a cheerful letter.
Say that it's all OK.
Tell him that you've ne'er felt better,
Though it's all the other way.
Don't send a word of sorrow,
Send him a page of joy,
And don't let your teardrops
Fall upon the kisses
When you write to your Soldier Boy.

A song that was popular in Britain in 1916.

1. How useful is **Source A** to an historian studying British propaganda in the early years of the war?
Explain your answer using **Source A and your own knowledge.**
2. **Source B** is from a novel written nearly 50 years after the events it describes. How much does this affect its value as an interpretation of attempts to recruit soldiers in 1914?
Explain your answer using **Source B and your own knowledge.**
3. The general public at home expected the cavalry to lead the charge to victory. How reliable is **Source C** for investigating the part played by cavalry during the war?
Explain your answer using **Source C and your own knowledge.**
4. Study **Sources D and E.** Which of these two sources is the more useful as evidence about the part played by women in encouraging men to fight in the war?
Explain your answer using **Sources D and E, and your own knowledge.**
5. 'Source F is only a cartoon; therefore it is of little use as evidence about British Home Front attitudes to the war at the end of 1917.' Do you agree or disagree?
Explain your answer using **Source F and your own knowledge.**
6. 'The use of propaganda helped Britain to avoid defeat in the First World War.' Do you agree or disagree with this interpretation?
Explain your answer using **all the sources and your own knowledge.**

Source F

Gradually, but remorselessly, the war has drawn us all into the vortex. The luxury and lightheartedness of 1914 have vanished, but the spirit of the nation, like that of the Brown family, grows the more determined as the struggle intensifies.—(By Mr. G. M. Payne.)

A cartoon drawn at the end of 1917.

CHAPTER 7

The USA, 1918–41

Society in the 1920s and 1930s

Isolationist attitudes after the First World War

The USA joined the First World War in April 1917 and played an important part in bringing about the defeat of the Germans and in establishing a peace settlement afterwards. Indeed, President Wilson's Fourteen Points (see page 9) provided a basis for establishing peace. He wanted to set up a League of Nations, which would be used to preserve peace and so prevent the outbreak of another war. The Allies were happy to accept this idea at the Paris Peace Conference, and the League of Nations was closely associated with the Treaty of Versailles, signed in 1919.

However, many Americans did not share Wilson's idealism. They liked neither the Treaty of Versailles nor the idea of a League. US public opinion had become strongly isolationist. Americans had no wish to get involved in world problems, and European conflicts in particular. They did not want more US soldiers being killed in what they saw as a remote and troublesome Europe. Nor did they want to have to pay for the cost of keeping world peace. So the Senate (the upper house of the US parliament) refused to accept the Treaty of Versailles in March 1920 and the USA never joined the League of Nations. Warren Harding, the new President, won the election promising to put 'America first'. From then until it joined the Second World War in 1941, the USA followed a policy of isolation.

SOURCE A

We seek no part in directing the destinies of the world.

Part of a speech by Warren Harding, 1920.

Developments in entertainment

In the 1920s, young people wanted to forget about the First World War and have a good time. They were better off and had more leisure time than their predecessors. They spent vast amounts of money enjoying themselves and so stimulated industry and business. The decade became known as 'the Roaring Twenties' largely because of the pace of social and economic development.

The jazz age

Jazz was a new form of music that developed from early kinds of black music. It was played in night clubs like the well-known Cotton Club in New York, by black musicians such as Duke Ellington and Louis Armstrong. It appealed to young people because it was often played in 'speakeasies'. These bars and clubs sold illegal alcohol and were therefore seen as daring and exciting places. The jazz too seemed wild and dramatic and it soon became a craze.

The radio

Young men and women listened to jazz on the radio. In 1920 only $2 million worth of radios were purchased. By 1929 this figure had increased by over 300 times and 10 million homes had their own radio. Local and national commercial stations were set up. They made money by advertising and, as people bought the consumer goods they heard about on the radio, so industry and business boomed.

SOURCE B

The parties were bigger, the pace was faster, the shows were broader, the buildings were higher, the morals were looser and the liquor was cheaper.

From Echoes of the Jazz Age by F. Scott Fitzgerald, 1931.

New fashions and crazes

Young people turned away from old-fashioned dances such as the waltz. New dances like the Charleston, the sexually suggestive Tango and the Bunny Hug became very popular. Young Americans went to the cinema and watched basketball, baseball and American football. Many young women became 'flappers'. Their hair was short and bobbed. They wore skirts that rose to the knee and tried to achieve a flat-chested appearance. They used lipstick and rouge, smoked cigarettes and drove cars such as Henry Ford's Model T 'Tin Lizzy'. Young men wore pin-stripe suits, trilby hats and spats on their shoes.

The older generation disliked what was happening. The Anti Flirt Association was set up to try to control the excesses of the young by distributing badges and making speeches.

This was a time of 'crazes' and 'fads', when youngsters joined in never-ending dance marathons, or sat on top of a flagpole for weeks just to break a record. Popular heroes appeared, such as Charles Lindbergh, who in 1927 became the first man to fly solo across the Atlantic. Other famous personalities included sportsmen, such as the boxer Jack Dempsey and the baseball player 'Babe' Ruth.

SOURCE C

A painting showing heavyweight champion Jack Dempsey being knocked out of the ring by his opponent, Luis Firpo. Dempsey climbed back into the ring and beat Firpo in the second round.

A flapper.

Film and Hollywood

The movie industry was established before the First World War, but its popularity soared during the 1920s when 'going to the movies' became a national habit. Soon nearly every town had its own cinema. By 1929, over 110 million Americans were going to the cinema each week. At first they watched silent films in black and white. Words were shown on the screen and cinemas employed piano players to provide the background music. In 1927, people flocked to see *The Jazz Singer* starring Al Jolson, which was the first 'talkie'. By the mid-1930s, films were also being produced in colour and Walt Disney had made cartoon characters like Mickey Mouse and Donald Duck into household names.

Most of the films shown were made in the USA. The new film industry mushroomed in Hollywood, which became the film capital of the world. Great movie companies such as United Artists, MGM and Paramount churned out over 500 new films annually. They created international film stars like Charlie Chaplin, Gloria Swanson and Mary Pickford. When the heart-throb Rudolph Valentino died in 1926, thousands of fans attended his funeral. However, some of these famous stars had their careers destroyed by technological developments. They had looked good on the screen in silent films, but their voices were unattractive and their careers ended when sound arrived.

QUESTIONS

1. Explain the meaning of the following terms:
   - a isolationism
   - b flappers
   - c talkies.
2. Why had US public opinion become strongly isolationist by 1920?
3. Why was the decade from 1920 to 1929 known as 'the Roaring Twenties'?

SOURCE D

A poster of the film star Charlie Chaplin in *The Kid*.

Prohibition and abolition

The origins of Prohibition

Since the nineteenth century, there had been a campaign to persuade state governments to ban the making, transportation, sale and consumption of alcoholic drinks. Campaigners often had religious or moral reasons for wanting alcohol banned. Many people in the small-town and rural USA believed that 'demon drink' caused wide-ranging social problems like poverty, physical abuse and crime. Nonconformist groups such as the Baptists and Methodists were traditionally hostile to liquor and were particularly strong in the mid-western states.

SOURCE E

> The drinking habits of most of my patrons appeared frightful ... intoxication to the point of senselessness – and this not once in a while but frequently or daily ... My unmarried patrons spent about 75% of their earnings on drink.
>
> *New York saloon keeper's comments in* McClure's Magazine*, 1908.*

Opponents of alcohol began to form protest groups. Organisations such as the Women's Christian Temperance Union and the Anti-Saloon League saw the prohibition of alcohol as the only way to end the evils of drunkenness and alcoholism. The founder of the Anti-Saloon League, Wayne Wheeler, used advertisements, magazines, pamphlets and meetings to attack saloons and promote prohibition. He won the support of many politicians too. They argued that drink was a waste of grain, which could be better used as food. Drink also led people to take time off work, causing a fall in production, and it caused social problems at home. The influential car-maker Henry Ford pointed out that alcohol was causing more accidents on the roads.

SOURCE F

A painting of the Women's Christian Temperance Union, who were part of the Anti-Saloon League.

Prohibition, prejudice and racism

Prejudice and racism were sometimes behind the campaign against alcohol in traditional, rural areas of the USA, where people were White, Anglo-Saxon and Protestant (so-called WASPs). They saw liquor as a social evil spreading out from the cities, which were filled with 'wet' Catholic immigrants. They may have wished to reform the working classes, but they were also motivated by anti-Catholic, anti-foreign prejudice. In the southern states, campaigners spread alarm by suggesting that blacks might be stirred up into violence and rebellion under the influence of liquor. They might start to question their inferior social position and seek to change it.

The effect of the First World War

The First World War gave the 'drys' a big boost. Prohibitionists said that the USA could not afford the illness and absence from work caused by drunkenness. Armament workers, in particular, would need to be discouraged from drinking too much because it might interfere with arms production. As a result, alcoholic consumption was seen as a very unpatriotic activity. Since 1917 it had been illegal to sell liquor to US soldiers. If American soldiers could not drink liquor, should civilians back home be doing so? Anti-drink campaigners also pointed out that many breweries were owned by families who had originally come from Germany. In the widespread anti-German feeling of 1917, there was a strong desire to close down these German-run breweries.

Prohibition is passed

In 1917, 18 states were 'dry' and most other states had introduced measures aimed to control the sale of 'booze'. But the anti-drink reformers realised that any state could pass a law to go 'wet' again. They also knew that drink from 'wet' areas was continuing to flow into 'dry' areas. This is why they believed that any anti-alcohol law had to apply to the whole country if it was to be a success.

In 1919 they achieved their aim when the US government passed the 18th Amendment to the Constitution, which was backed up by a new law called the Volstead Act. Together they banned the making, transportation, sale and consumption of alcoholic drinks. This law, known as Prohibition, applied to all liquor – that is, any drink that contained at least 0.5 per cent alcohol. So from 16 January 1920, the USA went 'dry', and it remained so for the next fourteen years.

The impact of Prohibition

Prohibition was intended to prevent alcohol abuse, but it clearly failed. Instead, consumption increased in all social groups. Even those close to the president drank liquor at poker parties held in the White House. Ordinary Americans began to make their own 'moonshine' in illegal stills hidden away in cellars and attics. Much of it was very strong; some was even poisonous.

'Bootleggers' were people who smuggled illegal liquor and often made a lot of money out of it. Liquor was secretly imported from nearby Canada and Mexico for consumption in illegal drinking saloons. The saloons were called 'speakeasies' because customers had to speak quietly to avoid discovery by the police. Speakeasies mushroomed throughout the USA during the 1920s. Before Prohibition there had been 15,000 saloons in New York. By 1932 the number had more than doubled to 32,000 speakeasies. (There were 200,000 speakeasies across the USA.)

Selling alcohol became big business and gangsters operating from the big cities did much of it. They supplied the booze, set up speakeasies and ran 'protection rackets' – threatening to damage property unless they received money to 'protect' it. Prohibition therefore led to a boost in organised crime, as gangsters fought each other to gain supremacy.

SOURCE G

The police discover an illegal still for making moonshine.

Al Capone

Al Capone became a very wealthy man as a result of Prohibition. He took control of Chicago by bribing local officials, politicians and the police. He operated without any real fear of arrest. In four years, 227 gangsters were murdered, but no one was convicted of the crimes. Capone's mobsters, disguised as policemen, gunned down six members of the rival Bugs Moran gang during the St Valentine's Day Massacre of 1929. Al Capone finally went to prison not for his gangster activities, but for tax evasion.

	1921	1925	1929
Illegal distilleries seized	9746	12,023	15,794
Gallons of distilled spirit seized	414,000	1,103,000	1,186,000
Arrests	34,175	62,747	66,878

Attempts by the authorities to enforce prohibition, 1921–9.

The government never put in enough resources to be able to enforce Prohibition effectively. Only 1500 additional agents were appointed. Among them were Izzy Einstein and Moe Smith, who enjoyed considerable success in arresting bootleggers, but they could not hope to contain the problem of illegal drinking. Alcohol became more attractive and consumption increased. Clearly large sections of the US public were unwilling to accept Prohibition. They saw nothing wrong with having a drink and were prepared to ignore the law in order to do so. The result was gangsterism and increasing lawlessness.

SOURCE H

Al Capone on the cover of a popular US magazine, 1930.

Abolition

It became clear that Prohibition was not working. It was also doing enormous damage to US society. As the country fell into economic depression, it seemed silly for the government to spend money on enforcing an ineffective law when the money could be spent on helping the unemployed. It was also pointed out that by making alcohol legal again, jobs would be created and tax revenues would increase. This is why Franklin D. Roosevelt, the Democratic candidate in the 1932 presidential election, promised to repeal the 18th Amendment. His policy was popular and helped him to win the election. The 21st Amendment to the Constitution therefore ended Prohibition in 1933. Roosevelt celebrated with a beer!

QUESTIONS

1. Explain the meaning of the following terms:
   a bootleggers
   b speakeasies
   c moonshine.
2. Why did prohibitionists want to ban alcohol?
3. Why did Prohibition fail?

SOURCE I

They call Al Capone a bootlegger. Yes, it's bootleg while it's on the trucks, but when your host hands it to you on a silver tray, it's hospitality. What's Al Capone done then? He's supplied a demand. Some call it bootlegging. Some call it racketeering. I call it a business. They say I violated the prohibition law. Who doesn't?

Al Capone's attitude towards Prohibition, described by a writer in 1931.

The economy in the 1920s and early 1930s

Growth in the economy in the 1920s

The total production of US industry increased by nearly 50 per cent during the 1920s. This period was one of economic boom in most but not all areas. Agriculture remained particularly depressed and so did some traditional industries, such as textiles, coal mining and shipbuilding. The boom particularly affected the north-east and the west coast of the USA, where the new industries were located. The south, on the other hand, was largely agricultural and fared badly.

Some of the reasons for this boom go well back into the nineteenth century and are associated with the USA's wealth:

- The population of the USA was large and the people, many of whom were recent immigrants, were ambitious and very hard working.
- The land was fertile and there were abundant natural resources, such as coal, iron, oil and wood.
- There had been significant developments in communication, which had opened up the continent. These included the expansion of railways and the use of the telegraph.

Such factors had helped to establish the USA as the world's leading industrial country by 1918.

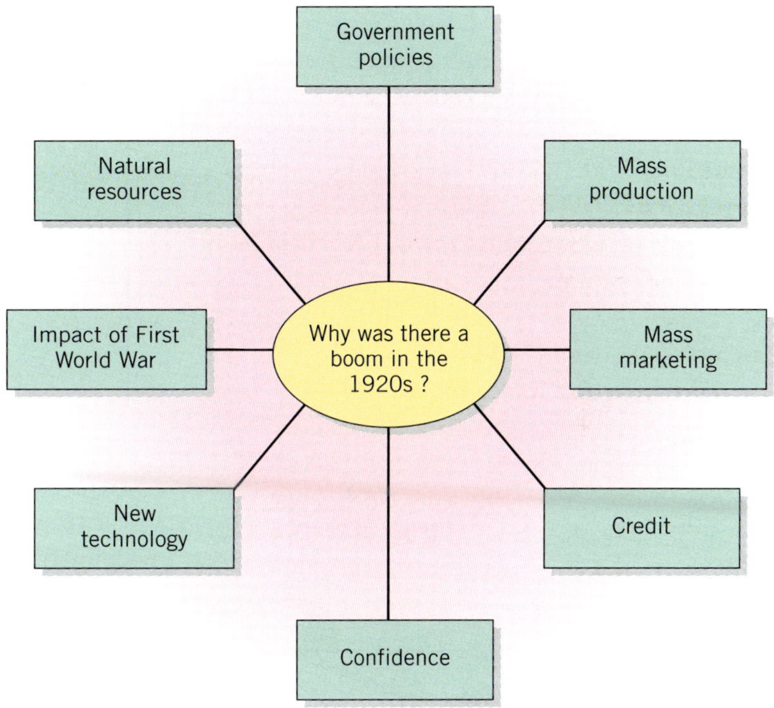

Why was there a boom in the 1920s?

Other reasons were more recent and were associated with developments during and after the First World War.

Impact of the First World War

The First World War seriously weakened the economies of the European powers, but the USA became an industrial giant. It had suffered far less physical and financial damage and had boosted its industrial production to supply the European powers with food, raw materials and weapons. The USA gained the overseas markets that the warring European states lost, and US banks lent money to the European countries at high rates of interest.

New technology and innovation

Over 80 per cent of all the world's inventions in the 1920s were developed in the USA. New technology and new inventions were introduced into industry. New materials such as rayon (an artificial fibre), bakelite and cellophane appeared. The use of electricity increased dramatically. In 1914 electricity powered only 30 per cent of factories. By 1929 this had risen to 70 per cent. Electricity became widely used in the home too, so electrical domestic goods also became widely available. The greatest innovation, however, was mass production, first applied to the car industry.

Mass production and the car industry

One reason for the boom was the mass production of goods. This was particularly true of car production, where Henry Ford worked hard to find ways of making things more quickly and cheaply. He had invented the 'assembly line' in 1913 to produce his 'Model T' cars. Instead of a worker making a whole car, the worker stayed in one place, doing just one or two jobs, and the car moved on to the next worker.

The cost of the car came down as more were bought. Even ordinary people could hope to buy their own car during the 1920s. The first model T, in 1908, had cost $850, but by 1924 the price had dropped to $260. By 1930 car manufacture was the most important US industry, accounting for 13 per cent of US manufacturing. Over 4 million jobs depended on it.

Assembly-line work could be boring, but workers received fairly good wages and so they prospered too. They could buy the consumer goods that were rapidly appearing. The car industry stimulated the development of other industries, such as petrol, rubber, glass, leather, steel and paint. Roads were built, and garages, petrol stations, hotels and restaurants were opened as people travelled by car to work or on holiday. All this increased the country's prosperity.

SOURCE A

It is the work, not the man, that manages. That work is planned on the drawing board and the operations subdivided so that each man and each machine do only one thing ... The thing is to keep everything in motion and take the work to the man and not the man to the work ... If a machine breaks down, a repair squad will be on hand in a few minutes. The men do not leave their work to get tools – new tools are brought to them ... All we ask of the men is that they do the work which is set before them. The work is never more than a man can do without undue fatigue in eight hours. He is well paid – and he works.

Henry Ford writing about the principle of the assembly line in 1926.

SOURCE B

Part of the Ford assembly line. The car body is being lowered on to the chassis.

Consumer industries, advertising and credit

Other goods were also produced on assembly lines. These included sewing machines, vacuum cleaners, washing machines, typewriters and cookers. They were often widely advertised on billboards, in mail-order catalogues, on neon signs, in newspapers and on the radio. A whole new advertising industry grew up to sell these new products. Advertisers made it possible to buy goods on credit by using hire purchase. People simply paid a small deposit and then paid off the rest by regular instalments. New chain stores like Woolworth, opened with a branch in most towns and cities. They were large shops which stocked a wide variety of goods and sold them very cheaply. These became very popular with ordinary Americans.

All these developments created a sales boom which meant busier factories, bigger profits and better wages. The extra money in people's pockets was used to buy more consumer goods and this fuelled the economic boom.

SOURCE C

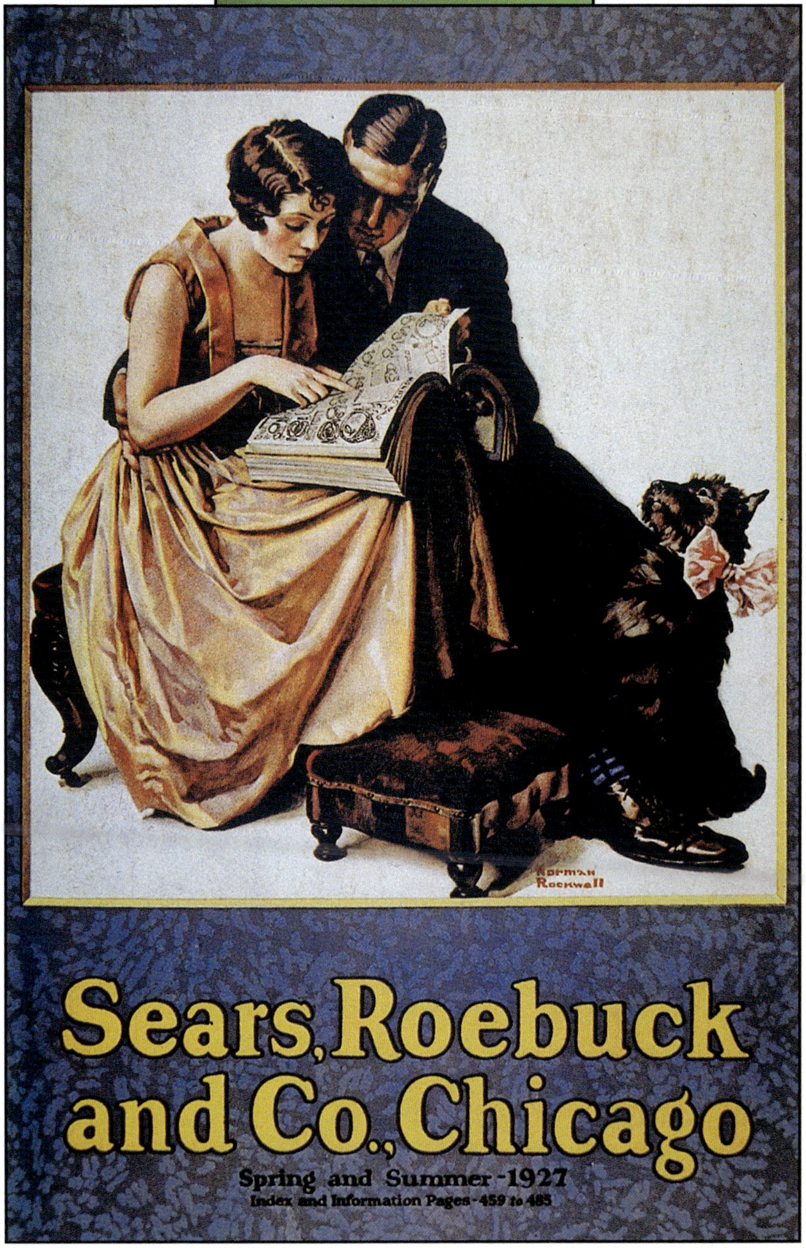

A page from the Sears, Roebuck & Co. catalogue, 1927.

Urbanisation

By the 1920s, most Americans lived in cities rather than in the countryside. This urbanisation led to a boom in the building trade, as people migrated to the cities and needed homes. Land became increasingly expensive, so buildings tended to become taller. Skyscrapers sprang up in urban centres and completely changed the skyline of many cities. The Empire State Building in New York, finished in 1929, was the tallest building in the world.

	1920	1929
Motor cars on the roads	9 million	26 million
Kilometres of roads	620,000	1 million
Radios	60,000	10 million
Telephones in homes and offices	13 million	20 million

Some changes in the USA during the 1920s.

Government policy

The first three Presidents of this period – Warren Harding, Calvin Coolidge and Herbert Hoover – belonged to the Republican Party. They believed in creating favourable conditions for US entrepreneurs. The Democratic Party believed in paying more attention to the conditions of life for the ordinary working person.

President	Term
Warren Harding (Republican)	1921–23
Calvin Coolidge (Republican)	1923–29
Herbert Hoover (Republican)	1929–33
Franklin D. Roosevelt (Democrat)	1933–45

Presidents of the USA, 1920–45.

At the end of the First World War in 1918, the USA turned its back on Europe and the outside world. This policy of isolation allowed the country to concentrate on building up its economy. Tariffs were imposed on foreign goods entering the USA, to give US goods an advantage. The Fordney–McCumber Tariff of 1922 made imported goods more expensive and so protected US industry from foreign competition. This helped the economy to boom in the 1920s. However, foreign states retaliated by putting their own taxes on US goods. This made it more difficult for US businesses to sell abroad and created economic difficulties at the end of the 1920s.

Another aspect of US isolationism was that immigration into the country was dramatically restricted. Americans resented the prospect of an influx of cheap labour that would take work away from them. They disliked the growth of ghettos – slum areas occupied largely by immigrant groups – and the spread of political extremism, especially after the communist revolution in Russia in 1917. The traditional 'open door' policy was ended. From 1917, new laws required immigrants to take a literacy test in English. In 1921 the Immigrant Quota Act limited the annual number allowed into the USA and discriminated in favour of western Europeans. By 1929 the annual quota was only 150,000 and no Asian immigrants were allowed.

The Republican Party was the party of big business and it formed the government throughout the 1920s. Warren Harding's government stimulated the economy by cutting back on government supervision and interference in industry. Everything was done to help economic expansion. Taxes were cut so that people had more money to spend and industry had more money to invest. Technological advances and government policy helped to keep production costs low, so prices remained steady or fell. This meant that people in work were able to afford to buy more goods. This stimulated the boom of the 1920s.

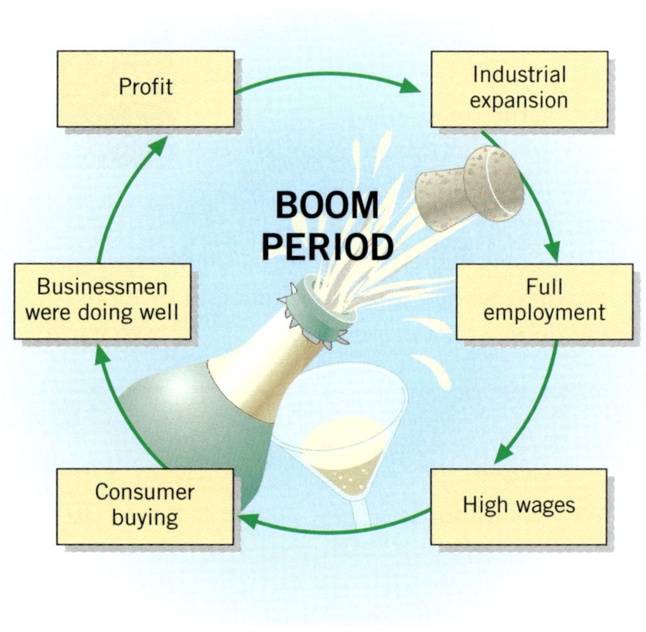

The cycle of prosperity.

Trade unions

The Republicans were hostile to trade unions because they saw them as interfering in the working of business. So Republican governments discouraged the development of unions and, as a result, union membership fell during the 1920s. Trade unionists were excluded from the motor car industry until the 1930s. Employers were allowed to use violence to break up strikes and encouraged not to employ trade union members. Laws controlling working conditions, minimum wages and hours of work were scrapped. Employers were therefore able to keep wages down and working hours long. This made industry more competitive. Enlightened attitudes such as those of Henry Ford, who offered good wages and sensible working hours, were uncommon during the 1920s.

1920	5 million
1932	3 million

Trade union membership, 1920 and 1932.

The stock market boom

Wall Street in New York is the home of the US Stock Exchange, where people can buy and sell shares. Companies sell shares on the Stock Exchange in order to raise money for investment. These shares are bought and sold by investors, who hope to make money for themselves. Shareholders usually receive a six-monthly dividend (payment) on their shares, and shares can also be sold to make a profit if a company is doing well. Share prices can go down as well as up, but during the 1920s the movement was usually upwards. It has been estimated that $100 invested in 1920 was worth over $300 in 1929. This reflected the boom in the US economy and the general atmosphere of confidence at the time.

It seemed as if anyone could make a profit, and so many ordinary Americans started to invest in shares. To them it appeared easy money. As more people bought shares, so the price of the shares increased. Shares were often bought 'on the margin'. This means that they were only partly paid for. The investor relied on selling them quickly in order to cover the outstanding debt but still make a handsome profit. All went well until October 1929, when confidence disappeared and share prices plummeted (see pages 216–17).

SOURCE D

'Say, Doc, do me a favour. Just keep your eye on Consolidated Can Common, and if she goes bearish [down] tell my broker to sell and get four thousand shares of P & Q Rails Preferred on the usual margin. Thanks.' A cartoon from *New York Magazine* in 1927 comments on Americans' obsession with the stock market in the 1920s.

Farming in the 1920s

Despite the economic boom of the 1920s, many Americans continued to live in poverty. The USA was getting richer, but this increasing wealth was shared unevenly. In 1929, about one-third of all the country's income was shared among only 5 per cent of its people. Many farmers struggled because of overproduction. They had lived well during the First World War, selling their produce to Europe. However, the tariff barriers and increased competition in the 1920s meant that it was impossible to sell their surplus produce abroad. The price of their produce collapsed and with it their incomes. Many farmers could not repay their debts and lost their land. Agriculture was already in depression. Other industries and businesses would follow.

QUESTIONS

1. Explain the meaning of the following terms:
   a assembly line
   b skyscrapers
   c economic boom.
2. Why was there a stock market boom in the 1920s?
3. Explain why agriculture and some traditional industries in the USA did not experience an economic boom during the 1920s.

The Depression, 1929–33

At the start of 1929, it seemed as though the boom of the 1920s would never end. The US economy appeared to be on a very sound footing, as share prices on Wall Street confirmed. President Hoover was promising prosperity for all and an end to poverty. However, the health of the economy was not quite as strong as it seemed. All looked good on the surface, but there were serious weaknesses that had been present for some time.

SOURCE E

This German cartoon from 1927 attacks the disregard of the poor by the world's financiers, while they themselves were on the brink of a massive crash.

The causes of the Depression

- Some traditional industries and farming had been depressed throughout the 1920s. This created an unequal distribution of wealth, so many families were unable to participate in the boom.
- Foreign trade was in decline. Other countries reacted to the policies of the US government by placing high tariffs on US goods. Therefore businesses in the USA could not sell effectively abroad.
- Industry and business began to run out of buyers. They could not export abroad and they could not sell to those people in the USA who were already suffering economic hardship. As a result, businesses began to cut back on the number of workers they employed. This meant that fewer families could afford to buy consumer goods, so even fewer goods needed to be produced. Industry reacted by making more cutbacks in the workforce. This seemed like a vicious circle from which it was impossible to break free.
- As long as there was confidence in the US economy, the boom continued. Shareholders, encouraged by banks to borrow, forced share prices up. But the US economy was rather like an expanding balloon – once pricked it would collapse. The end of confidence would result in the collapse of the financial markets. This was to happen at the Stock Exchange on Wall Street in October 1929.

The Wall Street Crash

On 24 October 1929, the Wall Street Stock Exchange crashed. On this 'Black Thursday', over 13 million shares were sold as prices moved down rapidly and panic selling occurred. In the week before, a number of businessmen had decided that share prices were too high and chose to sell. This caused a collapse in confidence. The banks tried to restore some stability by buying up vast numbers of shares. But this tactic worked only for a short time and within days share prices started to fall dramatically again. They continued to fall until 1932, by which time shares on average had lost 80 per cent of their 1929 value.

Thousands of investors were ruined overnight. Many lost all their possessions, and some committed suicide. Over 100,000 companies went bankrupt during the period 1929–33 and were forced to close. Others survived only by cutting back on production and so reducing their workforce.

Banks also suffered because many had chosen to invest their customers' money in shares that became worthless. As a result, people began to lose confidence in the banks. The banks tried to recover by demanding that the loans they had made to companies and individuals were paid back immediately. But this meant that even more businesses were forced to close, leading to yet more unemployment.

The Wall Street Crash sparked off the Depression that followed. It led to bankruptcies, industrial slowdown and widespread unemployment as the US economy started to spiral downwards. The USA was the first country to be affected by the Depression, but, as international trade suffered, so too did the rest of the world.

Company	3 September 1929	13 November 1929
Anaconda Copper	162	70
General Electric	396	168
General Motors	182	36
Radio	505	28
United States Steel	279	150
Woolworth	251	102
Electric Bond & Share	204	50

Changes in the price of shares in some leading US companies, 1929 (cents) .

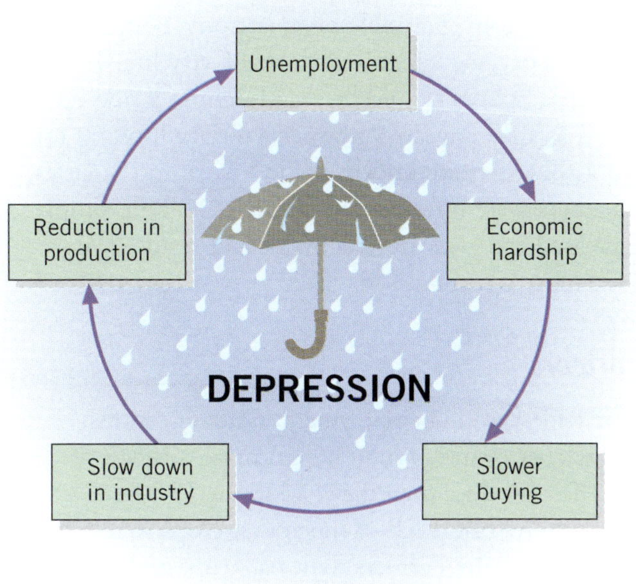

The cycle of Depression.

The effects of the Depression in the USA

As industry and business struggled to sell goods, many were forced to reduce production or even to close down. By 1933, production of manufactured goods was less than one-fifth of the level in 1929. The result was widespread unemployment – there were over 12 million jobless by 1932, about 25 per cent of the workforce. Even those in work faced massive pay cuts and a drop in their standard of living.

Most families were affected in some way. Many lost their homes because they could no longer afford to pay rents or mortgages. The homeless unemployed built their own homes in shanty towns located in cities or on the edge of towns. People blamed the policies of President Hoover for their plight, so the shanty towns were known as 'Hoovervilles'.

Unlike in Britain, there was no welfare available from the state. Some US cities tried to help the unemployed, but they were not always able to. For instance, in 1932 Philadelphia ran out of funds and could no longer offer support. The unemployed were often reduced to begging or to queuing in 'breadlines' for handouts from charitable organisations. Soup kitchens became a regular feature of city life. Tramps (hoboes) could be seen hitching a ride on trains as they migrated from city to city looking for work. Blacks moved north to find work in the cities, but there were no jobs. The influx of people simply increased the level of resentment and resulted in even more racial tension.

SOURCE F

He drove his old car into a town. He scoured the farms for work. Where can we sleep the night? Well, there's a Hooverville on the edge of the river ...

The rag-town lay close to water. The houses were tents, weed-thatched enclosures, paper houses, a great junk pile. The man put up his tent as near to water as he could get ... He scoured the countryside for work, and the little money he had went for petrol to look for work.

In this extract from the novel The Grapes of Wrath *by John Steinbeck (1939), poor farm workers drive to look for work.*

Farmers

The widespread unemployment in urban centres meant that farmers found it even more difficult to sell their produce than they had in the 1920s. Agricultural prices fell so much that crops were left rotting in the fields. It was simply no longer worthwhile harvesting them. Farmers went bankrupt and were evicted. They migrated to the cities or to the fruit farms of California seeking work.

In the mid-west, the farmers suffered an additional blow. Overfarming led to soil infertility and erosion. In the droughts and strong winds that were a feature of the early 1930s, the topsoil turned to dust and was blown away. The land turned into desert. Farmers had to abandon this 'dust bowl' and find work elsewhere.

SOURCE G

A painting of unemployed men queuing in a breadline during the Depression.

SOURCE H

Famous firms went bankrupt. Brokers jumped to their deaths from the top of skyscrapers ... People I knew were down and out. Some put up their houses for sale, a useless act as no one was buying anything, or boarded them up and left because they could no longer afford to live there ... An old couple who lived not far from us lost everything in the Crash ... so they committed suicide.

Recollections of the Depression, written in 1977.

SOURCE I

There is not an unemployed man in the country that hasn't contributed to the wealth of every millionaire in America. The working classes didn't bring this on, it was the financial big boys ...

We got more wheat, more corn, more food, more cotton, more money in the banks, more everything in the world than any nation that ever lived ever had, yet we are starving to death. We are the first nation in the history of the world to go to the poorhouse in an automobile.

From the play Brother Can You Spare a Dime?, *written in 1976 about the 1930s.*

Response of the Republican administration

The Republicans disliked government interference in business and President Hoover was no exception. He believed that business itself, not the government, would pull the USA out of the Depression, so he was prepared to wait for an improvement. But Hoover misjudged the true depth of the Depression and finally intervened.

In 1931 Hoover set up the Reconstruction Finance Commission to make loans to banks and finance companies in danger of collapse. He encouraged some limited public works programmes in order to create new jobs, and his Federal Farm Board bought surplus crops from struggling farmers to try to keep up the price of farm produce.

However, such action did not go far enough. Hoover did not introduce any unemployment benefit, and matters were made worse with the increase in tariffs in 1930 on foreign goods. This Hawley–Smoot tariff merely encouraged other countries to raise their own tariffs against US goods.

Hoover's popularity declined because he was not willing to use the full resources of government to deal with the Depression. Ordinary people felt that he had deserted them.

Bonus Marchers

Men who had served in the First World War had been promised a 'bonus' payment by an Act of 1924. The bonus, around $500, was not due until 1945, but the ex-servicemen wanted it now. When Hoover would not agree, the 'Bonus Marchers' demonstrated in the capital, Washington, and set up camps there. The government saw this as a threat and ordered soldiers to break up the camps and force out the marchers. Hoover lost any remaining sympathy. He appeared heartless and the US people displayed their anger when they voted against him in the 1932 presidential election.

SOURCE J

We have been passing through one of those great economic storms which periodically bring hardship and suffering to our people. I am convinced we have now passed the worst and we shall recover. There is one certainty in the future of a people such as ourselves and that is, prosperity.

President Hoover speaking in 1930.

QUESTIONS

1. Why did Wall Street 'crash' in October 1929?
2. What effects did the Crash have on the US economy?
3. Explain the meaning of the following terms:
   a Hoovervilles
   b breadlines
   c the dust bowl
   d Bonus Marchers.

The Presidencies of F. D. Roosevelt to 1941

Reasons for his election in 1932

During the campaign for the 1932 presidential election, Hoover was greeted with hostility because he made it clear that he was prepared to wait for the Depression to sort itself out. Roosevelt, however, promised direct and immediate action from the government – a 'New Deal' for the US people. He was convinced that the government must play an active role in helping people to get back to work and lifting the US economy out of the Depression.

Roosevelt made 'whistle stop' tours across the country by railway to deliver his message. He promised to end the banking crisis and provide aid for those needing food and shelter. He also aimed to set up government schemes that would provide jobs. His confidence and vision offered hope to the people and they voted for him in overwhelming numbers. In the 1932 election, Roosevelt won a landslide victory, winning in 42 of the 48 states.

The New Deal and the Hundred Days

A period of dramatic government activity followed in which a series of reforms was introduced to help banks, businesses, farmers and the unemployed. This intense period of reform was known as 'the Hundred Days'.

SOURCE A

> I pledge you, I pledge myself, to a New Deal for the American people. This is a political campaign; it is a call to arms. Give me your help, not to win votes alone, but to win in this crusade to restore America.
>
> *Roosevelt's New Deal pledge, 1932.*

Roosevelt's government was determined to put money into the economy in order to provide new jobs. With work, people would have money to spend on goods. As a result of this higher demand, businesses would employ more people. In this way, 'priming the pump' would get industry moving again by creating a cycle of recovery. Congress provided Roosevelt with emergency powers. He used these powers to set up a number of agencies, which would introduce the reforms necessary to deal with the Depression. The names of these agencies were abbreviated to their initials, so they became known as the 'alphabet agencies'.

The impact of the New Deal on the US economy and society

Helping the banks: the Emergency Banking Act (EBA)

Roosevelt first had to deal with the banking crisis. During the Depression, people had little trust in the banks and so withdrew their savings. This resulted in the closure of more and more banks, which reduced confidence even further. An additional problem was that the banks themselves lost confidence and would not buy shares. This forced share prices lower and made the Depression even worse. Roosevelt

	Failed businesses	Farm income ($bn)	Average weekly earnings in manufacturing ($)
1930	26,355	4.1	24.77
1931	28,285	3.2	not available
1932	31,822	1.9	16.21

The US economy under Hoover.

used the EBA to help. Passed in March 1933, this Act forced all banks to close for a four-day holiday. Government inspectors were then sent in to check on the banks. Those that were effectively managed were reopened, supported by government loans. Those that weren't remained closed. Confidence returned and Americans began to deposit their money with banks once again.

SOURCE B

A cartoon from 3 March 1933, showing President Roosevelt throwing out the policies of the previous government.

Helping farmers: the Agricultural Adjustments Administration (AAA)

In order to help farmers, it was necessary to force food prices to rise. This would increase farmers' incomes. However, it could be achieved only by encouraging farmers to cut production. The AAA did this by offering them government subsidies to produce less. The move was controversial because many people thought that it was morally wrong to reduce the production of food when so many Americans were hungry. Farmers also received government help with mortgage repayments and financial support to buy machinery and fertiliser. The policy of the AAA led to an increase in the standard of living for US farmers. Their average income doubled between 1933 and 1939.

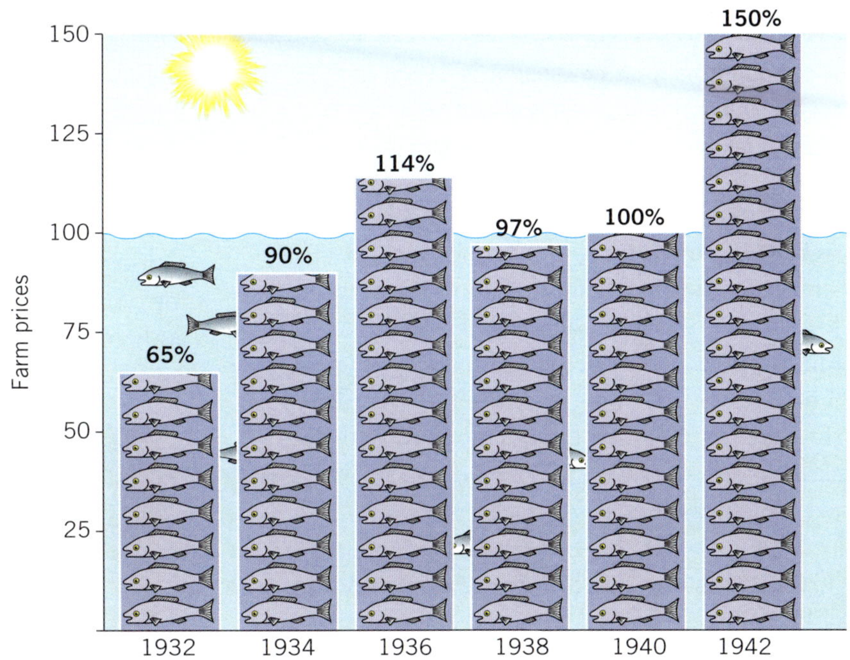

Changes in farm prices, 1932–42. The price that farmers had been getting between 1900 and 1914 is given the value of 100 and prices in other years are compared with that.

Helping the unemployed: the CCC, FERA, PWA and WPA

In March 1933 the Civilian Conservation Corps (CCC) was set up to provide work for single young men between 18 and 25 for a limited period. The unemployed were encouraged to join and during the 1930s the CCC gave work to 3 million men. They lived in camps and were provided with food and shelter and a dollar per day in wages. They

SOURCE C

A cartoon from a US newspaper in 1933. After he won the election, Roosevelt outlined his plans to the US public on the radio. These broadcasts were known as 'fireside chats' and they were very popular.

worked on environmental schemes such as strengthening river banks, creating fire lanes in forests and clearing beaches. They planted 200 million trees, which helped to reduce soil erosion. The rates of pay were criticised for being low, but the schemes provided the unemployed with the skills and experience they needed to gain permanent work.

The Federal Emergency Relief Administration (FERA) made $500 million of grants available to state and local governments to help them provide relief to the unemployed. The Public Works Administration (PWA) provided employment for skilled workers on huge construction schemes all over the country. They built, for example, dams, hospitals and schools. The Works Progress Administration (WPA), set up in 1935, was similar to the PWA but provided work for the lower skilled on much smaller schemes. It also provided work for artists, writers and actors. Murals were painted on public buildings and actors and singers toured the country giving regular performances.

Helping home owners: the Home Owners Loans Corporation (HOLC)

This provided much needed help for people who were unable to pay their mortgages. By providing loans at very low rates of interest, the HOLC prevented many Americans from losing their homes.

Helping industry and workers: the NRA, the Wagner Act and the Social Security Act

Roosevelt was not only interested in recovery from the Depression. He also wanted to lay the foundations for long-term security. To do this he intended to create a true partnership between industry and workers. The National Recovery Administration (NRA) was such a partnership. Through the NRA, the government hoped to tackle low pay and poor working conditions. Industry was encouraged to accept codes of employment in return for government contracts. These codes would guarantee a minimum wage and other workers' rights, such as the ending of child labour and a fair working day. In 1935 the Wagner Act established the right of workers to join trade unions and the Social Security Act introduced a national scheme for old age pensions and employment insurance.

QUESTIONS

1. Why did Herbert Hoover lose the 1932 presidential election?
2. Look at Source B. What is the message of the cartoon? Explain your answer referring to details in the cartoon.
3. Explain the meaning of the following terms:
   - **a** the Hundred Days
   - **b** alphabet agencies
   - **c** fireside chats.

Helping depressed areas: the Tennessee Valley Authority (TVA)

Roosevelt believed that the valley of the Tennessee River had become 'the nation's number one economic problem'. The whole region suffered from huge problems. The land had been overfarmed and the soil was exhausted. This resulted in widespread erosion, made worse in spring by the frequent flooding of the river, which washed away topsoil. Farming was in a terrible state and there was little industry in the region. The area was in deep depression and the people lived in poverty. Fewer than 2 per cent of the farms in the valley had electricity. Since the river ran through a total of seven states, each concerned about its own problems, it was difficult to take any positive co-ordinated action at a regional level.

The TVA was set up in April 1933 to plan and implement a strategy for the whole area. The government provided aid. Millions of trees were planted to prevent soil erosion. Twenty-one dams were

SOURCE D

The Watts Bar Dam on the Tennessee River showing the hydro-electric plant.

constructed to control the river and so prevent flooding, as well as making it more navigable. The lakes that were formed behind the dams became centres for water sports and leisure. Power stations were built using hydro-electricity to provide cheap power for industry and the home. This attracted new businesses to the area and led to the growth of new industries such as chemicals, aluminium smelting and flour milling. With this modernisation, jobs were created and the Tennessee Valley became much more prosperous.

The end of Prohibition

In 1933, during the first Hundred Days of the Roosevelt administration, the Beer Act was passed. It allowed the manufacture and sale of beers and wines. The 21st Amendment to the Constitution made the USA 'wet' again. It was a necessary measure to control gangsterism, but it also removed a law that most Americans did not respect. When the repeal had been completed, Roosevelt said, 'I think this would be a good time for a beer.' Many Americans would have agreed with this sentiment.

Successes of the New Deal

Much was achieved by the New Deal and many millions of Americans were helped to recover from the effects of the Depression. They were found work and given relief and their homes were saved. They could join trade unions and enjoyed improved workers' rights. Large-scale farmers benefited particularly as their incomes rose. The obvious general success of the New Deal led to Roosevelt's overwhelming victory in the 1936 presidential election and gave him a mandate for carrying on his policies.

Criticisms of the New Deal

However, 16 million Americans had not voted for Roosevelt. Some considered his policies too radical. Others felt they did not go far enough. Indeed, whole sections of society, including blacks and poor farmers, missed out. Many farmers in the mid-western states were defeated by the effects of both the Depression and the 'dust bowl' and had to leave their homes.

Although the New Deal reduced unemployment, it did not eliminate it. In 1937, Roosevelt made a serious error by trying to cut back on the amount of government financial help. The economy slipped once more into depression as industrial production fell and unemployment rose. The government quickly had to increase spending again. In fact, it was not until the outbreak of the Second World War that the US economy recovered. It was stimulated first by supplying Britain and France with manufactured goods and food and then by the USA's direct entry into the war in 1941. War, rather than the New Deal, finally lifted the USA out of depression.

The struggle with the Supreme Court

The nine judges in the Supreme Court check government legislation. If they find that a measure is against the US constitution, they can declare it illegal. Most of the judges in Roosevelt's time were Republicans, who disliked the New Deal policies. From 1935, starting with the National Recovery Administration and the AAA, they declared a number of alphabet agencies illegal. Roosevelt planned to increase the number of judges from nine to fifteen and ensure that the additional six supported his ideas to give him control of the court.

His move was a serious error because he needed the support of Congress to get it through. Most Americans opposed his attempts to tamper with the constitution and he was forced to withdraw his plan. But the judges realised that they must tread more cautiously and stopped blocking Roosevelt's policies.

SOURCE E

Our President evidently has noted the apparent success of Adolf Hitler and is aiming at the same dominance.

A US political commentator writing in 1937 about Roosevelt's decision to reform the Supreme Court.

SOURCE F

A cartoon from 1933 criticising Roosevelt's policy of 'priming the pump'.

Radicals, however, claimed that Roosevelt's measures did not go far enough. Father Charles Coughlin, the 'radio priest', used his popular broadcasts to demand more social justice. Huey Long, the popular governor of Louisiana, criticised Roosevelt for being too cautious. He wanted to strip the wealthy of their fortunes and give their money to the masses. His views made him a serious political rival to Roosevelt until his assassination in 1935.

The attitudes of Americans to the New Deal

Although many Americans supported the New Deal, Roosevelt faced opposition from all sides. There were those, particularly Republicans, who disliked too much government involvement in people's lives and saw the New Deal as a threat to individual freedom. They preferred people to stand on their own feet and help themselves. Roosevelt's policies seemed like unnecessary government interference and were denounced as 'socialist'.

In particular, many people in business disliked the increasing role played by government in their affairs. They disliked the NRA and the government's support for trade unions. The wealthy resented paying higher taxes and saw many of Roosevelt's policies as a waste of money. Many of these groups criticised the New Deal for being unconstitutional and un-American.

The role of Roosevelt

Roosevelt made some mistakes and there is little doubt that his New Deal ran out of steam from 1936 onwards. However, his policies had started to bring the USA out of the Depression. Most people were better off in 1938 than they had been in 1932 and they understood that much of this was due to Roosevelt. By using the power of government, he had restored confidence in the USA and its way of life.

SOURCE G

Any jackass can spend money. Any crackpot with money at his disposal can build himself a dictatorial crown. It takes no brains to be liberal with other people's money.

From a speech by Father Coughlin in 1937.

There is little doubt that the federal government now had much more control over people's lives, but many of Roosevelt's policies protected rather than weakened individual rights. Whereas much of Europe reacted to unemployment in the 1930s by destroying democracy, Roosevelt showed that great problems could be overcome without removing individual liberties.

Race relations, 1918–41

Immigration and the ethnic composition of the population

As we saw on page 214, there was a reaction against immigration during the 1920s. The First World War had stirred up nationalism and a dislike of foreigners. This increased with the policy of isolation. There was a feeling that mass immigration needed to be controlled – even ended. Americans disliked the influx of new people who threatened jobs, spoke little English, lived in urban ghettos and seemed to favour extreme political ideas such as communism.

The strikes in US cities in 1919 started an anti-communist scare. Anti-communist feelings reached their height with the execution of two Italian immigrants, Sacco and Vanzetti, in 1927. Immigration seemed to threaten traditional US life, particularly as people were now coming from eastern and southern Europe and Asia, and were not White Anglo-Saxon Protestants (WASPs).

SOURCE H

A cartoonist's view of the effects of Roosevelt's policies. He gave Americans a new faith in their country and its way of life.

QUESTIONS

1. Why did Roosevelt believe that the Tennessee Valley had become 'the nation's number one economic problem'?
2. How successfully did Roosevelt's government deal with the economic problems of the Tennessee Valley?
3. On what grounds has the 'New Deal' been criticised?
4. Look at Source F. What criticism is the cartoonist making of the New Deal?

The causes and nature of racial discrimination and segregation

Many whites regarded the blacks, who formed 10 per cent of the population, as inferior. They attempted to exclude them from the opportunities and rights that whites enjoyed. The 'Jim Crow' laws, introduced by many states in the southern USA by 1919, aimed to segregate whites and blacks. They were not to mix in public places such as schools and restaurants and on public transport.

During the First World War, many blacks had migrated from the south to northern cities, such as Chicago, to look for work. They lived in poor housing and had the lowest-paid jobs. Pressure on housing and employment created racial tension and there were riots in many northern cities between 1918 and 1920.

However, at least those blacks in the north did not live in fear of lynching – being executed without a trial. In the south, on the other hand, blacks were murdered for no reason. Many of those responsible escaped arrest because the police and judges were white and unwilling to take action. In addition, since most blacks in the south were involved in agriculture, they suffered in the farming depression of the 1920s.

Despite the fact that many blacks did receive financial help from the government, prejudice and segregation did not end with the New Deal, but continued up to 1941.

The activities and impact of the Ku Klux Klan

The Ku Klux Klan (KKK) had been set up after the American Civil War in 1866 to try to maintain white supremacy over blacks. It was therefore strongest in the southern USA and in rural areas where most blacks lived. Its popularity declined in the early years of the twentieth century, but its fortunes revived during the 1920s as isolationist, anti-immigrant and anti-black ideas grew. From a membership of 100,000 in 1920, it had expanded to 5 million by 1925.

Members of the KKK were often poor whites, who felt threatened by both blacks and immigrants who were willing to work for lower wages. Members were attracted by the KKK's extreme racist views and its promise to save the USA from Jews, Catholics, immigrants and, in particular, blacks. The KKK organised secret meetings and its members dressed in white robes and hoods. They were prepared to attack those whom they disliked and resorted to torture, violence, intimidation and even lynching. They were frequently protected by the authorities rather than prosecuted.

After 1925, membership began to decline. Many Americans were sickened by the reports of the KKK's more violent activities. Additionally, its leadership was involved in a number of unsavoury scandals, which created a reaction against it.

SOURCE A

The KKK parading through the streets of a town. This organisation used terror tactics against black people in the Southern States of the USA.

SOURCE B

```
There are three great racial instincts
which must be used to build a great
America: loyalty to the white race, to
the traditions of America and to the
spirit of Protestantism ... The pioneer
must be kept pure. The white race must
be supreme.
```

From a speech in the 1920s by Hiram Wesley Evans, the Imperial Wizard (leader) of the Ku Klux Klan.

QUESTIONS

1. Explain the meaning of the following terms:
   - a 'Jim Crow' laws
   - b WASPs
2. Describe the purposes and activities of the Ku Klux Klan.
3. The USA had traditionally welcomed immigrants under the 'open door' policy. Why then did the USA start to impose restrictions on immigration after 1917?
4. Does Source B have any value to historians studying race relations in the USA in the 1920s?

Coursework/Paper 1–style questions

The USA, 1918–41

Assessment Objective 2

Aspect 1 Causes and/or consequences

1. During the 1920s why did the US economy only bring prosperity to some Americans?
2. Was the Great Depression caused by the Wall Street Crash? Explain your answer.
3. Many people in the USA saw Prohibition as a 'Noble Experiment' when it was introduced in 1919. Why by 1933 had it failed in its aims?
4. Explain why the USA seemed to become increasingly intolerant over racial issues during the 1920s.

Aspect 2 Change and continuity

1. To what extent did the role of women change in the USA during the 1920s?
   Explain your answer.
2. Had the USA recovered from its economic problems by December 1941?
   Explain your answer.

Aspect 3 People's ideas and attitudes

1. Explain the reactions of people in the USA to the ending of Prohibition in 1933.
2. Did all Americans welcome the 'New Deal for the American People' during the 1930s?
   Explain your answer.

Aspect 4 The role of the individual

1. Does President Herbert Hoover deserve the blame for failing to deal with the Great Depression and its effects on the American people?
2. Were the policies of President Roosevelt the most important reason why the USA made some recovery from the Depression during the later 1930s?
   Explain your answer.

Assessment Objective 3

The USA in the 1920s – did it really roar?

Source A

A photograph of bootleg liquor being dumped, taken in the 1920s.

Source B

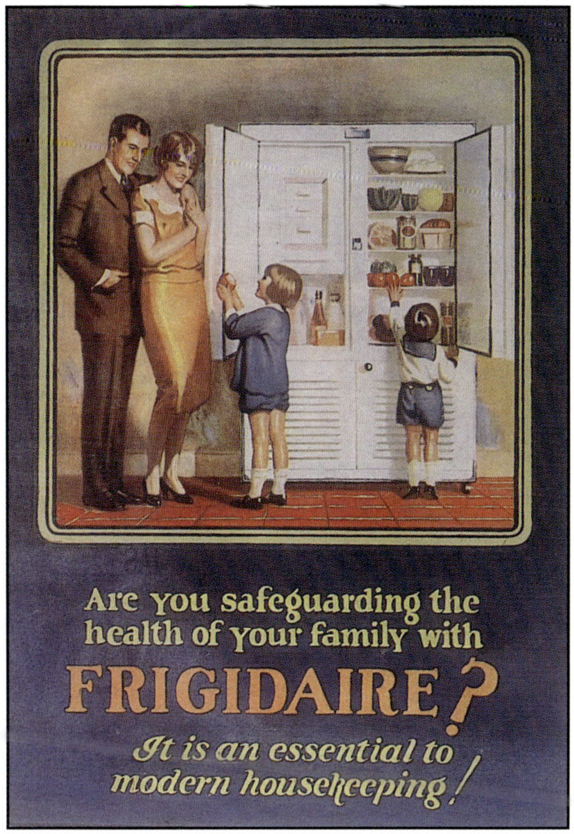

An advertisement from 1926.

Source C

A Chicago nightclub in the 1920s.

Source D

> Liberation did not much affect the daily lives of most American women in the 1920s. Though a few young upper-class women in the cities talked about throwing out the older ideas – they were called 'flappers' – most women kept to more traditional attitudes concerning their 'place'. Few middle-class women, in fact, tried to find steady employment outside their home. Though contraception and new, time-saving household appliances seemed to give them more freedom to enter the job market, most concentrated on managing the home. Their daughters, far from taking to the streets against sexual discrimination, were more likely to prepare for careers as mothers and housewives.

From *America in the Twentieth Century* by James T. Patterson (1989).

Source E

> **Section 1.** From now on it shall be unlawful for any man or woman, male or female to be guilty of committing sexual intercourse within this town …
>
> **Section 3.** Section 1 of this law shall not apply to married persons committing intercourse with their husband or wife, unless of a grossly improper nature.

From a local law passed in an Arkansas town in the 1920s.

Source F

> 'Our daughters (eighteen and fifteen) don't use our car much because they are always with somebody else in their car when we go out motoring,' lamented one middle-class mother. And another said, 'The two older children (eighteen and sixteen) never go out when the family motors. They always have something else on.' 'In the 1890s we were all much more together,' said another wife. 'What on earth do you want me to do? Just sit around home all evening!' retorted a popular high school girl of today when her father discouraged her going out motoring for the evening with a young man. 348 boys and 382 girls in the three upper years of the high school placed 'use of the automobile' fifth and fourth in a list of twelve possible sources of disagreement between them and their parents.

By Robert and Helen Lynd from their book *Middletown*. Written in 1929, this was a study of everyday life in the USA at that time.

1. Does **Source A** give a reliable view of attitudes towards Prohibition in the USA in the 1920s?
   Explain your answer using **Source A and your own knowledge.**
2. How useful is **Source B** to an historian studying changes in US home life during the 1920s?
   Explain your answer using **Source B and your own knowledge.**
3. **Source C** is a photograph from the time. **Source D** is an interpretation written many years later. Which of these two sources is the more reliable evidence about how 'liberated' the lives of US women were in the 1920s?
   Explain your answer using **Sources C and D and your own knowledge.**
4. **Source E** became law in only a small part of the USA. Does this mean it is of little use as evidence about US attitudes towards sexual behaviour in the 1920s?
   Explain your answer using **Source E and your own knowledge.**
5. **Source F** was one of the first detailed attempts to study the everyday life of ordinary Americans. How useful is this source for investigating the impact of the motor car on US life in the 1920s?
   Explain your answer using **Source F and your own knowledge.**
6. Why is it difficult to make an accurate assessment of how much US society was changing in the 1920s?
   Explain your answer using **all the sources and your own knowledge.**

Assessment Objective 3

The achievements of President Roosevelt from 1933 to 1941

Source A

Roosevelt visiting a Civilian Conservation Corps in Virginia, 1933.

Source C

The King is in the White House
Handing out the money
The Queen is on the front page
Looking very funny
Their knave is up in Boston
Picking up the plums
While the nation alphabetically
Is feeding all the bums.

A poem, about Roosevelt and his family, written during the New Deal.

Source B

A cartoon about Roosevelt's policies, from the 1930s.

Source D

President Roosevelt is the first statesman in a great capitalist state who has tried deliberately to use the powers of such a state for certain social purposes. He is the first statesman who has volunteered, without being forced to do so, to give organised workers a weapon which is bound to improve their bargaining power with their employers. He has also tried to use the state to share out the national income more fairly.

No unbiased spectator can hold back his admiration for the courage such an effort has needed. Success or failure, it shows great leadership. Put together in haste, and in a grim crisis, in an atmosphere of panic and confusion, Roosevelt's policy stands out in remarkable contrast to the policy of other capitalist governments in the world today.

The views of Harold Laski, a British socialist, in the late 1930s.

Source E

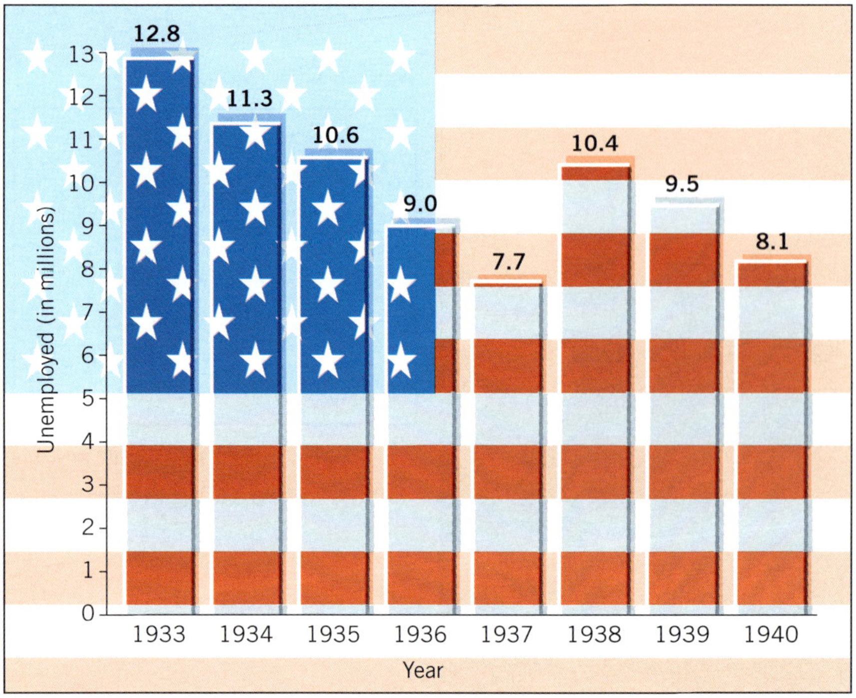

Unemployment in the USA, 1933–40, based on US government figures.

Source F

> He was concerned with more than improving his own position (though he cared very much about that). He wanted to help ordinary people and he expressed their needs in simple language they could understand. In his 'fireside chats', his numerous press conferences and his attention to the avalanche of mail that poured into the White House, he projected the image of a man who cared ... His air of confidence gave people hope and restored their faith in democracy.

From *America in the Twentieth Century* by James T. Patterson (1989).

1. Study **Source A**. How reliable is this photograph for assessing the success of Roosevelt's New Deal policies?
   Explain your answer using **Source A and your own knowledge**.
2. **Source B** is an exaggerated cartoon showing Roosevelt working to help the USA recover from the Depression. Does this mean that it is of little use as evidence about Roosevelt's part in the recovery?
   Explain your answer using **Source B and your own knowledge**.
3. **Sources C and D** give very different views on Roosevelt's achievements during the 1930s, even though they were written around the same time. How do you account for these differences?
   Explain your answer using **Sources C and D and your own knowledge**.
4. **Source E** was put together from information collected by the US government. How much can you learn from this source about Roosevelt's employment policies in the 1930s?
   Explain your answer using **Source E and your own knowledge**.
5. Study **Source F**. This is an account written in a textbook for US college students. What are the strengths and weaknesses of this interpretation for a study of Roosevelt's approach and methods as President of the USA?
   Explain your answer using **Source F and your own knowledge**.
6. In 1982 a survey of US historians ranked Roosevelt as one of the two greatest presidents in US history. How far do these sources help you to assess Roosevelt's achievements as President from 1933 to 1941?
   Explain your answer using **all the sources and your own knowledge**.

CHAPTER 8

The Second World War, 1939–45

The war against Germany

German military successes in Poland and western Europe, 1939–40

German and Soviet conquests, 1939–40.

The nature of blitzkrieg warfare

Blitzkrieg is German for 'lightning war', and it was the key to the rapid German successes in the early part of the Second World War. The Germans wanted surprise and speed, using tanks and planes. Their importance had been seen at the end of the First World War (see pages 181–2).

Attacks were carried out by firstly bombing key targets, such as enemy headquarters and centres of communication. At the same time, parachutists were dropped behind enemy lines. Then tanks and trucks containing infantry (foot soldiers) carried out the main attack. The tanks and infantry would start by attacking all the enemy's weak points, so that the enemy's strongholds could be encircled while more troops were arriving. Meanwhile, the tanks and infantry would advance further.

Using this tactic meant that the Germans concentrated their tanks in large groups in a few places, to very great effect. On the other hand, the British and French were still using tanks to back up each infantry division and not using tanks as a spearhead.

The conquest of Poland, September–October 1939

The Germans invaded western Poland on 1 September 1939 (see pages 34–5). Following the terms of the Nazi–Soviet Pact of August 1939, the Russians invaded eastern Poland on 17 September, and Poland was faced with two enemies attacking on two fronts. Britain and France had declared war on Germany on 3 September, but the French did not invade Germany and the British were still assembling troops and beginning to transport them to Europe when the Germans completed their defeat of the Polish army on 19 September.

Blitzkrieg methods were very successful across the flat Polish plains, and the Poles had only one tank brigade against Germany's eleven. The Polish air force was also small – 210 bombers compared with Germany's 850 – and many of their aircraft were destroyed on the ground anyway. Initially, some people living in Poland welcomed the Germans. After all, there had been a large German minority living there since the Treaty of Versailles had re-created Poland as an independent country. Poles who opposed the Germans had no chance of success against the joint attack of Germany and the Soviet Union. Poland was divided between them.

The German invasion of Norway, April 1940

The period after the defeat of Poland is known as the 'Phoney War'. Although there were battles at sea, the expected attack on Britain and France did not occur. Many civilians were relieved but puzzled at this lack of activity.

The Phoney War ended in April 1940 when Germany attacked Norway. The Germans relied on Norway and neighbouring Sweden for over half of their iron ore imports. The British Prime Minister, Neville Chamberlain, had considered occupying Norway to cut off Germany's vital supplies, but feared that world opinion would be against Britain as Norway was a neutral country. He lost his chance. Hitler ordered a *blitzkrieg* attack by sea, and seized points along the Norwegian coast as far north as Narvik. German paratroops were dropped to capture places inland, such as bridges and airfields. The British and French were unable to provide sufficient help to prevent Norway being defeated.

However, perhaps the most important result of the British failure to help Norway was the resignation on 10 May 1940 of the Prime Minister, Neville Chamberlain.

SOURCE B

A British poster from May 1940.

Winston Churchill was chosen to lead a coalition government for the duration of the war. He took office just as Hitler began the invasion of France.

SOURCE A

I have nothing to offer but blood, toil, tears and sweat. You ask, what is our policy? I will say: It is to wage war, by sea, land and air, with all our might. You ask, what is our aim? I can answer in one word: Victory – victory at all costs, victory, however long and hard the road may be.

Winston Churchill speaking in the House of Commons, 13 May 1940.

QUESTIONS

1. What is meant by '*blitzkrieg*'?
2. In the first year of the war, where was *blitzkrieg* most important in explaining German success? Explain your answer.
3. What difference do you think the Phoney War made to Hitler's chances of winning?

The German invasion of the Netherlands, Belgium and France, May 1940

In May 1940, Hitler launched his attack on western Europe (see the map on this page). Again the German *blitzkrieg* was hugely successful. The peoples of the Netherlands and Belgium were easily overwhelmed. The French had built an elaborate set of fortifications – the Maginot Line – along their border with Germany. The French knew that the Germans were unlikely to attack there as the border was so well defended. They believed that the main German attack would come through the lowlands of Belgium, as had happened in 1914. In fact, the Germans seriously considered this option, but the German general, Guderian, persuaded them that they could create routes through the Ardennes Forest in southern Belgium and attack there.

The French also believed that the German tanks would not be able to get through the Ardennes, so Germany's tactic ensured that it achieved maximum surprise. With the rapid German advance, both French troops on the Belgian border and the British Expeditionary Force that had just arrived in France had to retreat rapidly to avoid being cut off from the rest of the French armies.

Dunkirk, May–June 1940

The Germans planned to race to the Channel ports and seize them. The 380,000 British and French troops who had been fighting in Belgium and in north-eastern France retreated to Dunkirk, and were surrounded by the Germans. For nine days between 27 May and 4 June, the German air force (Luftwaffe) pounded the beaches as the Royal Navy evacuated men back to England. Hundreds of small, privately owned boats went to the beaches of Dunkirk to rescue as many as possible and transfer them to bigger Royal Navy vessels waiting off-shore. The British government hoped that at least 50,000 men could be rescued – possibly 100,000. In fact, around 340,000 men were rescued in 'Operation Dynamo'. The escape was referred to as a miracle, but huge amounts of military equipment had to be abandoned, including 475 tanks, 1000 heavy guns and 400 anti-tank guns.

Within a month of the Dunkirk evacuation, Paris had been captured and France had surrendered to Germany. Instead of occupying the whole of France, Germany allowed southern France to set up a government at Vichy run by General Pétain. This Vichy government was really controlled by the Germans.

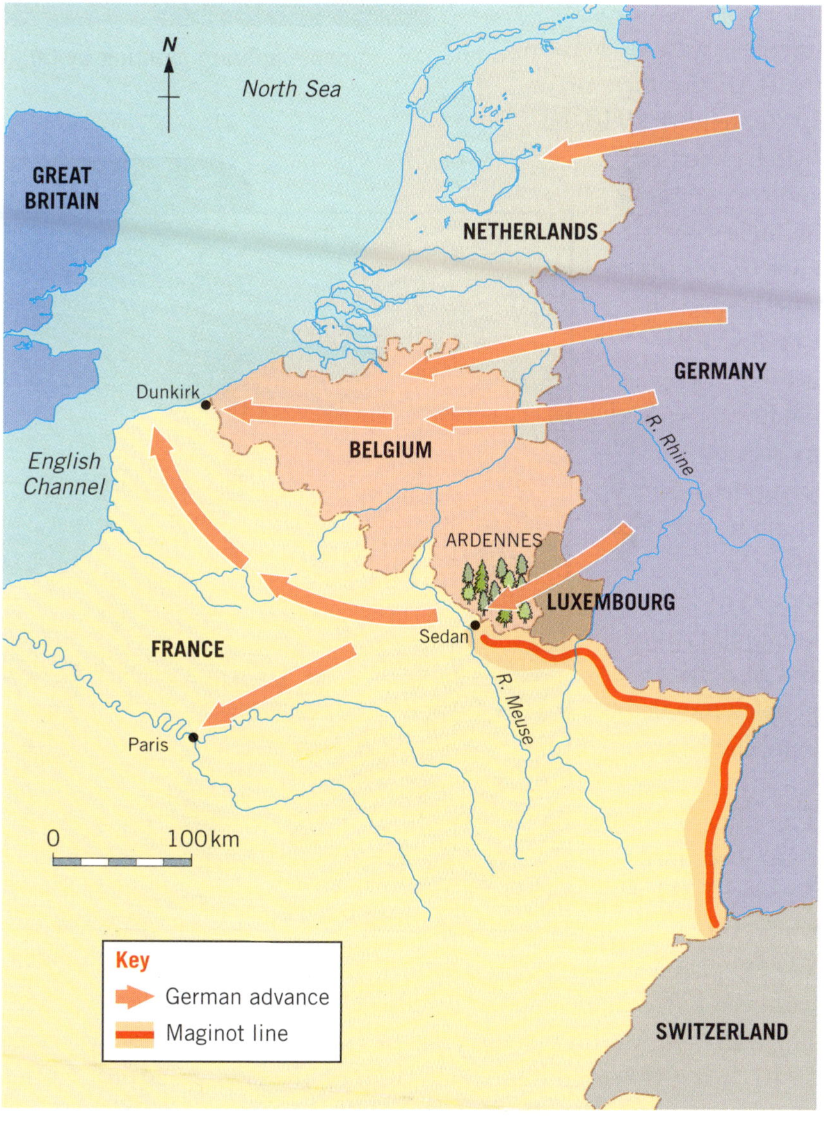

The German invasion of the Low Countries and France, May 1940.

The Battle of Britain, 1940

Hitler wanted to invade Britain, but he knew that he could not succeed until he had destroyed the Royal Air Force (RAF). Between July and September 1940, the RAF and the German Luftwaffe fought the Battle of Britain in the skies over England. In the first week of September, the British lost 185 aircraft and 300 airmen. New planes had to be built rapidly, but it took longer to train new airmen. Hitler did not realise how near the Germans were to defeating the RAF. But then, on 17 September 1940, he switched tactics and concentrated on night-time air-raids on British cities, especially London. This became known as the Blitz. It aimed to disrupt transport by bombing railways, to damage industry by bombing factories and to destroy people's morale by bombing homes.

The Blitz continued until summer 1941, by which time 43,000 people had been killed in air-raids in Britain. The worst single air-raid was on Coventry on 14 November 1940. It lasted for ten hours; one-third of the city was destroyed and 4000 people were killed. However, the bombing made British people even more determined to carry on fighting the war against Hitler.

SOURCE C

A contemporary painting by Charles Cundall showing British troops being rescued from the beaches of Dunkirk.

SOURCE D

Air-raid damage in London leaves a bus leaning against a building.

Germany's offensive and initial success in the Soviet Union

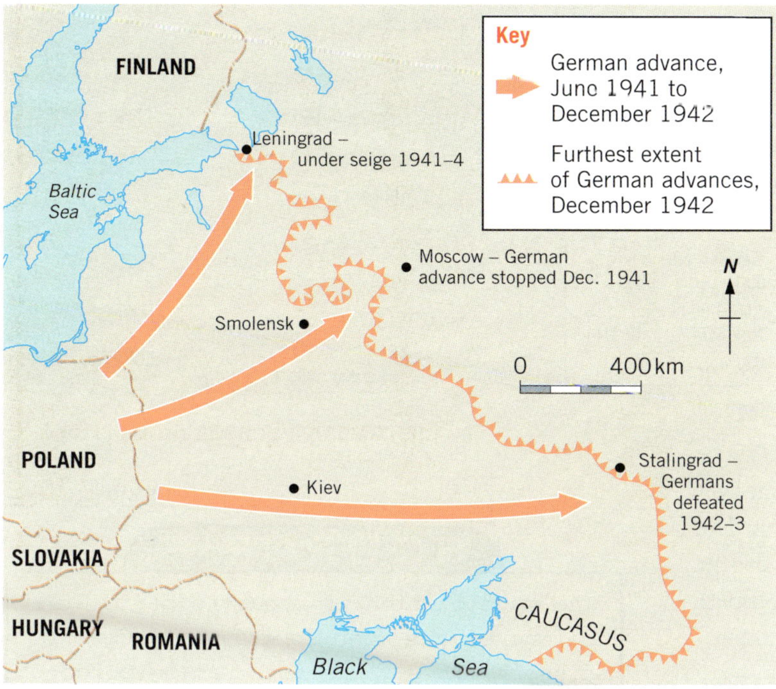

Germany's invasion of the Soviet Union, 1941–2.

In spite of signing the Nazi–Soviet Pact in August 1939, Hitler regarded the Slav peoples of the Soviet Union as sub-human and he hated communism. In addition, he wanted control of the grain areas of the Ukraine and the valuable oilfields of the Caucasus, and more living space (*Lebensraum*) for the German master race.

Hitler had planned to start 'Operation Barbarossa', his attack on the Soviet Union, in April 1941, but it was postponed until 22 June 1941. In April he had to assist Mussolini in the Mediterranean. Mussolini was trying to extend his empire in north Africa and Greece. Hitler also took the opportunity to invade Romania to gain access to the valuable oil supplies there. The delay proved to be critical. Even though the German tank units advanced up to 30 kilometres a day, by November they had only reached the outskirts of Moscow, Leningrad and Kiev. The temperature dropped rapidly, and the Germans were badly prepared. As they had been equipped only with summer uniforms, over one million German troops suffered from frostbite. Oil froze in the tanks. The Germans were also short of food and other essentials, as the Soviets had destroyed as much as possible as they retreated – a scorched-earth policy.

The Germans were forced to dig in for the winter, and this allowed the Soviets to launch a series of counter-offensives, led by Marshal Zhukov. They also moved and created many armaments factories further east, safe from the Germans. By late 1942 these factories were producing vital supplies for the Soviets, who were also aided by US and British tanks and aircraft.

SOURCE E

Soviet troops using a tank as cover to fire on the enemy in 1941.

Major events of the war against Germany

El Alamein, October 1942

In north Africa, Britain was fighting Italian and German forces for control of the Mediterranean coast and the Suez Canal. This canal route was vitally important for shipping going to and from India and the Far East, and for controlling access to Middle East oil reserves. The British defeated the Italians, and Hitler was forced to send a German army under General Rommel to help them. The British were helped by troops from Australia, New Zealand, India and South Africa, but by May 1941 they had been forced to retreat into Egypt, except for the area around Tobruk, which is on the north African coast, west of Egypt.

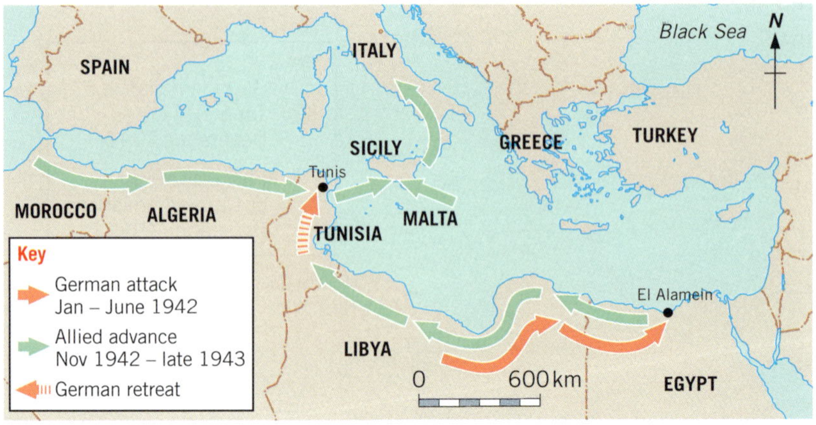

The campaign in north Africa, 1942–3.

In 1942 Tobruk also fell to the Germans, and Churchill appointed General Montgomery to lead the British Eighth Army against Rommel. Montgomery built up his forces until he had over 200,000 men and over 1000 tanks. He knew that the forthcoming battle would decide who controlled north Africa. The Battle of El Alamein lasted over a week, until Rommel's forces were forced to retreat from Egypt. This was the first major victory for Britain in the war and proved, as Montgomery had hoped, to be a turning point in its fortunes.

SOURCE F

The battle which is about to begin will be one of the most important battles in history. It will be the turning point of the war.

Montgomery speaking to his men, 23 October 1942.

From November 1942 onwards, US troops began arriving in north-west Africa to support the Allies against Germany. Rommel wanted to take his troops out of north Africa before they were trapped by the advancing Allies, but Hitler refused. In May 1943, 130,000 German and Italian soldiers surrendered.

Once the German and Italian forces had been defeated in Africa, Allied troops were able to cross into Italy and began to fight their way northwards towards Hitler's Germany.

SOURCE G

Australian soldiers at the Battle of El Alamein, 1942.

Stalingrad, 1942–3

During 1942 Hitler made new plans to defeat the Soviet Union. Increasingly, he refused to allow his generals to make any decisions themselves. He decided that the priority was to gain control of the Caucasus oilfields by switching the main force of German attacks to the south of the Soviet Union around Stalingrad.

Hitler wanted to capture Stalingrad as top priority. Not only was it 'the city of Stalin', which meant that its capture would harm Soviet morale, but also Hitler believed that the city was strategically important. The Soviets, led by General Zhukov, were seriously outnumbered but their total determination to defend the city stopped them from giving in.

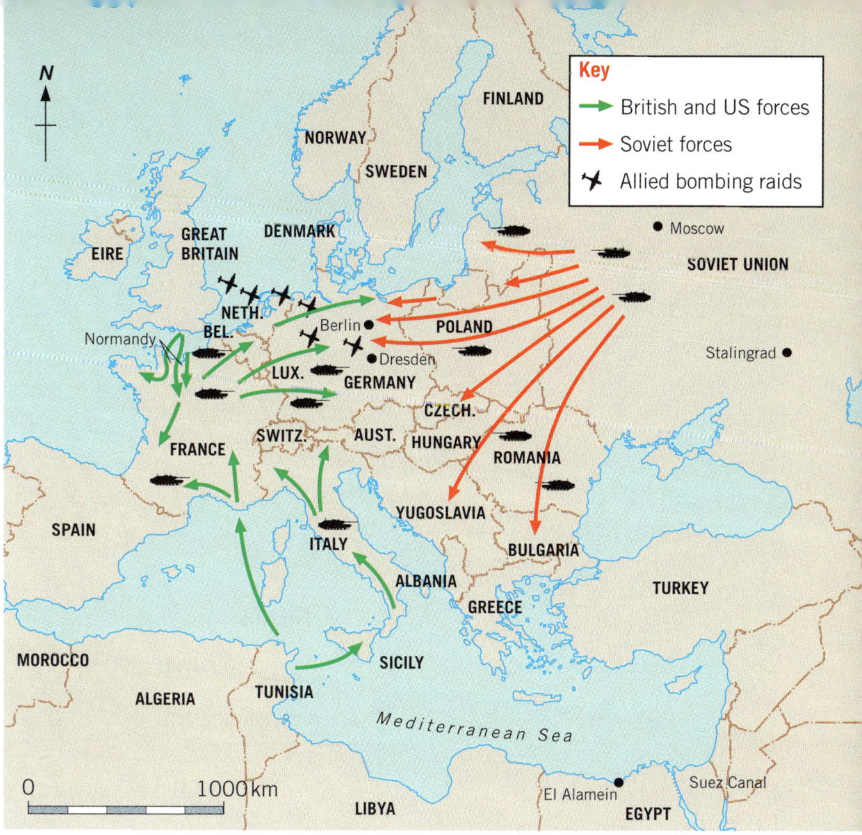

The defeat of Germany 1944–5.

The German army, led by General Von Paulus, began attacking Stalingrad at the end of June 1942. The battle for the city was fierce, with the Soviets trying to regain at night the control of streets, ruins, cellars and sewers lost during the day.

Then, in November 1942, the Soviet armies managed to break out from Stalingrad, and it was the Germans' turn to find themselves surrounded. Their supplies of food and fuel were diminishing just as winter established its full grip. Von Paulus wanted to retreat from the city, but Hitler repeatedly refused permission. He demanded that German troops resist to the end.

On 31 January 1943, Von Paulus disobeyed orders. He told his men – nearly 100,000 of them – to surrender. About 150,000 had already been killed in trying to capture Stalingrad.

The siege of Stalingrad, together with Germany's failure to capture Moscow and Leningrad, proved to be the turning-point in the Soviet Union. The Germans were able to launch only one more serious offensive against the Soviets, at Kursk in July 1943. When that failed too, the German armies, lacking reserves and essential supplies, were forced to retreat rapidly. By summer 1944 they had been driven from Soviet territory altogether. Soviet troops followed them into eastern Europe and headed for Berlin.

QUESTIONS

1. Why did Hitler invade the Soviet Union in June 1941?
2. Why did this blitzkrieg attack not produce another victory for Germany?

D-Day landings, June 1944

Ever since the German invasion of the Soviet Union in 1941, Stalin had been asking Britain and the USA to launch an invasion by sea of German-occupied western Europe. This would force the Germans to transfer some of their 3 million troops from the Soviet Union to the west. Churchill agreed in principle, but decided to concentrate first on north Africa. Stalin believed that this was done so that the communist Soviet Union was weakened first, before it received much help from the western allies.

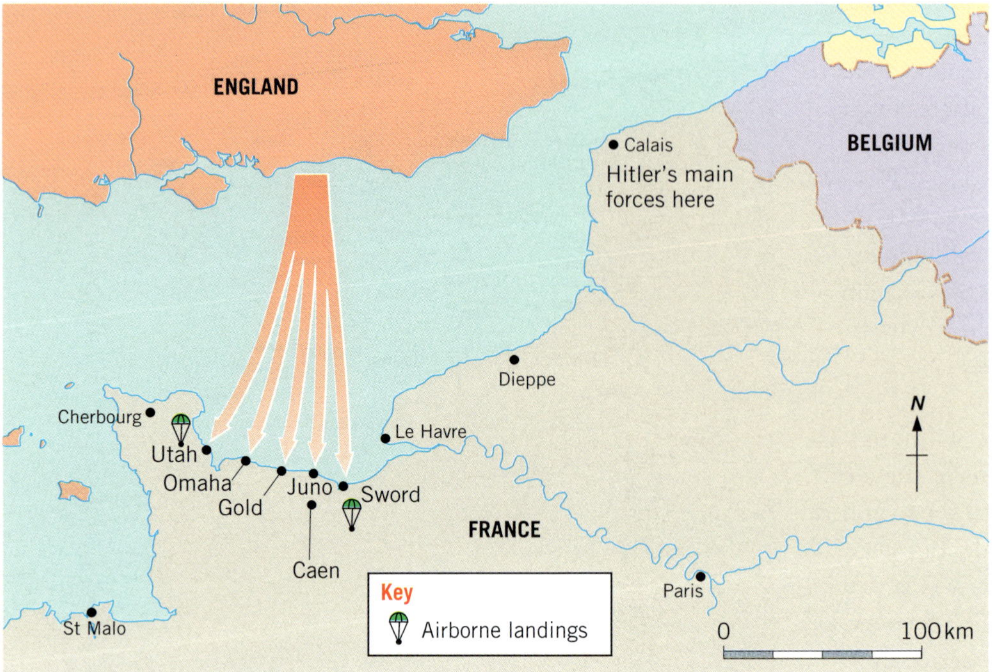

D-Day landings in France, June 1944.

However, in 1944 preparations for landings in France were made on a huge scale. Dwight D. Eisenhower, the US general, was in overall command of 'Operation Overlord'. He led the Germans to believe that the landings would take place near Calais – the shortest Channel crossing-point. The Allies repeatedly bombed the city of Calais. Dummy military camps were built in Kent, complete with wooden tanks. Only a few Germans believed that the invasion would happen in Normandy.

The invasion occurred on 6 June 1944 – D-Day – and its scale took the Germans by surprise. The plan involved five separate landings, in areas code-named Utah, Omaha, Gold, Juno and Sword. The first two were the responsibility of the Americans; the other three, the British and the Canadians. Even when he had realised the full extent of the invasion in Normandy, Hitler refused to move tanks and troops from the Calais area, fearing that another major attack was planned there.

Landing on the Normandy beaches was grim on the first day. About 3600 British and Canadian soldiers were killed or wounded. The Americans lost 6000 men. However, over 150,000 Allied soldiers had landed. In the next few days, they established their positions on the five beaches, and began to move inland to liberate France. By 12 June 325,000 Allied troops were in France.

The Germans fought hard. For example, it took nearly a month for the Allies to capture Cherbourg, an important port. But once the Germans began to retreat, the pace of liberation quickened. On 25 August 1944, Paris was freed and its new leader was Charles de Gaulle, who had been in exile in Britain.

The advance into Germany

In September 1944 the Allies reached the important river crossing, the Rhine, and began capturing bridges held by the Germans. Although most of France had now been liberated, the Allies had problems progressing into Germany. In December 1944 the Germans launched a counter-attack in the Ardennes. At first it achieved remarkable success, but by the end of January 1945 the Germans were once again in retreat.

While German troops were retreating out of western Europe, the Soviets were moving in from the east. The Germans were also retreating out of Italy. Allied bombing raids on German cities were stepped up. Cities such as Hamburg were destroyed. Apart from targeting German industries and communications, the RAF bombed civilian areas in the hope of breaking German morale. The bombing of cities such as Dresden was far worse than the Luftwaffe's attacks on British cities.

Resistance movements in Europe

In countries occupied by the Germans, there were groups of people who were prepared to carry on resisting the Nazis by fighting an underground war. These members of the Resistance were important in undermining the German war effort. They carried out acts of sabotage – for example, blowing up railways, roads and factories. They also passed on information about enemy plans to other countries, such as Britain, by using secret radio transmitters. During the D-Day landings, members of the French Resistance worked with the Allies by cutting telephone wires and disrupting the Nazi movement of troops. In some countries, such as Denmark, Resistance workers prevented many Jews from being captured. In south-east Europe and the Soviet Union, the Resistance fighters were called partisans. There were about one million members in Yugoslavia alone. They were very active in Poland too, as Source I shows.

SOURCE H

The woman fumbling in her bag is taking a photograph with a hidden camera. The lens can be seen just below the centre of the two rings.

The British Special Operations Executive (SOE) trained men and women in Britain to help set up Resistance groups in occupied Europe. It also provided weapons, radios and explosives. Trained agents were then parachuted into an occupied country such as France.

The Nazis took strong action following acts against their rule. For example, in September 1944, Dutch railway workers went on strike to help the Allied advance against the Germans. During the next few months food supplies were denied to western Holland and 16,000 people died of starvation. At Lidice in Czechoslovakia in June 1942, the local SS General, Reynhard Heydrich, was assassinated. Nearly 200 local men were shot, and the women and children were taken to concentration camps or gas chambers. The village was then razed to the ground.

The activities of the Resistance in various countries did not defeat the Nazis, but they contributed to that defeat. More importantly, they helped to retain local pride and morale in occupied areas. The Nazis also had to keep substantial numbers of troops in these occupied areas – troops that could otherwise have been used in combat against the Allies.

SOURCE I

Locomotives damaged	6930
Transport derailed	732
Railway wagons damaged	19,058
Military vehicles damaged	4326
Defective parts for aircraft engines produced	4710
Defective artillery shells produced	92,000

Activities of the Polish partisans. From *The Polish Underground State, 1939–45* by Stefan Korbonski (1978).

Causes of the German defeat and the Allied victory

By early 1945, Soviet troops had advanced on to German soil and Allied troops in the west were crossing the River Rhine. The Germans continued to put up strong resistance, but the tide of the war had turned and the Germans were only postponing the inevitable defeat.

By late April, Soviet troops were in the suburbs of Berlin. On 30 April, Hitler committed suicide, and in the next few days all German forces surrendered. The Soviets were the first to reach the Reichstag, and a soldier hung the Soviet communist flag from the building.

The Nazis had seemed in an invincible position in early 1941. Why had it all turned sour?

QUESTION

1. Choose from the box the **three** reasons that you think are most important to explain Germany's defeat. For each reason, explain carefully why you think it was important.

Causes of Germany's defeat

1. Hitler failed to invade Britain. This was essential in 1940–1 when Britain was the only major power actively fighting against him.
2. The leadership of Churchill was crucial for maintaining British (and world) morale in the most difficult stages of the war.
3. Even before the USA officially joined the war, President Roosevelt organised a scheme called 'lend-lease', by which Britain could borrow or hire military equipment. This helped Britain with essential war materials until the USA officially joined the war after the attack on Pearl Harbor in December 1941 (see page 244).
4. Hitler's attack on the Soviet Union was a costly mistake. Because he detested communism, he underestimated the ability and determination of the Soviets to defend themselves. Mistakes in planning and Hitler's refusal to allow local generals to make decisions for themselves led to German defeat in the east.
5. Resistance groups in many occupied countries made life difficult for the Nazis, and many German troops were used in controlling them. The Nazis' treatment of Jews meant that many people in occupied countries would never accept the Germans. It also increased the determination of the Allies to defeat Hitler.
6. Hitler had to help Mussolini in Africa. Indeed, Hitler claimed that this was the reason why he lost the war. But although he did have troops and generals in Africa, they were only a small fraction of the number of German troops fighting against the Soviet Union.
7. Germany suffered increasingly from a lack of oil supplies, which were needed to fuel the German war effort. For example, Romania (which had been conquered by Germany) quit the war in August 1944, causing Germany to lose 23 per cent of its oil supplies. By 1944, Germany's total oil supplies were about one-fifteenth of the Allies'. Its coal production was nearly half.
8. The military might of the Allies overwhelmed Germany. The Soviet Union produced an amazing number of war goods considering the desperate state of parts of the country. The USA, however, physically mostly untouched by the war, had a seemingly endless capacity for stepping up production of tanks, aircraft, guns, ammunition, food and other essential war materials.

The war against Japan

Japanese expansion in the Pacific and the Far East, 1941–2

During the 1930s, Japan had begun to build an empire in China. Obtaining more land was essential to gain access to the basic raw materials that Japan lacked, such as oil, rubber, tin, iron and coal (see page 245).

In 1937 Japan had started a full-scale invasion of China, and had joined an alliance against communism with Italy and Germany. This was called the Anti-Comintern Pact. The invasion of China was still in progress when events in Europe brought about the defeat of France and the Netherlands by Germany, with Britain the next target for invasion. The Japanese believed that this provided an excellent opportunity to seize British, Dutch and French colonies in Asia. They believed that the USA would take no action. After all, the USA was following a policy of isolationism, and Roosevelt was promising the US people that they would not get dragged into another world conflict.

In July 1941 Japanese armies occupied French Indo-China. However, by then, President Roosevelt was becoming alarmed about the growing threat of the Japanese to US colonies in the Far East, such as the Philippines. In the same month, he demanded the withdrawal of Japanese forces from occupied areas and banned the sale of oil from the USA to Japan. This would have a devastating effect on Japan's military plans, as Japan relied on the USA for 80 per cent of its oil, and at the current rate of use would run out by April 1942.

Major events of the war against Japan

The plan to attack Pearl Harbor

On 1 November 1941, Japan's Prime Minister, General Tojo, discussed the possibilities with his ministers and military leaders. They decided to take military action to seize control of raw materials in Asia. The European powers were too preoccupied to act, but the US navy was powerful and could prevent the Japanese from succeeding. Therefore, the Japanese decided to launch a surprise attack on the US Pacific Fleet at Pearl Harbor in Hawaii. They would then be in a good position to take over south-east Asia before the Americans could rebuild their navy.

The Americans had been expecting an attack, but they assumed that the target would be the Philippines, a US colony. So even when, the day before the attack took place, the Americans received warnings that it was imminent, they still did not believe that Pearl Harbor would be the target.

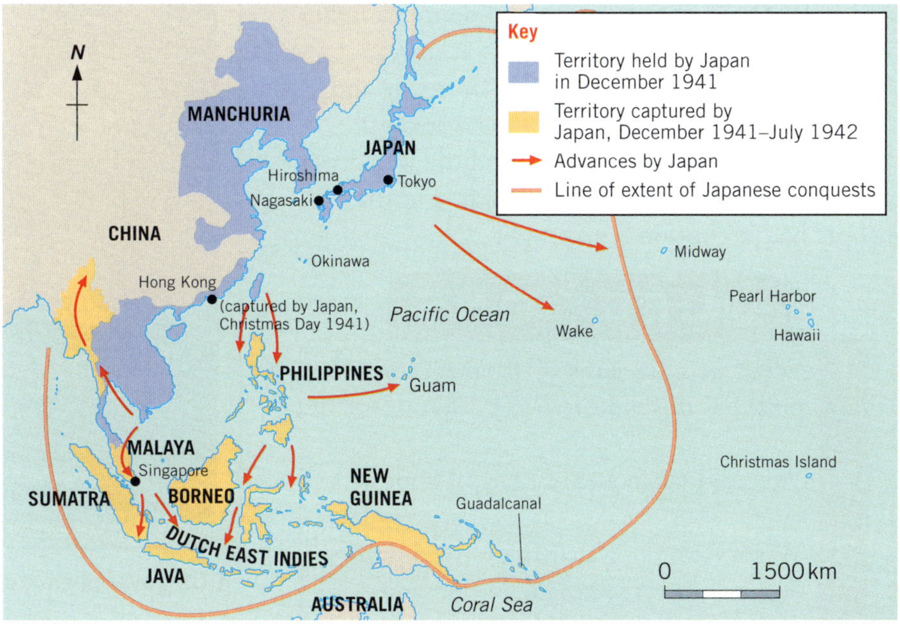

The war in the Pacific, 1941–2.

The attack on Pearl Harbor, 7 December 1941

At 8 a.m. on Sunday, 7 December 1941, Japanese aircraft pounded the American Pacific Fleet of 70 ships in its harbour. The Japanese were pleased with their success. Six US battleships were sunk, another three were put out of action, and nearly 200 aircraft were destroyed. Over 2000 Americans had been killed. The Japanese had lost just 29 of their 384 aircraft.

However, none of the three US aircraft carriers had been destroyed; they were away from Pearl Harbor on exercises. Nor were the ship repair yards or the huge oil tanks damaged.

SOURCE A

US sailors man their boats at the site of the burning USS *West Virginia* to fight the flames started by Japanese torpedoes and bombs in the raid on Pearl Harbor.

Consequences of the attack

The immediate effect of the attack on Pearl Harbor was that Japan was at war with the USA – and also with Britain, as the Japanese had attacked the British colonies of Hong Kong and Malaya on the same day, as well as other US possessions in the Pacific. It was not automatic that the USA would also declare war on Germany and Italy. Many Americans had no desire to fight what they saw as two separate wars at once. However, on 11 December 1941, Germany and Italy settled the matter by declaring war on the USA. The separate conflicts around the world were now officially part of one global war, and the US people had no option but to fight.

SOURCE B

A US government poster reminds people of the attack on Pearl Harbor.

QUESTIONS

1. What were the aims of Japanese foreign policy at the end of the 1930s?
2. Why did Japan attack Pearl Harbor?
3. Was it surprising that the USA did not declare war on Germany in the same month (December 1941)?

Events from December 1941 to mid-1942

In the next few months, the Japanese had two main objectives. One was to capture the lands that would supply the raw materials they needed. The other was to secure and fortify a defensive line to protect their new empire.

Within five months both objectives had been achieved. They had access to plenty of oil, to 70 per cent of the world's tin and most of the world's rubber. They captured Hong Kong (Christmas Day 1941), Singapore (February 1942), the Dutch East Indies (March 1942) and the Philippines (May 1942). They threatened Ceylon (now called Sri Lanka) and dropped bombs on Darwin in Australia, so Australia also felt threatened. The Japanese took huge numbers of prisoners, and forced them to work in terrible conditions.

By mid-1942 the Japanese had gained almost total control of the Pacific region.

The Battle of Midway, June 1942

In late 1942, the Allies achieved victories in other parts of the world that proved to be turning-points: El Alamein in north Africa, and Stalingrad in the Soviet Union (see pages 238–9). But there was an equivalent turning point against the Japanese earlier in the year. It happened in June 1942, and proved that the Japanese could be beaten.

The Japanese had planned to seize the US island colony of Midway. However, the Americans knew of the plan, as they had deciphered Japan's secret code. US aircraft, launched from aircraft carriers, attacked the Japanese fleet and sank four of their aircraft carriers. The Americans lost only one aircraft carrier. The Battle of Midway was the first sea battle in history when the opposing fleets never met each other, but the effects were devastating for the Japanese. The Japanese only managed to build seven more aircraft carriers in the next two years, while the Americans built 90. Aircraft carriers proved to be vital for the war in the Pacific.

The nature of warfare against Japan

The Americans took command of the Allied campaign in the Pacific, with General MacArthur leading the land forces and Admiral Nimitz leading the naval forces across the Pacific.

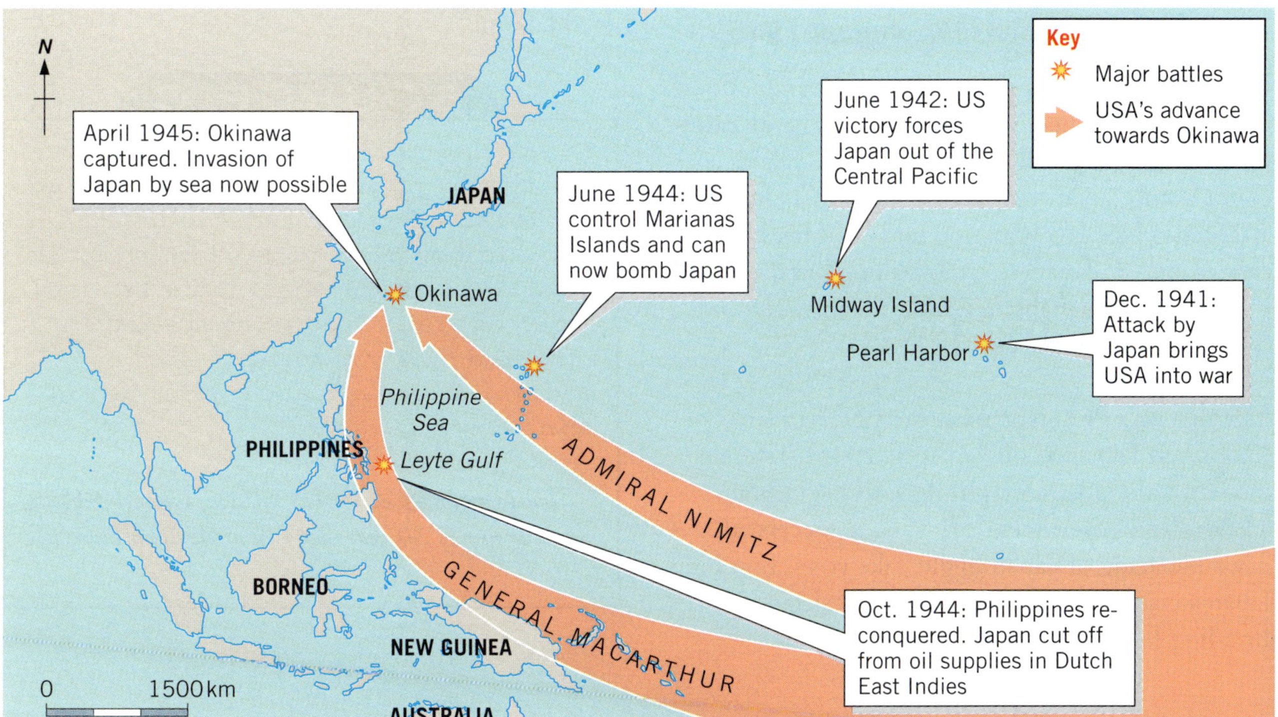

US advance towards Okinawa, 1942–5.

The Americans developed an 'island-hopping' or 'leapfrogging' strategy. It was similar to Hitler's blitzkrieg, in that strongly defended islands were bypassed and isolated from supplies and reinforcements, so that they would eventually be easy to capture. This speeded up progress across the vast distances and hundreds of islands held by the Japanese. It also limited US casualties.

Even so, progress was costly in terms of US men. The Japanese fought fanatically and refused to surrender. To be captured in battle was thought to be shameful, so most Japanese fought to the death. Some Japanese volunteered to be *kamikaze* (suicide) pilots. From October 1944 onwards, over 5000 pilots flew their planes, packed with explosives, into US ships. The high number of US casualties in capturing islands worried the US government enormously. How many Americans would be killed in the invasion of Japan?

The war in Europe had already ended by the time Okinawa, close to Japan, was captured in June 1945. But it was captured only after two months of vicious fighting and the deaths of 13,000 US soldiers and sailors. Now the Japanese mainland could be attacked.

Hiroshima and Nagasaki, August 1945

By July 1945, Japan's position was desperate. Food was scarce, and there was a great shortage of raw materials such as coal, iron and oil. US planes could bomb Japan with little danger of being attacked. Huge US bombing raids had been carried out on Japanese cities, killing hundreds of thousands of civilians. Yet Japan's leaders refused to consider surrendering.

The new US President was Harry S. Truman (Roosevelt had died on 12 April 1945). Truman discussed the possible options with his military advisers and government officials. A successful naval blockade of Japan might take years. Bombing Japan would only encourage heroic resistance. Invading Japan would be extremely costly. MacArthur reckoned that the Americans would need at least 5 million men to invade, as the Japanese still had 2 million troops and thousands more volunteering to be *kamikaze* pilots.

The US government decided to use the atomic bomb. It had been tested earlier in the summer, and it was expected that one bomb would destroy most of a city. But the exact results of the atomic bomb were not known. The US government hoped that its use would force Japan to surrender, ending the war as quickly as possible and keeping US casualties to a minimum.

At 8.15 a.m. on 6 August 1945, a US B-29 bomber, the Enola Gay, dropped an atomic bomb on Hiroshima. There was no sound, but the centre of the explosion was hotter than the surface of the sun. Nearly 13 square kilometres of the city were totally destroyed. At least 80,000 people died instantly, and many others died in the following days, weeks and years from radiation sickness.

The Japanese government was shocked, and initially refused to admit the extent of the devastation to the Japanese people. But the US Secretary of War had already sent a message to President Truman, telling him of the total success of the bomb.

SOURCE C

We saw this cloud coming up. The cloud, two minutes after the explosion, was at our height of thirty-three thousand feet. It continued to go right on up in a boiling fashion. Where there had been a city with distinctive houses and buildings, now you couldn't see anything except a black boiling debris down below.

The commander of the US mission, Colonel Tibbetts, speaking nearly 30 years later in a television interview.

SOURCE D

Damage at Hiroshima after the dropping of the atomic bomb, 6 August 1945.

The Americans hoped that the Japanese would surrender instantly. They did not. On 9 August another bomb was dropped, this time on the city of Nagasaki. Around 40,000 people died instantly, and many more died later. Emperor Hirohito of Japan at last faced up to reality. Japan would have to surrender. Even then, the Japanese argued for one concession – that the Emperor be allowed to stay on the throne. This was agreed by Truman, and the Japanese surrendered on 14 August 1945.

Was the use of the atomic bomb justified?

People have argued about the dropping of the atomic bomb ever since the event. We can say that it ended the war quickly, but we cannot say how long the war would have lasted if it had not been used. We only have people's estimates.

Although the use of atomic bombs on Hiroshima and Nagasaki resulted in over 100,000 deaths straight away, it has to be remembered that earlier in the year the Americans had fire-bombed cities such as Tokyo. In the attack on Tokyo on 9 March 1945 over 80,000 people were killed and 40,000 wounded. One million were made homeless. Therefore, the immediate extent of destruction caused by the atomic bombs did not seem so much more catastrophic than that caused by fire-bombs.

Some Japanese commanders later said that their country would have had to surrender soon through lack of arms and food. However, that did not seem to be the prevailing mood at the time, with kamikaze pilots and soldiers refusing to surrender as a matter of honour.

SOURCE E

Any weapon that would bring an end to the war and save a million lives was justified ... It was our duty to bring the war to an end at the earliest possible moment.

US Secretary of State, James Byrnes, in an interview in 1965.

SOURCE F

The use of this barbarous weapon at Hiroshima and Nagasaki was of no material assistance in our war against Japan. The Japanese were already defeated and were ready to surrender because of the effective sea blockade and the successful bombing with conventional weapons.

Admiral Leahy, Chief of Staff to the US President in 1945, writing in his memoirs in 1950.

President Truman was under pressure in the USA to protect the hundreds of thousands of prisoners of war held by the Japanese in terrible conditions. With food shortages throughout Japanese-held territory, it was the prisoners who were likely to suffer most.

Truman was also worried about Stalin. Now that the war had ended in Europe, Stalin was consolidating Soviet control of eastern Europe and planning to establish communist governments. The conference held at Potsdam in July 1945 (see pages 42–4) had shown up serious disagreements between the USA and the Soviet Union. Truman wanted to defeat Japan before the Soviets could claim any credit for the victory. He wanted to ensure that Soviet influence did not extend to Asia as well as Europe.

Whatever judgement about the use of the atomic bomb is reached by historians now, their attitudes are bound to be influenced by events since 1945.

SOURCE G

We remind you of the report sent to President Roosevelt in 1940. It spoke of the danger of radiation which will kill men, women and children for several miles around the explosion. They will go on dying after the bomb has fallen. This will be a completely new horror in war. We began to build this bomb because we feared Hitler, who is now defeated. You want to use it against Japan. We believe this is wrong. The USA should not be the first to use the atom bomb. The military advantage and saving of lives by dropping the bomb could be outweighed by the horror and revulsion that would sweep the world if we used it. We recommend dropping a bomb on an island in Japan, to show the Japanese the power of the bomb and give them a chance to surrender before it kills thousands.

From a secret report sent to President Truman in April 1945 by the scientists who made the bomb.

At the height of the Cold War, most people thought that the atomic bomb had given the USA a vital breathing-space to establish itself as the major superpower in the late 1940s.

SOURCE H

Our agents all report an amazing will to fight among the Japanese. If we invade Japan we can expect that no one will surrender. There are nearly 2 million soldiers in Japan and we will have to kill them all, one by one. The Japanese have been told by their government that the invading Americans will kill everyone in Japan, so they will fight to the death.

From secret reports made by US intelligence agents, given to President Truman in June 1945.

SOURCE I

Dropping the atomic bomb was no 'great decision'. For your information there were more people killed by the fire bombs in Tokyo than by these bombs. It was merely another powerful weapon in the arsenal of righteousness. The dropping of those two bombs stopped the war and saved millions of lives. It was just the same as getting a bigger gun than the other side, to win the war. That's what it was used for.

President Truman talking to students at Columbia University in the USA, 1959.

QUESTIONS

1. Look at the sources on pages 247 and 248. What were the reasons why Truman ordered the atomic bomb to be dropped on Hiroshima?
2. What reasons have some people used to argue that Truman was wrong?

The Home Front in Britain, 1939–45

Attitudes of the British people towards the war

When war was declared in Britain on 3 September 1939, almost everyone accepted the need to fight. But, in contrast to the mood in August 1914, there was very little cheering. In 1939 most people hoped that a last-minute solution could be found to avoid war, as it had apparently at the Munich Conference almost a year earlier. Even after the invasion of Poland on 1 September, people hoped that Hitler would compromise. But they had not understood the significance of the Nazi–Soviet Pact. Hitler now appeared to be determined to fight, regardless of the odds.

By the time war broke out, Britain had begun its preparations. Over one million shelters made out of corrugated iron had been issued, together with gas masks and leaflets explaining their use. Plans for air-raid precautions had been introduced in 1938 and 100,000 air-raid wardens were ready for duty. From 1 September 1939 it was an offence to allow any light to be visible in the street from any buildings at night – the 'blackout' had begun. In the first few days of September, one and a half million children were evacuated from the cities to the countryside, where they would be safe from bombing.

SOURCE A

A Ministry of Information poster from early in the war. Some people thought this reinforced a 'them and us' attitude. The workers would win the war; the upper classes would benefit from the victory.

Censorship and propaganda

People in Britain were limited in what they could hear and read. Government officials checked written and printed materials, films and photographs to ensure that they contained nothing that might aid the enemy. For example, newspapers were not allowed to print stories that emphasised defeats, or show pictures of dead air-raid victims. Newsreels at cinemas could not suggest despair, but could show Londoners struggling valiantly through the rubble on their way to work.

The Ministry of Information was the government department responsible for keeping the British public informed about the war and keeping up morale. Near the beginning of the war, the Ministry did not always succeed in creating a positive mood. Its early posters were uninspiring and were sometimes misinterpreted (see Source A). Later posters (such as Source B) were more artistic and used humour to keep up morale.

As the war progressed, radio, cinema and newspapers all became essential tools for the government, maintaining morale among the British people, so that they would fight on with determination.

SOURCE B

One of a series of posters intended to stop people carelessly giving away secret information to enemy spies.

Internment

There was a worry that there were lots of secret spies in Britain. Soon after the war started, German and Italian citizens living in Britain were arrested and put in prisoner-of-war camps – even though some of them had fled Germany and Italy to escape fascism. By the summer of 1941 the scare had died down, and only about 5000 were kept in prison.

The role of women in civilian and military life

War work

In September 1939 all men aged between 18 and 41 were called up for military service. As a result, there was a shortage of labour and women were encouraged to fill the jobs that men used to do. There was no tradition of 'respectable' women working in many jobs, so the government used propaganda to encourage them. After 1941 the government said that women between 18 and 40 (except those with young children) had to work in war industries. From December 1941, women between 20 and 30 could be conscripted into the women's armed forces – though not for actual fighting.

By 1943 nine out of ten single women were doing war work, and so were many married women. Some worked in industry, and those who worked in dangerous conditions, such as in a munitions factory, were well paid. Men were usually better paid for doing the same jobs but, even so, women were earning a lot more than before the war.

The Women's Land Army

On the land, there was a shortage of workers as many men had joined the armed forces. About 80,000 women joined the Women's Land Army (WLA) to make up the difference. Some men doubted whether women would be able to do the physically demanding parts of the job, especially as many came from the cities and had little knowledge of country life. They were given lodgings in remote areas, sometimes with very basic conditions. However, most of them did cope with the tough jobs, and afterwards many spoke with pride of their achievements.

Social freedom

Life for many women had been very strict during the 1930s. Now, with clothing shortages, what women wore was more varied – and sometimes less uncomfortable. There was a shortage of younger men at home, and there tended to be more freedom in sexual relationships. Some women argued, with bombs dropping in the cities, that they should enjoy themselves while they could – and take their minds off the grim realities of life during the war.

SOURCE C

"Now, Miss Fforbes-Wattson, have you had any experience of agricultural work?"

A wartime cartoon from *Punch* about women joining the Land Army.

SOURCE D

These women are servicing a 6-ton truck.

The services

Women who were conscripted after 1941 could join one of three organisations. However, the Women's Royal Naval Service (WRNS – known as Wrens) and the Women's Auxiliary Air Force (WAAF) already had waiting lists. Therefore, many had no choice but to join the Auxiliary Territorial Service (ATS), which offered less glamorous jobs.

By 1944 there were 450,000 women working in these three services, almost half of them in the ATS. This allowed many men to concentrate on fighting while women did other essential jobs. Many women worked as mechanics, welders, pilots, carpenters, and gunners on anti-aircraft guns – though they were not allowed to fire them.

However, traditional attitudes towards women were well established. Most women in the services worked as cooks, cleaners or secretaries, or in other jobs far away from the fighting front. Women who did get close to military action were often regarded suspiciously by the men, who expected them to look and behave in ways that men thought were feminine. Some people criticised the way that women sometimes had to share accommodation with men and work close to them.

SOURCE E

I was called up in 1941. I did not mind being called up. I think all of us were eager to do some sort of war work. I chose the Land Army as a result of a chance remark from my brother-in-law who was in the Royal Welsh Fusiliers. He said that I would not like any of the women's services, as I was a bit on the quiet side. I always liked gardening and decided to apply for a job to do with the horticultural side of the Land Army. In due course I got this.

From an interview with Lily Halford, a member of the Women's Land Army.

After the war

When the war ended, fewer women wanted to work. Many saw work as a wartime emergency, and believed their proper place was in the home. Many had delayed having children during the war and now wanted to start their families. However, some of these women did seek work in the 1950s when their children were growing up. Attitudes towards married women working were clearly changing, even if their career opportunities were often very limited and they did not receive equal pay. It was only in the 1960s that some women began to campaign for equal opportunities and equal pay.

SOURCE F

The war was the best thing that ever happened to us. My generation had been taught to do as we were told. At work you did exactly as your boss told you; then you went home to do exactly what your husband told you. The war changed all that. The war made me stand on my own two feet.

From an interview with Mona Marshall in 1986.

Food supplies and rationing

Before the Second World War, Britain imported over half of its food. However, once the war started, German U-boats (submarines) began sinking ships bringing essential supplies, such as food, clothing, metals and oil, to Britain. This quickly led to shortages.

Rationing

The government had used rationing in the last year of the First World War. This time it acted more quickly. Rationing was introduced in January 1940. Ration books containing coupons were issued and the prices of rationed goods were controlled.

People could not buy rationed goods wherever they wanted. They had to use the shopkeeper where they were registered. The shopkeeper received supplies according to how many customers had registered at the shop. At first, only butter, sugar and bacon were rationed, but by 1941 other items, such as clothes and petrol, were also included.

Alternatives to rationing

To begin with, rich people avoided the coupon system by eating in restaurants. However, from 1942 restaurants were not allowed to charge more than 25p for a meal (the equivalent of a few pounds now).

People were encouraged to use alternatives to rationed goods. Some goods came from abroad, such as powdered milk and Spam (Supply Pressed American Meat) from the USA. People tried new recipes, such as carrot marmalade.

The government encouraged people to grow their own food, using every available piece of land as vegetable gardens. This 'Dig for Victory' campaign was very successful. The number of allotments increased from 815,000 in 1939 to 1.4 million in 1943. People were also resourceful in catching animals, such as rabbits, for meat.

A less patriotic way of gaining food supplies was to buy them on the 'black market'. These arrived in Britain as 'extras' that by-passed customs officials, and were sold at high prices either by traders or 'under the counter' by shopkeepers.

Many people developed cravings for foods that were rarely seen in shops, such as bananas, oranges and lemons. But it has been suggested that, in spite of the shortages, many people had a much better diet during the war than before.

SOURCE G

A wartime poster issued by the British government.

The effects of air warfare

Evacuation

SOURCE H

Children being evacuated to the country by train. Their teacher is on the left of the picture.

In September 1939 the government expected British cities to suffer immediate bombing from the German Luftwaffe and over 1.5 million children were evacuated to the countryside. But this was the time of the Phoney War (see page 234), and, when the bombing did not happen, many children gradually returned to their homes. Then, when the Blitz started in summer 1940, many of these children were re-evacuated, not necessarily to the same areas as before. A third evacuation happened in 1944 when German V1 and V2 rocket attacks were launched from northern Europe.

Evacuation was not compulsory, and some parents refused to let their children go. However, many children did leave, and they found the move a strange experience. They left their mothers behind (many fathers had already been called into the armed forces), and had to adapt to a new way of life.

When they arrived in their new town or village, evacuees were lined up for the host families to inspect. These families often chose which children they wanted, and clean-looking girls and strong-looking boys were the most popular. Dirty or weak-looking children were often left until last. Some evacuees found living in the countryside delightful; others, usually from well-off families, found life in the countryside backward, with houses often lacking hot-water taps and flushing toilets.

Relations between the evacuees and their host families also varied. Some families took in evacuees out of a sense of duty or because they welcomed the small allowance paid or the manual work that the evacuees could do. Some evacuees were not used to basic hygiene, had skin diseases or head-lice, and were not used to taking baths.

In other cases, evacuees developed a close relationship with their host families, and hated the idea of going home. They enjoyed the healthy fresh air of the countryside. There are cases of evacuees returning to their host families to work (for example, on a farm) once the war was over.

QUESTIONS

1. Did the plan to evacuate children in September 1939 work well? Explain your answer.
2. What might evacuees have liked and disliked about being away from home?

The Blitz

The Blitz destroyed large parts of many cities between September 1940 and summer 1941. At first, London was the only target; then other cities were included. From February 1941 onwards, the main German targets were ports in the west of England, such as Bristol, which were important for supplies. Many people had to sleep in underground shelters. In London, many people slept on the platforms of underground stations.

Air-raid precautions

At first, defences against air-raids were very limited. Radar on the east and south coasts of Britain provided warnings of approaching enemy aircraft. However, searchlights were limited in their range, and the German bombers simply flew above them.

Air-raid wardens were active in enforcing the blackout regulations that had been issued before the war started, together with gas masks and instructions about air-raid warnings. The ARP (air-raid precautions) Wardens, mostly part-time volunteers, organised preparations for air-raids and were also active when bombing actually began.

The Home Guard

In May 1940, the British government realised that, if France was defeated, Britain was in danger of invasion next. It therefore hurriedly set up the Local Defence Volunteers (LDVs). These were intended to act as a second line of defence behind the official armed forces. They consisted of men either too old or too young to fight in the regular army, or men exempted from fighting because their civilian jobs were too important, such as bank managers. By June 1940 nearly 1.5 million men had joined the LDVs. Churchill decided to give them an easier name – the Home Guard – but because of their age, they were commonly referred to as 'Dad's Army'.

SOURCE I

Damage in the centre of Canterbury, Kent, after heavy bombing in 1940.

SOURCE J

Lighting restrictions

All windows, sky-lights, glazed doors, or other openings which would show a light, will have to be screened in war time with dark blinds or blankets, or brown paper pasted on the glass, so that no light is visible on the outside. You should obtain now any materials you may need for this purpose.

No outside lights will be allowed, and all street lighting will be put out.

Instructions will be issued about the dimming of lights on vehicles.

Fire precautions

An air attack may bring large numbers of small incendiary bombs, which might start up so many fires that the Fire Brigades could not be expected to deal with them all. Everyone should be prepared to do all he can to tackle a fire started in his own house. Most large fires start as small ones.

Clearing the top floor of all inflammable materials, lumber, etc. will lessen the danger of fire, and prevent a fire from spreading. See that you can reach your attic or roof space readily.

Water is the best means of putting out a fire started by an incendiary bomb. Have some buckets ready.

Extracts from a civil defence leaflet, issued in July 1939 by the British government.

Members of the Home Guard gathered in the evenings after work, and were trained in weapons handling, unarmed combat and anti-tank warfare, even though to begin with they had hardly any weapons or equipment. They acted as lookouts – for example, on the coast to spot an invading fleet and in the sky for German parachutists or bombs being dropped. They also removed local signposts that might help invading forces, guarded important buildings and manned road blocks.

SOURCE K

The Home Guard practising drill in Kent, 1940.

SOURCE L

We shall defend our island, whatever the cost may be, we shall fight on the beaches, we shall fight on the landing grounds, we shall fight in the fields and in the streets, we shall fight in the hills; we shall never surrender.

Churchill speaking in the House of Commons, 4 June 1940.

QUESTIONS

1. List the ways in which Britain tried to defend itself from attack.
2. Why do you think so many people joined the Home Guard?

The effects of the war on British society

Winston Churchill had been wartime Prime Minister since he took over in May 1940. He was an inspiring speaker and most people admired him for what he had achieved. However, many had concerns about his ability to make Britain a better place to live in after the war ended. People were sensing that life had changed during the war – and would not return to how it had been in 1939. Churchill lost the election in July 1945, and Clement Attlee led a Labour government for the next five years.

There were also changes in attitude towards social class. People became aware of the huge differences in standard of living between social groups, and came to accept that there should be a certain minimum standard of health and housing for everyone. The Beveridge Report of 1942 had said that everyone should have the right to certain benefits when they were unemployed or ill, and pensions when they retired. After suffering so much during the war, people expected a better life afterwards and welcomed the 'welfare state' that was set up between 1945 and 1951.

Yet Britain also faced many problems in the late 1940s. Much rebuilding had to be done (some by German prisoners of war, who were kept in Britain until 1946 or 1947), and Britain owed a huge amount of money to the USA. Many families came back together painfully, with discoveries of illegitimate children born during the war, and some returning husbands suing their wives for divorce because of adultery.

What many British people did not want to face was the fact that the glorious days of the British Empire were over. India was about to receive its independence, and Britain was only a junior partner in the US-led alliance against communism in the developing Cold War.

Coursework/Paper 1–style questions

The Second World War 1939–45

Assessment Objective 2

Aspect 1 Causes and/or consequences

1. In the late summer of 1940 Britain prepared for an expected German invasion. Why, despite its victory in western Europe, did Germany decide not to attempt an invasion of Britain at that time?
2. Why were the Allied summer offensives in 1944 able to bring about the rapid collapse of German resistance by April 1945?
3. Explain the consequences of the bombing of civilian targets in Britain between 1940 and 1945.
4. 'A tactical triumph but a strategic disaster.' Why did the Japanese attack on Pearl Harbor fail to bring victory for Japan in the Second World War?

Aspect 2 Change and continuity

1. How great were the changes in aerial (**or** naval) warfare during the Second World War?
2. The Second World War had many important effects on British life. Did it completely change women's lives between 1939 and 1945? Explain your answer.

Aspect 3 People's ideas and attitudes

1. It was widely expected that bombs would destroy civilian's will to fight.
   Explain the reactions of the British people to the Blitz in 1940 and 1941.
2. In the early years of the Second World War, many British people had come to see the Soviet Union as at best an unfriendly neutral. Yet in December 1941 Britain became the ally of the Soviet Union. Explain the reactions of British people to this change of policy.

Aspect 4 The role of the individual

1. Adolf Hitler increasingly attempted to control the Nazi military campaigns during the Second World War. How important was his role in causing Germany's defeat?
2. Churchill became British Prime Minister at a disastrous time. How important was his part in bringing about the recovery in Britain's position between 1940 and 1943?
   Explain your answer.

Assessment Objective 3

The Japanese attack on Pearl Harbor, 7 December 1941

Source A

THE MOST UNLIKELY THING IN THE WORLD!

A Japanese attack on Hawaii is regarded as the most unlikely thing in the world, with one chance in a million of being successful. Besides having more powerful defences than any other post under the American flag, it is protected by distance.

From a newspaper, printed in Honolulu, Hawaii, on 6 September 1941.

Source B

This dispatch is to be considered a war warning. Negotiations with Japan ... have ceased. An aggressive move by Japan is expected within the next few days. The number and equipment of Japanese troops, and the organisation of their naval task forces, indicates an amphibious expedition against either the Philippines, Thailand, Malaya or possibly Borneo. Carry out appropriate defensive deployment.

A message sent to Admiral Kimmel, Commander of the US Pacific Fleet, from the military intelligence headquarters in Washington, on 27 November 1941.

Source C

A photograph taken from a Japanese aircraft at the start of the attack. The two circled aircraft are attacking 'Battleship Row'.

Source D

As usual, there was a warm breeze that Sunday morning. We had just finished breakfast and drifted out of the compartment to get a little air. This was our normal routine on weekends, as we had no work station to report to. It was fortunate for us that we were able to sleep in until 6.30 as many of us had been out the night before. Just as we left the mess area we heard this noise. We went outside to take a look because it's usually very quiet. When we arrived we could hear and see there were airplanes. I looked across the bow of the ship and could see large plumes of smoke coming up from Ford Island. At first, we didn't realise it was a bombing. It didn't mean anything to us until a large group of planes came near the ship and we could see for the first time the rising sun emblem on the plane wings. The bombing was becoming heavier all around us and we knew this was REALLY IT!

At first there was a rush of fear; the blood started to flow real fast. My battle station was on a forward 5-inch gun and it was standard practice to keep only a limited amount of ammunition at the guns. There was only one ready gun crew on each side and mine wasn't one of them. There we were, the Japanese dropping bombs over us and we had no ammo. All the training and practising for a year and when the real thing came we had no ammunition where we needed it.

An eyewitness account of the Pearl Harbor attack, written many years later. These are the memories of George Phraner, who was serving on board the battleship USS Arizona.

Source E

It was a typical Sunday morning breakfast for the first weekend after payday ... Warden was just going back for seconds on both hotcakes and eggs when this blast shuddered by under the floor and rattled the cups on the tables. Warden stopped in the doorway and looked back at the mess hall. He remembered the picture for the rest of his life. It had become very quiet and everybody had stopped eating and looked up at each other.
'Must be doin' some dynamitin' down at Wheeler Field,' somebody said.
'I heard they was clearing some ground for a new fighter strip,' somebody else agreed. That seemed to satisfy everybody. They went back to their eating. That was when the second blast came ...
'This is it,' somebody said quite simply.
Warden ran through the porch into the street. Down the street over the trees a big column of smoke was mushrooming into the sky.
A red headed boy was down the street.
'What's up, Red?' Warden hollered at him.
'The Japs is bombing Wheeler field! I seen the red circles on the wings!'

Extracts from a novel, *From Here to Eternity* by James Jones (1952).

Source F

The Japanese attack was brilliantly planned and flawlessly carried out. It involved a bold new use of aircraft carriers. ... The attack required extraordinarily well-trained aircrews with commanders capable of co-ordinating 150 planes in each wave of the attack. The scale and complexity of the attack greatly exceeded anything that had been done before. American military experts underestimated Japanese capability.

From a recent official report on Pearl Harbor, the Dorn Report (1995). This was made for the US government.

1. Study **Source A**. How useful is this source for investigating the US preparations for an attack on Pearl Harbor?
   Explain your answer using **Source A and your own knowledge.**
2. At the time there was a great deal of argument over whether Admiral Kimmel had been taken too much by surprise by the Japanese attack. Does **Source B** help to explain why there was so much argument over this issue?
   Explain your answer using **Source B and your own knowledge.**
3. How much can you learn from **Source C** about the Japanese attack on Pearl Harbor?
   Explain your answer using **Source C and your own knowledge.**
4. **Source D** is an eyewitness account of the first minutes of the attack. **Source E** is from a novel describing this time. They broadly agree on what happened. Does this mean these sources are reliable evidence for US reactions when the attack began?
   Explain your answer using **Sources D and E, and your own knowledge.**
5. **Source F** is from a recent US government report. Does this mean Source F is an accurate interpretation of why the Americans were surprised at Pearl Harbor?
   Explain your answer using **Source F and your own knowledge.**
6. 'Pearl Harbor was deliberately left unprepared to face the Japanese in the hope that it would shock American opinion into supporting war.' Is this a fair interpretation?
   Explain your answer using **all the sources and your own knowledge.**

Assessment Objective 3

The role of women in military and civilian life in Britain during the Second World War

Source A

> British women often give orders to men. The men obey smartly and know it is no shame. For British women have proved themselves in this war. They have stuck to their posts near burning ammunition dumps, delivered messages afoot after their motor cycles have been blasted from under them. They have pulled aviators from blazing planes. They have died at their gun-posts, and as they fell another girl has stepped directly into the position and 'carried on'. There isn't a single record of any British woman in uniformed service quitting her post, or failing in her duty under fire. When you see a girl in uniform with a bit of ribbon on her tunic, remember that she didn't get it for knitting more socks than anyone else.

An extract from a booklet issued by the US War Department to every US soldier entering Britain during the war.

Source B

Drawn by Joan Zeephat, who served in the Royal Engineers, a unit of the British army.

Source C

> This place is really horrible ... We sleep on stone floors in old disused army huts. To start with I had an awful night's sleep, not being used to sleeping on the floor – how my shoulders ached! There are 66 new recruits in the charge of an officer, who calls us by blowing his whistle at 6.15 each morning ... Breakfast is from 7 to 7.15 and lorries depart after that ... We started picking spuds until it rained at 4.30 p.m. then packed it in and walked most of the way back. It really rained then and I got soaked to the skin. I've had a hot bath in a filthy tub and some half-cold grub. I can't find anywhere to hang my wet clothes, so they are in the hut at the moment, which is not exactly a healthy state to sleep in – what a life! So picture Beryl and me lying on our stomachs on our divan-like beds, with the smoke of the oil lamp, our only light, getting up our noses, and the rain falling hard on the tin roof. I've already killed two spiders – again what a life!

From a letter written by a new Land Army recruit to her boyfriend.

Source D

A photograph showing a Land Army information office in a London store, March 1941.

1. How much can you learn from **Source A** about the roles of women in British military life during the war?
Explain your answer using **Source A and your own knowledge.**

2. **Source B** was drawn by a female cartoonist, during the war. Does this make it reliable evidence about the military training of women during the war?
Explain your answer using **Source B and your own knowledge.**

3. Study **Sources C and D.** They give very different views of the Women's Land Army. Which is the more useful source for investigating women's lives in the Land Army?
Explain your answer using **Sources C and D, and your own knowledge.**

4. **Source E** is a set of statistics, put together many years after the war. Does this mean it is reliable as evidence about changes in women's employment during the war?
Explain your answer using **Source E and your own knowledge.**

5. Study **Source F.** Does the author's claim that the factory in the source is 'fictional' make it useless as evidence about the views of women working in a munitions factory during the war?
Explain your answer using **Source F and your knowledge.**

6. 'Women made a major contribution to Britain's war effort.' Do Sources A–F provide enough evidence to support this interpretation.
Explain your answer using **all the sources and your own knowledge.**

Source E

Changes in numbers of women employed, 1939–43

Distribution	–6,000
Services	+58,000
Textiles	–165,000
Clothing	–149,000
Admin/clerical	+480,000
Engineering/aircraft/ships	+1,197,000
Manufacturing	–48,000
Food	–18,000
Chemicals	+220,000
Agriculture	+102,000
Transport	+147,000
Other	+531,000

From *Life in Wartime Britain* by Richard Tames (1993).

Source F

Over ten hours a day, six days a week that BROWNED-OFFNESS begins to creep in on the munitions workers. Hardly noticeable at first, and then steadily growing till, aided by other factors like lack of sleep, petty illnesses and factory disturbances, it takes over your whole life. Always there is one eye on the clock, to see if it has moved an inch nearer to teatime, or to 7.30 p.m. and the release to go home, eat, and sleep. If a statistician took the trouble to record how many times the word 'browned off' was used in a munitions factory, he'd get so browned-off himself he'd give it up. 'Browned-off', as anyone must have guessed by now, means totally and completely bored. Bored with turning handles, the same old faces, the same old jobs, the same old dried peas and leftovers in the canteen, the same woman supervisor; bored with the day shifts and the night shifts, in fact thoroughly and wholeheartedly BROWNED-OFF.

From a book, *Ladies May Now Leave Their Machines*, published during the war. It was written by Diane Murray Hill, who said the factory described was fictional, but based on her first-hand experience.

Glossary

Appeasement A policy of conciliating (pleasing) a potential aggressor by making concessions, e.g. the policy followed by Britain in the 1930s to try to avoid war with Nazi Germany.

Bolsheviks Members of the political party led by Lenin who favoured revolutionary tactics.

Capitalist (country) One where the production and manufacture and trade of goods is run by private people or companies who can try to make a profit for themselves.

Communist A supporter of the political theories first outlined by Karl Marx advocating class war and a society in which all property is publicly owned.

Conscientious objector Someone whose principles prevent him or her from fighting in a war.

Conscription Compulsory military service.

Demilitarised zone An area where no military forces are permitted.

Democracy System of government in which the whole or majority of the population has had a say in choosing the people who make the decisions of government.

Détente The improvement in relations between East and West in the Cold War.

Disarmament The deliberate reduction of military strength.

Discrimination Treating somebody unfairly on the basis of their colour, religion or sex.

Duma The Russian Parliament.

Embargo A government order suspending trade or commerce, or ships to enter or leave a port.

Entrepreneur A go-ahead business person willing to back new ideas and take risks.

Hyperinflation A period of rapid and extreme price increases, especially in Germany in 1923/4.

Immigrants People who leave their country of birth to live permanently in another.

Mandate (in the Treaty of Versailles) A country previously governed by Germany.

Moonshine Illegal alcohol.

Propaganda Information altered or presented in such a way as to make a special impression or influence the way people think.

Reparations Payments demanded from Germany by the victorious countries after the First World War in compensation for the damage caused.

Sabotage Deliberate damage, especially to factories, railways etc.

Sanctions Actions taken by one country against another (often in the form of stopping trade or the shipment of supplies) as a sign of protest.

Satellite (country) A small country controlled by a greater power, e.g. Hungary was controlled by the Soviet Union after 1945.

Socialism Political and economic theory which states that the people should own and control the means of production, i.e. factories, etc.

Spanish Civil War The war of 1936–9 between Spain's left-wing republican government forces and General Franco's right-wing 'fascist' forces.

Superpowers The capitalist USA and the communist Soviet Union who were the two most powerful countries after the Second World War.

Tariff A tax or duty on goods imported into a country from another.

Wall Street Crash The sudden and spectacular collapse of the US stock market (based in Wall Street, New York) in October 1929, leading to the economic depression in the USA and Europe.

War of attrition A war in which one side wins by gradually wearing the other down with repeated attacks.

Index